Grand Strategy and the Presidency

This book examines the role and importance of the Presidency in the formulation and conduct of US grand strategy.

The text discusses US strategic history, with particular emphasis on the period from the end of the Cold War to the present day. While the United States periodically has enjoyed exceptional presidential leadership in the past, this book argues that few future presidents will meet high standards of leadership in foreign affairs. In turn, this will undermine the ability of the United States to construct and maintain a coherent grand strategy appropriate to the multipolar world of the twenty-first century.

Grand Strategy and the Presidency explores the role that the holders of the presidential office have played in the past development of the United States as a great power. Drawing upon examples from history, the textual analysis is shaped around the description of the long-term strategic development of the United States. The author then considers what the events of recent decades portend for the future of US strategy and foreign policy.

This book will be of interest to students of presidential studies, US foreign policy, strategic studies, and international relations/security studies in general.

C. Dale Walton is a Lecturer in International Politics and Strategic Studies at the University of Reading, UK. He is the author of *Geopolitics and the Great Powers in the Twenty-First Century: Multipolarity and the Revolution in Strategic Perspective* (Routledge, 2007) and *The Myth of Inevitable US Defeat in Vietnam* (Frank Cass/Routledge, 2002).

Series: Strategy and History
Series editors: Colin Gray and Williamson Murray
ISSN: 1473-6403

This new series will focus on the theory and practice of strategy. Following Clausewitz, strategy has been understood to mean the use made of force, and the threat of the use of force, for the ends of policy. This series is as interested in ideas as in historical cases of grand strategy and military strategy in action. All historical periods, near and past, and even future, are of interest. In addition to original monographs, the series will from time to time publish edited reprints of neglected classics as well as collections of essays.

1 **Military Logistics and Strategic Performance**
Thomas M. Kane

2 **Strategy for Chaos**
Revolutions in military affairs and the evidence of history
Colin Gray

3 **The Myth of Inevitable US Defeat in Vietnam**
C. Dale Walton

4 **Astropolitik**
Classical geopolitics in the space age
Everett C. Dolman

5 **Anglo-American Strategic Relations and the Far East, 1933–1939**
Imperial crossroads
Greg Kennedy

6 **Pure Strategy**
Power and principle in the space and information age
Everett C. Dolman

7 **The Red Army, 1918–1941**
From vanguard of world revolution to US ally
Earl F. Ziemke

8 **Britain and Ballistic Missile Defence, 1942–2002**
Jeremy Stocker

9 **The Nature of War in the Information Age**
Clausewitzian future
David J. Lonsdale

10 **Strategy as Social Science**
Thomas Schelling and the nuclear age
Robert Ayson

11 **Warfighting and Disruptive Technologies**
Disguising innovation
Terry Pierce

12 **The Fog of Peace and War Planning**
Military and strategic planning under uncertainty
Edited by Talbot C. Imlay and Monica Duffy Toft

13 **US Army Intervention Policy and Army Innovation**
From Vietnam to Iraq
Richard Lock-Pullan

14 **German Disarmament After World War I**
The diplomacy of international arms inspection 1920–1931
Richard J. Shuster

15 **Strategy and History**
Essays on theory and practice
Colin S. Gray

16 **The German 1918 Offensives**
A case study in the operational level of war
David T. Zabecki

17 **Special Operations and Strategy**
From World War II to the war on terrorism
James D. Kiras

18 **Science, Strategy and War**
The strategic theory of John Boyd
Frans P.B. Osinga

19 **US Defense Strategy from Vietnam to Operation Iraqi Freedom**
Military innovation and the new American way of war, 1973–2003
Robert R. Tomes

Grand Strategy and the Presidency

Foreign policy, war and the American role in the world

C. Dale Walton

Routledge
Taylor & Francis Group
LONDON AND NEW YORK

First published 2012
by Routledge
2 Park Square, Milton Park, Abingdon, Oxon OX14 4RN

Simultaneously published in the USA and Canada
by Routledge
711 Third Avenue, New York, NY 10017

Routledge is an imprint of the Taylor & Francis Group, an informa business

First issued in paperback 2013

British Library Cataloguing in Publication Data
A catalogue record for this book is available from the British Library

Library of Congress Cataloging-in-Publication Data
Library of Congress Cataloging-in-Publication Data
Walton, C. Dale, 1971–
Grand strategy and the presidency : foreign policy, war and the American role in the world / C. Dale Walton.
p. cm. – (Strategy and history, ISSN 1473-6403 ; 25)
Includes bibliographical references and index.
1. United States–Foreign relations–1989– 2. United States–Foreign relations administration. 3. Strategic culture–United States.
4. Presidents–United States–History–20th century.
5. Presidents–United States–History–21st century.
6. Executive power–United States–History–20th century.
7. Executive power–United States–History–21st century. I. Title.
E840.W355 2012
327.73009'048–dc23 2011035944

ISBN: 978-0-415-59832-3 (hbk)
ISBN: 978-0-415-73122-5 (pbk)
ISBN: 978-0-203-12622-6 (ebk)

Typeset in Baskerville
by Wearset Ltd, Boldon, Tyne and Wear

For Shelley, with love

Contents

Preface

The great bulk of *Grand Strategy and the Presidency* was composed before 19 March 2011, when the United States, alongside a coalition of allies, began to involve itself militarily in an ongoing civil war in Libya. Thus, this work makes only passing references to the Libya War, and that conflict has played very little role in shaping the analysis. While the US enterprise in Libya ultimately may prove to have a satisfactory outcome, the author would note his view that, for reasons that the main body of this work hopefully makes clear, the Obama administration's decision to intervene in Libya's civil war was reflective of the deep flaws in US grand strategy that are discussed in this book.

Acknowledgments

I have benefited from the knowledge of a multitude of colleagues and students at the University of Reading Department of Politics and International Relations. I would like especially to recognize the contributions of Simon Anglim, Alan Cromartie, Sadaf Farooq, Philip Giddings, Christina Hellmich, Beatrice Heuser, Jeremy Lester, Patrick Porter, Alan Renwick, Geoff Sloan, Oisín Tansey, Richard Rubright, and Dominik Zaum. Many other friends worldwide also have helped to make this book possible. These include, among many others, Martin Alexander, Steve Cimbala, Eric Grove, Chris Harmon, Tom Kane, James Kiras, Dave Lonsdale, Peter Pham, Chris Tuck, and John Sheldon. I also thank Andrew Humphrys, my longtime editor at Routledge, for his support throughout the publication process, and Penny Harper for her outstanding copyediting.

Three individuals stand out for particular recognition in regard to this book. Colin S. Gray's contribution to this, and all, of my work is incalculable; he has been a friend and mentor throughout my career. Col. Michael "Coyote" Smith deserves particular recognition for his special contribution as a boon companion and the sounding board for many of the ideas herein—his thoughtful questions and insightful comments surely made this a better work. Finally, my wife Shelley contributed a great deal as an eagle-eyed copyeditor, tireless index organizer, and, most importantly, deeply loving spouse.

The financial assistance of the Leverhulme Foundation, through its Liberal Way of War project, is acknowledged gratefully.

Introduction

At the present historical moment, the President of the United States has no true peers: he leads the most powerful polity on earth, and in regard to foreign policy and national security decision making his personal authority is enormous and only lightly moderated by law and custom. The US Constitution places deep constraints on presidential influence over domestic affairs, but the power to act as commander-in-chief of the armed forces and control of the machinery of the Executive branch have allowed presidents to minimize Congress' role in foreign policy making, while the Supreme Court has prudently tended to practice self-marginalization by refusing to interfere overly in matters relating to defense and foreign policy.[1]

In general, the vesting of "strategic authority" in the Oval Office has proven beneficial, as the other two branches of the US government are not capable of providing coherent strategic leadership. A Congressionally led foreign and defense policy would be whimsical and confused, with over 500 representatives and senators—most of them having little knowledge of strategic theory, military history, or similar relevant subjects—tinkering with policy. (Congressional oversight hearings provide an insight into how problematic Congressional leadership in strategic affairs surely would be. Such hearings often consist of a weird mixture of partisan cheerleading and accusatory questions reminiscent of a show trial; oftentimes, committee members use all of their allotted question time to make elliptical speeches that do not even contain a clear question.) Given its respect for precedent and relative insulation from partisan politics, the Judicial branch might be somewhat less chaotic if it had responsibility for strategic decision making. However, when the structure of the US court system is considered, it is difficult to imagine how the judiciary might provide timely and coherent strategic leadership even if all judges were defense and foreign policy experts—the American legal process is organized in such a fashion as to make "strategic juristocracy" impractical. Even if this were not the case, for the unelected branch of the federal government to make the key decisions regarding war and peace would be constitutionally and politically unpalatable.

Given the lack of viable alternatives, vesting the president with the right to direct foreign and defense policy is a practical necessity if the United States is to function effectively as a great power, much less the greatest of powers. However, doing so inevitably carries a very considerable risk, as it makes a single individual largely responsible for the success or failure of foreign policy at any given time. This is an enormous potential problem, as a single poor president serving at a pivotal moment in history may immediately and gravely damage the strategic fortunes of the United States. Fortunately, however, such moments are rare. At least for the foreseeable future, a possibly more significant risk for the United States is presented by the possibility of a slow degradation of its international position resulting from a succession of bad decisions by strategically uninspired presidents, with new errors building on the old ones to cause a cycle of failure that, over time, very seriously degrades Washington's global position.

The circumstances that lead to cycles of strategic success or failure are key to the analysis herein, and this work intentionally takes a very long-term view; this is not a "policy book" in any usual sense of the term and does not provide advice on specific future US decisions regarding, for example, Afghanistan or the size of the defense budget. Rather, it focuses on how the United States came to occupy the position that it today has in the global system, how it might decline, and the critical role of the presidency in the rise, and quite possibly the eventual radical degeneration, of US power. The book, therefore, is divided between the past and the future, with the argument regarding the latter deeply dependant on the discussion of the former.

Strategic success considered

This book endeavors to provide an explicitly strategic analysis of the role that the holders of the presidential office have played in the past development of the United States as a great power, and what this history indicates regarding the future of US strategy and foreign policy. The historical examples presented are intended to illustrate the general trajectory of US strategic history and how certain individual presidents have shaped the development of their polity, not to provide a general historical survey. The analysis relies on the description of the long-term strategic development of the United States to provide a foundation for discussion of more recent developments (the period from the Cold War to the present) and then, in turn, to consider what recent decades portend for the future.

The international rise of the United States was, by virtually any standard, extraordinarily rapid, with the country moving in less than 200 years from colonial status to being one of only two global superpowers. This achievement is all the more striking when one considers that the United States was not overtly militaristic (even if it had a pitilessly efficient policy regarding internal political consolidation). The Constitution was constructed with an eye toward *preventing* the central government from welding the nation's human resources into a mighty war-making instrument capable of endless conquest; the early United States was, in essence, defensively oriented in regard to external states—although, of course, expansion at the expense of Native American tribes was considered desirable. (In some respects, the foresight of the Founders was astonishing; very shortly after the drafting of the US Constitution, Revolutionary France would proceed to undergo precisely the sort of the convulsions that most American leaders feared—an internal bloodbath and the launching of aggressive, expansionist conflicts, both justified by abstract ideological goals, followed by Caesarism and *more* expansionist wars.) This is not to claim that the US government was above occasionally indulging in opportunistic military expansion at the expense of foreign states—northern Mexico did not affix itself to the United States through a mysterious, peaceful process. Nonetheless, the rarity of US expansion through foreign military conquest is notable because it is historically unusual—generally, great polities emerge at the expense of bordering states, either quickly conquering neighbors outright or vampirically draining them of territory and population until they finally are absorbed.

Surely, the largest part of the credit for America's anomalous rise is attributable to its unique geopolitical circumstances, which ensured that during its period of rapid geographical expansion Washington did not present a critical threat to the interests of any of the European great powers; it therefore largely avoided Old World entanglements and all which would result from these. One plausibly might say that, in its early years, America's foremost foreign policy strength was its irrelevance to the great powers; the United States simply did not matter enough that the most powerful states found it necessary to destroy it.

Britain was the only great power whose interests very regularly butted against those of the United States, and this chiefly resulted from the fact that Canada and the United States shared a long, and disputed, common border. Furthermore, British seapower presented a unique potential threat to the United States; as the possessor of the world's greatest naval instrument, Britain could, at will, damage American economic life enormously and, if it desired, threaten invasion by both land (via Canada) and sea. It was not coincidental that vast and underpopulated Canada did not again suffer American invasion after the War of 1812. Britain could make the price of a Canadian invasion prohibitive for the United States, while the inherent vulnerability of Canada and the immense expenses that would be incurred if it were necessary to defend (or, worse still, reconquer) it in a conflict encouraged London's conciliatory instincts.

Acting alone, any of the other great powers were far less potentially menacing to the United States—only France could present a major challenge, and, given the rivalry between Paris and London, a critical French threat to US security surely would have resulted in British aid to the Americans. Prussia and the Russian and Austrian Empires presented an even less plausible threat, having no major clashes of interest with Washington and, in any case, very little ability to act in North America. Finally, even before its near-complete collapse in the 1810s and 1820s, the decrepit Spanish Empire in the Americas was less a threat to the United States than the latter's potential mugging victim.

Nevertheless, while geography afforded the United States unusually rich strategic opportunities, it did not guarantee long-term success. The excessively reductionist notion that US geopolitical success was foreordained should not be taken seriously. Failure *was* an option for America; it merely was one which, because of fairly good overall strategic judgment, it did not pursue. However, that does not mean that it made no significant missteps; this work describes a number of these and could cite many more. Indeed, in the 1860s the United States government came perilously close to the sort of strategic disaster from which it would never have made a full recovery (and which, moreover, would have had changed world history in unknowable, but certainly radical, ways). Such errors underline the role of contingency in American strategic history.

Again, as noted above, this work uses the United States' past strategic success to illuminate its likely prospective challenges and the likelihood of future disappointment. For the sake of clarity, it is necessary briefly to describe the concept of "strategic success" as it is used herein. Unfortunately, this is not a phrase given to an uncomplicated and readily quantifiable definition. Total failure is easy enough to judge—when Hulagu's Mongols conquered Baghdad in 1258 and (at least according to legend) shortly thereafter rolled Caliph Al-Musta'sim in a carpet and trampled him with horses, it was fairly obvious that the Abbasids had suffered a strategic disaster. Above this baseline, however, there is a degree of ambiguity that is best addressed by examining the goals of the government in question. For any polity, however, assessing strategic success requires judging the degree to which it has been able to shape the global environment so as to enhance its security and influence—most importantly, this implies protection from foreseeable dangers and the power to shape the environment in a fashion that will protect against presently unforeseeable threats. That is at the core of this book's discussion.

Some of the ways in which American policy makers historically have sought to enhance US security are both obvious and, in some form, applicable to any polity at any time. These include diminishing, or, better still, eliminating the threat of foreign invasion; ensuring that the economy thrives—this allows, among other things, generous defense-related spending—and that prosperity is sustainable, thus allowing the state to cope with future threats; preventing the domestic overthrow of the current regime (in the US case, the constitutional order) or the splintering of the state; and so forth. There also, however, are other factors that are not shared by all states, most notably including the US belief that the spread of its democratic republican form of government would both enhance American security and improve the likelihood of great power peace.

It is not necessary for our purpose to create a highly precise definition and weighting of the factors that US policy makers have used to characterize strategic success over time. Indeed, it would be impossible to do so, as each leader individually assesses such matters somewhat differently, while general elite opinion changes over time: the generation that conducted the War of 1812 surely had a rather different vision of strategic success than did the one that directed the Korean War. Moreover, as noted, a degree of ambiguity is inescapable if one is to discuss such matters realistically—excessive precision actually is misleading, as it implies unattainable certainty in regard to the views and motivations of numerous, complex human beings. Indeed, while "grand strategy" is a highly useful concept,[2] it would be dubious to presume that most policy makers at most times even have a highly precise vision of how they would prefer the world to be organized.

With that said, it is obvious that, on the whole, the United States enjoyed enormous strategic success from the War of Independence through the end of the Cold War. The US government's ability to influence global events clearly increased exponentially.[3] In military terms, the United States of today is virtually unrecognizable when compared to the one that fought the Spanish–American War, much less the War of Independence; Washington undoubtedly possesses the world's most powerful overall military capabilities and an unmatched ability to deploy and sustain that force logistically. Diplomatically, it is the most powerful single state, though its dominance in this realm is far less secure (a fact demonstrated, for example, by its inability to secure broad global support for the 2003 invasion of Iraq). Moreover, the United States has either the world's largest or second-largest economy, depending on whether all of the European Union states are counted as a single unit, and its wealth can be leveraged for diplomatic and other influence.

The first two chapters herein concern the rise and changing global role of the United States. Chapter 1 draws out the major threads of the strategic "story" of the period from independence to the end of World War II, while Chapter 2 deals with the Cold War and the decade thereafter. Part of the reason for this particular division is that it is in the latter period that the American presidency transforms into the key Western leadership position in an ideologically charged superpower competition with no clear endpoint. (US presidents, as well as lesser policy makers, obviously hoped that the Cold War would end peacefully and that Moscow would abandon its errant ways, but precisely *how* that would occur was not at all obvious throughout most of the period.) The challenges of Cold War leadership placed a premium value on the strategic acumen of presidents, especially once the USSR came to possess a number of nuclear weapons sufficient to grant itself the option of destroying the NATO countries in a matter of hours. Nevertheless, the occupants of the Oval Office during the Cold War era do not stand out as a collective of Machiavellis and Tallyrands who all displayed dazzling strategic ability and outwitted their foreign counterparts, a point significant to this book's larger argument.

Missed opportunities and uncertain prospects

By the 1990s Washington enjoyed an unprecedented status: it was a global quasi-hegemon. It commonly is said that the United States was, or even still is, a world hegemon, or even empire, but this overstates the case, given the very real limits on Washington's power and its willingness to apply force in many situations. Still, though, the United States held (and, albeit to a lesser degree, still holds) a truly unique position.

The fundamental weakness with the strategic thinking of the post-Cold War period is that it was based on the fundamental assumption that US quasi-hegemony would continue long into the future. This was a fatally flawed premise. Rather, *the years immediately following the end of the Cold War were anomalous, and represented a fleeting strategic moment that could not have been made permanent even by the most talented policy makers.* Unique circumstances had made the Cold War itself possible—most critically, the world wars brought about the demise of the old multipolar great power system; the disintegration of the Western European overseas empires soon followed. With German power utterly destroyed and London and Paris militarily and financially exhausted, both Moscow and Washington enjoyed an unprecedented chance to expand their influence. (Though, at the time, the United States was far less focused on the opening that presented itself than it was on the threat of Soviet domination of Eurasia—its strategy clearly, and appropriately, was driven more by fear than perceived opportunity.)

The progressive collapse of the Cold War order over the three years from 1989 to 1991, with the Soviet imperium in East-Central Europe crumbling, to be followed by the splintering of the USSR itself, created a temporary unipolar condition. Even if American policy makers had possessed unsurpassed cunning and ruthlessness, they could not long have maintained US dominance worldwide: by the time of the USSR's dissolution, China already had been implementing serious (and highly successful) economic reforms for more than a decade; India was a significant regional power that long had been ambitious to be something considerably greater; the Japanese economy provided Tokyo with the option of playing a substantial global role, though it remained reticent in this regard; the process of European integration had been ongoing for decades and was accelerating; and so forth. Indeed, there is every reason to suppose that Soviet collapse merely permitted a brief period of unipolarity *that would not even have occurred if Moscow had been better able to manage its decline.*[4] Absent a globally devastating nuclear conflict, multipolarity—the usual condition of great power politics in recent centuries—would sooner or later reassert itself.[5]

Despite its ephemeral character, however, unipolarity offered American leaders a unique opportunity to shape the future of the global system. As Chapter 2 discusses, the period following the end of the Cold War offered a matchless opportunity to policy makers to use American influence to shape the security environment by building new institutions and/or altering existing ones. Given the inevitability of multipolarity, new global political arrangements ideally would have been able to accommodate the reasonable ambitions of rising powers while simultaneously creating an environment in which competition among major states could be channeled in ways that would diminish the possibility of the outbreak of great power war. However, the actual attempt to craft the international security environment was unfocused and desultory, with Washington remaining bogged down in day-to-day problems and displaying no realistic long-term vision—largely because policy makers did not understand that unipolarity was a rapidly wasting asset. The US failure to thoughtfully refashion the security environment when it was at the apex of its power and possessed the maximum ability to influence the process was a missed historical opportunity; as a result, it is entirely possible, if not probable, that the renewed multipolar system will be highly unstable and conflict-prone.

Of course, channeling great power competition is not easy under the best of circumstances, and there is no guarantee that American policy makers could have shaped the security environment in ways that would have been of long-term benefit. This does not, however, alter the disturbing fact that few US leaders appeared to have understood that relatively humble concerns related to the activities of rogue states, terrorists, and similar petty villains were a distraction from more enduring challenges facing their country. There was an absence of long-term strategic vision within the US policy making class, and no clear US strategic concept beyond the desire for "more": the further spread of democracy, greater global stability, and an ever-growing military advantage over potential foes. These objectives were vague, and the unfocused effort to achieve them distracted American policy makers from efforts that might be more significant over the long term.

Chapter 3 addresses the continuing failure of the United States to construct a grand strategy that would allow it to effectively shape the global security environment. A particular focus is the aforementioned progressive crumbling of unipolarity and the trend toward the rise of great power competitors capable of effectively challenging American power. The conflict known in the G.W. Bush years as the Global War on Terrorism (GWOT) and the Long War—and which in essence continues, though those terms have fallen out of fashion—also is addressed, particularly the problems that flow from making counterterrorism the central strategic focus of the US government.

The quiet crisis: presidents and strategy in recent decades

Chapter 4 of this work ties together many of the threads in the previous chapters to explore the unique role that the presidency has played historically in American grand strategy. As noted above, the Constitutional system gives the president a uniquely powerful role in the formation of foreign and defense policy, and over the course of US history the president has proven, time and again, to be *the* key figure in strategic decision making. While many governments—including, somewhat ironically, authoritarian or totalitarian ones such as the Argentinean junta that launched the Falklands War[6] and the post-Stalin Soviet Union[7]—had or have strategic decision processes in which power is dispersed among numerous players and coalition-building is central to policy making, the president is a singular figure in US strategic decision making. Bureaucratic wrangling is not unknown in Washington, of course, but the president has the legal and practical ability to drive policy in a chosen direction regardless of the views of his advisors and can do so without fear of overthrow, a privilege enjoyed by neither the British prime minister nor the chairman of Burma's (Orwellian-titled) State Leadership Development Council. Therefore, to a very considerable degree, American strategy is presidential strategy—a reality that has both enormous advantages and risks.

Voters, presidents, and the future of US strategy

Most likely, it is not merely the case that the American public chooses to place a premium on perceived domestic affairs competence while putting little value on perceived strategic acumen. In some elections (particularly the three immediately after the Cold War's end: 1992, 1996, and 2000) foreign and defense questions appear to have played a relatively modest role, but in others—such as the 1968, 1972, 1980, and, more recently, 2004 contests—views regarding the strategic talent of the presidential candidates likely were a significant factor in the election's outcome. (For instance, the outcome of the 1980 election—a landslide electoral college victory for Reagan—might have been different if Carter's handling of the Iran hostage crisis had not deeply undermined public perceptions regarding his strategic judgment.) Moreover, a voter possessed of even very modest foresight has an incentive to take strategic competence into account. If Americans believe that their state will, much less *should*, continue to act as a superpower over the long term (clearly, the prevailing opinion), then even in a period of relative international calm it is easy enough to see that good "strategic management" is valuable in preventing future problems and maintaining an amenable global environment. Thus, American voters have every reason to place a high value on strategic competence.

It is argued herein, however, that in the years following the death of Franklin Roosevelt a substantial number—indeed, a majority—of presidents have been strategic underperformers and this represents a discernable long-term problem, not a simple matter of bad luck. This outcome reflects the fact that, in regard to selecting for strategic competence, the modern US presidential electoral system is dysfunctional—*and it can be expected to remain so.* To put the matter in Darwinian terms, the electorate does a poor job of selecting for strategic excellence: lack of obvious promise as a grand strategist rarely is a fatal selection disadvantage for a candidate. *Demonstrable* incompetence might constitute such a disadvantage, but, except in the case of a president running for reelection, most presidential candidates (the occasional Eisenhower aside) have never had high-level directly personal responsibility in foreign affairs, and voters seem inclined to grant them the benefit of the doubt in regard to their (unproven) strategic competence.

As noted above, this does not necessarily mean that, in the abstract, US voters do not care about strategic competence.[11] However, it certainly seems that most Americans do not possess—or, if they do have, choose not to use—a very effective filter for separating the heroic from the hapless.[12] In part, this reflects the fact that relatively few Americans possess an especially nuanced understanding of foreign and defense policy, but it is possible to assess likely aptitude without oneself being especially knowledgeable—one can be ignorant of theoretical physics and yet appreciate that Edward Teller and Enrico Fermi were not.[13] However, for the purpose at hand, whether voters are indifferent to strategic acumen or value it but have difficulty ascertaining when a candidate actually possesses it is tangential. The important point is that in recent decades the US electoral system has not served as an effective mechanism for assuring a consistently high level of presidential strategic competence and it should not be expected to do so in the future.

There are two major potential criticisms that should be noted in regard to this claim. First, one could object that, in fact, the level of strategic competence displayed by US presidents in recent decades actually has been high; after all, the United States did emerge victorious in the Cold War and is the world's greatest power. This is not an inconsequential point, but it also is not a devastating one, if historical context is properly taken in account. Given the position that the United States occupied in 1945, there was, realistically speaking, only one foe capable of inflicting catastrophic damage to its national interests; this remained the case for more than four decades. The Cold War presidents—some vastly more than others—do deserve credit for avoiding any radical strategic failure, but it should be appreciated that the Soviet Union was not a consistently brilliant superfoe: it was a very real polity with not-inconsiderable strategic blind spots[14] and a decisively flawed ideology. The USSR *was* hostile and had the military assets to be remarkably dangerous, but the bipolar structure of the Cold War was unusually simple. By contrast, for instance, in the

Napoleonic Wars, London had to cope with a diplomatic kaleidoscope—an ever-changing line-up of allies, foes, hesitant neutrals, and so forth,[15] while the *ancien régime* environment that Fredrick the Great operated in a few decades earlier was unreservedly carnivorous.[16] Simply put, some threat environments simply are more difficult to navigate than others—and thus require great strategic sophistication and consistently excellent performance; the menace that Washington faced in the Cold War was grave, but relatively straightforward in character.

In retrospect, given the record of both Soviet and American mistakes, it seems implausible that unfailing strategic genius, or anything reasonably close to it, was necessary to fend off Moscow's challenge. It required, rather, a US grand strategy that was sufficiently simple and robust to be more-or-less consistently implemented by a superpower polity given to frequent error and intermittent self-doubt. Containment proved to be suitable to this purpose.[17] In short, the string of Cold War presidents performed adequately in the context of the circumstances,[18] but the completeness of the American victory was as much a result of Soviet actions (including, critically, the decision not to undertake significant domestic economic and political reform until it was so late that the medicine would kill the patient) as a demonstration of presidential wisdom.

While the United States performed adequately overall in meeting the Soviet test, its post-Cold War record has been far less impressive: as argued above, the record for the 1990s was a deeply unimpressive one overall, with Washington unable even to form a coherent, plausible set of strategic goals (or, perhaps worse, unaware that it needed to do so). Since 9/11, American strategic performance has been even more problematic, a point discussed in greater detail below. While the United States remains the world's greatest power, its position has deteriorated tremendously since the Soviet collapse.

A second potential criticism of this book's overarching thesis is that the number of relevant presidents is so small that there is insufficient evidence to demonstrate that the electoral system is not an effective quality filter. As of this writing, only twelve presidents have served since Franklin Roosevelt's death and only four from 1991 to the present. The sample certainly is small, but the author would contend that there are clearly discernable ongoing historical trends that can be explored usefully in a work such as this one and, in turn, the analysis of those trends offers insight regarding likely future developments. Forecasts of "the history of the future" rarely are both very specific *and* highly reliable. Herein, the latter attribute is privileged over the former one: the author hopes to provide a generally accurate map, and thus it is not an intricately detailed one. The global security environment is the product of an immensely detailed system of inputs; it literally reflects the sum total of human existence, with everything from commodity prices to theology playing a role. Such complex systems do not lend themselves to precise divination.

Short of a radical Constitutional overhaul of either the system for selecting presidents and/or the concentration of foreign policy and defense authority in the Oval Office—completely unrealistic prospects, and ones which would carry their own considerable hazards—there is every reason to believe that most presidents in the foreseeable future will, at best, possess modest strategic talents. Of course, some presidents will be relatively capable strategists, and a small number may even prove to be brilliant, but the general quality of presidential performance in this area should be expected to be unimpressive. (The myriad reasons for this are explored in Chapter 5.) Therefore, this work offers no simple panacea for this problem. However, this does not mean that it necessarily is entirely beyond amelioration—and the first step in doing so is undertaking a frank debate regarding it.

The management of predictable failure

The ability successfully to manage an unpleasant strategic reality is largely dependent on the recognition that such a problem exists. At present, the American policy elite still struggles with acceptance of the reality that unipolarity is breaking down; recognizing that the system for choosing presidents contains critical flaws and that this is not a fixable problem is even more difficult, as it cuts against the grain of US strategic culture, which is solution-oriented and reluctant to acknowledge the existence of unsolvable problems. Thus, while it is to be hoped that the United States will prove willing to confront this profound difficulty squarely, it should not be taken for granted that it will do so—rather, it is likely that recognition of this systemic flaw may only occur after it has extracted an enormous price.

Already, US interests have suffered greatly as a result of failures in presidential strategic decision making. Most strikingly, the United States has experienced much difficulty in translating its military prowess into long-term strategic advantage or even, astonishingly, into unambiguous military victory. Of the five most significant US conflicts since World War II—the Korean, Vietnam, and Gulf Wars, and the invasions and occupations of Iraq and Afghanistan—only the 1991 Gulf War was an unarguable military victory. The Vietnam War clearly was a defeat for the United States, while the Korean War was ambiguous—successful insofar as the initial war goal (securing the survival of the Republic of Korea) was attained, failed in that the more ambitious objective of eliminating Kim Il-Sung's regime was thwarted.[19] The situations in Afghanistan and Iraq still are unfolding, but for reasons discussed herein, it is likely that neither will prove strategically profitable overall: the first because it is a nation-building exercise almost surely doomed to futility, the second because even if Iraq becomes a stable democracy that is friendly to the United States, that victory will have been achieved at a Pyrrhic cost.

The difficulty that the United States has and is experiencing in successfully applying military force kinetically is especially conspicuous because the US military potentially is Washington's most potent strategic tool. Globally, no other force is remotely comparable with the US military in terms of overall quantity of assets combined with quality of personnel. The only militaries that might plausibly compete with the United States in the latter category (such as Britain, Japan, and Israel) are relatively small; the few military establishments that, in personnel quantity terms, stand alongside America in the "heavyweight division" are uncompetitive on a soldier-for-soldier basis. It is entirely sensible for the United States to attempt to leverage its military strength to strategic advantage, but the record indicates that it has great difficulty in actually doing so successfully.

Chapter 6 of this work argues that this US failure to use its military to good strategic effect is intimately related to the judgment of presidents: the US military is a powerful instrument, but one that is difficult to wield wisely. A great danger that accompanies the possession of awesome military power is the temptation to use it imprudently, not only too often but, even more importantly, with insufficient consideration of precisely how a desired end state is to be brought about. It is all too easy to treat a military force like a Rottweiler that simply can be released on troublemakers; yet, the purpose of the use of violence is not simply to shred foes, but rather to favorably alter the security environment, and the latter usually requires the setting of realistic goals and a plausible theory of victory. This chapter examines the similarities and differences between the wars in Vietnam and the occupations of Iraq and Afghanistan, illuminating how the United States entered all of these conflicts with fuzzy notions regarding the preferred ultimate outcome and no clear roadmap for achieving it through primarily military means.

Given the aforementioned reasons for pessimism regarding the strategic insight of future presidents, and the fact that the media, public, and Congress repeatedly have failed effectively to compel a sharpening of strategic goals, there is every reason to expect that the United States will continue to fail to use its military to anything approaching maximum strategic advantage. Given that the United States—again, for reasons that, in the abstract, generally are quite sensible—attempts to use its military power to shape the international security environment in an advantageous fashion, this is a very considerable problem in a world of great power competition. As Chapter 6 explains, in a unipolar world the damage that Washington could inflict on itself through imprudence was, in the short to medium term, quite limited as a practical matter. In an environment where the United States must contend with near-peers, however, it faces the possibility of a real and rapid loss of influence, to the benefit of competitors, or even the possibility of a great power war.

Conclusion

American culture, very much including its strategic culture, essentially is optimistic,[20] and this is reflected in much of the strategic analysis of US foreign and defense policy. Although "declineist" works sometimes do have an influence in elite circles,[21] the American orientation toward problem-solving very much is reflected in the foreign policy literature.[22] Diagnosing unpleasant chronic conditions is not a good formula for attaining lasting popularity in Washington, and this likely has been one of the factors undergirding American reluctance to acknowledge its "presidential problem." The mystique surrounding the presidency serves some useful purposes, but it undermines efforts to discuss the US strategic situation cogently.

To assert that the United States confronts a chronic systemic problem in regard to presidential strategic decision making is not, however, to counsel despair. First, Washington *does* have many strengths, and a state with the economic, diplomatic, and military resources of the United States has a very considerable margin for error. This can translate into a critical advantage; strategy is a competitive enterprise, and as noted above in relation to the USSR, America's potential competitors and foes have their own, potentially crippling, weaknesses. Unipolarity is dying, but if the United States is to retain its position as the single greatest power, its leaders need not be perfect in their judgment, or even nearly so.

Nevertheless, chronic underperformance can have a very real—and cumulatively devastating—impact on American power, which obviously would not be desirable for the United States; perhaps even more significantly, it could be grievously detrimental for the world system as whole. The United States plays a critical role in the maintenance of global peace and stability, and its self-marginalization would increase the hazards in a twenty-first century which already promises much danger. A responsible Washington can diminish the level of hazard caused by the rise of other great powers, while at the same time playing a key role in organizing multilateral efforts to deal with terrorism, proliferation, and other general threats.

Greater awareness regarding their country's inherent weaknesses can be very enlightening to American policy makers, and should be of real practical assistance—*when one recognizes systemic flaws, they can be taken into account in planning even if they cannot be solved.* Indeed, given greater discussion of the "presidential strategy problem" and sufficient time—measured, surely, in decades—this systemic flaw may be at least partially corrected by the American electorate.

1 Beyond all expectations

The American rise to preeminence

In the latter years of the eighteenth century, there was little reason to believe that the United States would become one of the world's most significant states. Though physically large, the US population was under four million, well below that of Great Britain and enormously smaller than that of an entity such as Qing China. If one subtracts slaves, who made up somewhat under one-fifth of US residents but were not citizens and did not possess fundamental rights, the US population was even less impressive.

The early United States was an overwhelmingly rural country, its people (again, slaves excepted) relatively prosperous and healthy by European standards, but scattered and rather libertarian in their inclinations. During the Seven Years' War (or, as the North American portion of that conflict is generally known in the United States, the French and Indian War) British governors and army officers had seen, and noted with contempt, the indiscipline of American militiamen and their seeming obsession with their rights—and their willingness to shirk what Britons saw as their lawful duties to their sovereign.[1] While contemporary Prussia demonstrated compellingly that a European state with a relatively small population nonetheless could function as a great power, the latter was located in a geographical position that both obliged it to participate in European controversies and granted Berlin little freedom for error. The American geopolitical position was a far happier one, and the American population, both elite and general, displayed a very un-Prussian attitude toward military prowess.

A huge variety of explanations have been offered for US success, and it very much is worth exploring why the United States attained superpower status when other formerly colonial states which enjoyed their own advantages—Argentina, Brazil, and Mexico being three interesting cases—did not. The purpose herein, however, is not to provide a definitive answer to the question of precisely why the United States was so successful in building its economic and military power.[2] That subject has been explored by many authors, and will always be a matter of debate—though most careful observers likely would agree that there was no single "magic" factor that assured the fortunes of the American polity. It would be reasonable to posit that a variety of governmental,[3] economic, geographic (both human and physical),[4] and other factors provided the foundation for long-term US success. However, regardless of how fortunate the United States was in these terms, its leaders—particularly its presidents—ultimately had to make prudent choices in order for the country to prosper, and the overall American strategic record from the nation's founding to the end of World War II is an enviable one. A brief examination of this history provides useful insight both into the development of US strategic culture and the critical role that key leaders from George Washington onward have played in American strategic history and that polity's attainment of superpower status.

Surviving: independence and state-building

The process of the creation of an American nation actually began long before the founding of the United States. There is no definitive point at which such nation-building began, but a convenient marker would be the establishment, in 1607 and 1620, respectively, of Jamestown in the Virginia Colony and the Plymouth Colony in what later became Massachusetts. (Jamestown, however, was not the first English settlement in what was to become the continental United States—several failed experiments already had been undertaken, beginning in the 1580s.)

Nations ultimately are creatures of the mind, having only as much reality as humans grant them. The nearly two centuries that separated Jametown's founding and the War of Independence provided ample time for the development of a distinct national identity, but so long as the American Colonies remained tied politically to the British crown, this process was very incomplete—and the continuous flow of immigrants from Britain no doubt further retarded the process of American identity creation. However, a sense of American apartness from the Old World developed during this time, though this largely expressed itself in identification with a specific colony rather than with the Colonies as a larger unit. This localism is understandable: British America was a diverse collection of political entities tied together politically by little more than the sovereignty of a geographically distant king.

The War of Independence was the first great strategic "test" that the United States endured. The audacity of the revolutionaries was, in retrospect, stunning: it is rare for elite individuals to be willing to risk so much on an issue of principle (even if many of them no doubt presumed that they would in some way benefit personally from independence), and the Second Continental Congress must be credited for its boldness. Yet, declaring independence was so daring that it would not be altogether unfair to call it injudicious; in the latter eighteenth century, there were few peoples anywhere in the world who were more prosperous and, in practical speaking, freer than the inhabitants of British America. The notion that one should not be taxed without receiving representation in Parliament was eminently defensible intellectually, but a cautious American of the events of 1775–76 reasonably could ask his or her contemporaries whether this and other grievances really were worth war, much less a war against a metropolis which had ruled rather benevolently by the standards of the day.[5]

With the benefit of hindsight—having seen how putatively democratic revolutions such as the French of 1789 and the Russian of 1917, among many others, turned out—prudence certainly would appear appropriate. Whatever the faults of British rule in America, it was not defined by guillotines or gulags. Of course, as the Americans pulled away from Britain, the bloodshed of what might be called the "Age of Ideological Madness" was still in the future; the Founders understood that a republic could degenerate into tyranny, but seem to have possessed little consciousness of the possibility of true mass terror. This perhaps is unsurprising, since past incidents of mass terror in Europe, such as the Albigensian Crusade and the oppression of the Huguenots,[6] typically were linked to religion, and the Revolution was an explicitly secular undertaking. Nevertheless, with the hindsight provided by the following two centuries, the Founders do seem curiously innocent.

Having decided upon its course, the Congress placed its enterprise in the hands of George Washington, appointing him general-in-chief of the Continental Army. Again, the good fortune of the revolutionaries is remarkable; although he was one of the few Americans who also was a fairly well-credentialed military officer, Washington's military career to that point had been uninspired. He began his military life with an embarrassing series of disasters that appears, as best one can reconstruct the incident, to have included involvement in an atrocious war crime: the murder of French prisoners, including a diplomat/officer, by Iroquois tribesmen who (at least nominally) were under his command.[7] Washington apparently was unable to prevent the incident, and certainly did not authorize it—but he subsequently distorted the character of the matter to his superiors, and the massacre resulted in an international scandal. While his subsequent career contained no similarly enormous failures of command responsibility, there was nothing in Washington's personal history to indicate that he was capable of leading an amateurish Continental Army to victory over a highly professional British one. Indeed, Washington never proved himself to be an operational commander of unarguable genius—the American Civil War produced several generals who likely had greater operational talent—though his exceptional strategic vision compensated amply for this weakness.

Washington's performance early in the War of Independence was unimpressive—most notably, in mid-1776 he led the near-catastrophic effort to save New York from British occupation, with the bulk of the Army only barely escaping capture on Long Island. But eventually he came to see that winning battles was far less important for the Americans than was not losing them. So long as the Army endured, the uprising lived, but if it were shattered, the Revolution was lost;[8] the Continental Army was the Revolution's center of gravity. He appears to have intuited that—unlike the Roman Republic, which repeatedly proved capable of generating new armies after Hannibal had destroyed an existing one—the proto-state created by the American revolutionaries was brittle; it lacked the history, customs, and ethno-national consciousness that buttressed Roman resolve in a time of awesome threat. The elites who led the conflict—the revolutionary vanguard, so to speak—might not surrender after a critical military loss, but if Americans in general came to see the rebellion as hopeless, they would not support it.

The most critical problem that Washington faced therefore was not, in the usual sense, a military one. The British could not compel obedience from the Americans because there simply were too many of the latter scattered over far too great a territory and consistent use of state terror—which may or may not have "worked" as a counterinsurgency strategy, but certainly would have transformed the war into a far uglier one—was not, in London's view, a politically acceptable means to direct the behavior of its wayward colonists.[9] Thus, Britain essentially had to rule by (at least passive) consent. Permanent military control of the American Colonies was not tenable financially or politically—Britain theoretically could maintain a large, permanent military force and "occupation" bureaucracy, but doing so would expend resources disproportionate to the perceived value of the Colonies themselves. The British Empire had a worldwide perspective;[10] ultimately, it would be prudent to grant the troublesome Americans independence if doing so permitted London to protect more vital interests elsewhere.[11]

Thus, Washington faced the challenge not of decisively defeating Britain militarily—that was impossible, as Britain could continue fighting indefinitely, if it wished—but to convince Parliament that acknowledging US independence was the most practical solution to a complicated problem. The British government had to be persuaded to accept the Americans' preferred outcome—*in essence, it had to agree to its own defeat.* Time was on the side of the revolutionaries, so long as they did not lose faith in the likelihood of ultimate success—the longer the war continued, the more the nascent American national identity could solidify and the more costs would mount, vexing Parliament and encouraging acceptance of US independence.

Washington understood, long before twentieth century theorists of insurgency argued the point, that even if government forces retained control of major cities this did not necessarily translate into defeat for the revolutionaries[12]—even if, as in the War of Independence, these were also centers of revolutionary agitation. Indeed, control of population centers was a decidedly mixed blessing for British commanders. On the one hand, it deprived the Continental Congress of human and material assets and, vitally, ensured the control of the key Atlantic port facilities necessary for British logistics, but on the other it tied troops down in garrison duties, removing them from the field of battle, where they might contribute to a military decision.

To most of the Revolution's leaders, specific actions by the British government had resulted in a loss of legitimacy and the withdrawal of the Americans' consent to be ruled by Parliament—a vision that owes more to a Lockean conception of the social contract than to a devotion to anti-monarchism as an abstract principle that trumps all others. Thus, although the Declaration of Independence is obviously republican in orientation (its author, after all, was Thomas Jefferson), it chiefly is devoted to indicting, in detail, the wrongs committed by George III and Parliament. Having criticized "the present King of Great-Britain" and laid out his "History of repeated Injuries and Usurpations, all having in direct Object the establishment of an absolute Tyranny over these States,"[13] the signers of the Declaration declared the bond between the British government and the American people dissolved. Strongly implicit in this was the understanding that the new government would not act tyrannically, instead defending the interests and liberties of citizens. As a result, there was no room intellectually for anything like a "dictatorship of the proletariat"—the revolutionaries' ideology was not one that could justify the use of despotic means to attain utopian ends. (Indeed, the Founders lacked utopian goals—they never intended that the old political order would be utterly destroyed and a perfected society constructed in its place. The "City upon a Hill" of American lore is a much earlier Puritan ideal that did not particularly drive the revolutionary generation.) This is a critical point, both because it created a basically level field between insurgents and counterinsurgents in regard to the use of terror and because the self-imposed limitations that the Revolution's leaders accepted go far toward explaining why that event did not degenerate into massacre and authoritarianism (and, therefore, why the United States developed as it did).[14] Terror was alien to the libertarian spirit of the Revolution and its use would destroy that enterprise's intellectual foundation.[15]

The revolutionaries needed to retain a functioning government and army, but it was not critical that the new government take excessive risks to rapidly eject every last British soldier from American soil. Simple possession of territory was not, in the vision laid out in the Declaration, the same as legitimate rule—the British Army, from this perspective, merely was an occupation force, and one that was far too small to fully control US territory. However, at the same time, consistent military losses would have the practical effect of convincing most Americans that the new government was ephemeral, and this perception quickly could become reality—some sense of military progress was necessary if the general public was to retain its support for the enterprise.

Washington thus faced a number of fairly strict intellectual and practical limitations on his actions. Given the "ethics of the revolution" and the temperament of the revolutionaries themselves, the American War of Independence, unlike many civil wars, could not be a near-total conflict. It was, in that regard, *a limited war even from the perspective of the revolutionaries.* While Washington and other key leaders personally could expect to be executed for treason if they failed to win the war, they were unwilling to destroy the society from which they had arisen—the Revolution was intended to create a government better suited to the expression of that society's Enlightenment values, and discarding those principles was not an acceptable price for victory. (This perspective was radically different from, for example, that of a Lenin or Mao, who were not only willing to act in ways contradictory to the standards of their respective societies, but whose projects themselves were intended to undermine traditional Russian and Chinese culture and restructure those societies into something new.[16])

Even after independence was established, the links between the colonies remained weak for some time. The Articles of Confederation was an accurately named document, as it did not create a state as centralized as the United Kingdom, much less France or Prussia. Intriguingly, it says something of the strategic horizons of the American elite that the Articles were so quickly abandoned. Although today there is a tendency simply to dismiss the Articles as utterly unworkable, the United States was not in fact on the point of collapse when the Philadelphia Convention occurred in 1787;[17] indeed, the Convention itself was organized under the pretense that its purpose was merely to revise the Articles, not to construct an entirely new government. The Anti-Federalists were not simply benighted reactionaries, and while history did not bear out some of their warnings—a standing army did not prove as dangerous to liberty as many of them feared—they certainly were more right than wrong in their prophecy that the central government eventually would eclipse the states.

The United States possibly could have survived permanently without a strong central government, although this is by no means certain. Weak polities—and a confederated United States almost certainly would have remained feeble militarily—sometimes have endured for long periods despite having much less favorable geography than the Americans enjoyed. However, without the approval of the Philadelphia Constitution or some other document creating a reasonably robust central government, it is exceedingly unlikely that the United States would have expanded nearly so vigorously; moreover, its fate would have rested much less in its own hands and far more in those of other powers. As it would require colossal naiveté to assume the consistent benevolence of other polities, this should, at minimum, give one pause when considering the eventual fate of a United States governed by the Articles. However, it is not possible to offer a trustworthy conjecture as to how events would have developed if the United States had remained a confederation—the adoption of the US

Constitution happened long ago and impacted global political, military, economic history profoundly. Perhaps the Americans never would have fought a Civil War and enjoyed far more peace and prosperity than actually has been the case—or perhaps the republican experiment eventually would have collapsed altogether, with anarchy followed by tyranny. In any case, the details of recent world history would have been enormously different.

Nevertheless, the rise of the United States to great power status would have been implausible. (In this regard, it is notable that the European Union, an entity in many respects more tightly centralized than the United States under the Articles, has not discovered how to be an effective global actor—Brussels has, heretofore, simply found it impossible to convince Europe's states to transform the Common Foreign and Security Policy into more than an impressive-sounding fiction.[18]) It is not mere coincidence that the great powers of the last two centuries have all been states with strong—sometimes, as in the Soviet case, excessively, and, in the end, self-destructively, strong—central governments capable of ruthlessly marshaling the resources of the nation so as to achieve military victory. A government lacking the capability to do this simply is incapable of functioning as a great power under modern conditions; thus, the acceptance of the Constitution was the second major strategic test that the Founders passed in the US rise to great power status.[19]

Thriving: the early expansion of the republic

The third great strategic test that the early United States faced was a curious one: the decision over whether to accept the French offer to sell Louisiana.[20] The Louisiana proposition was the ultimate outcome of extended diplomatic efforts that initially addressed only the acquisition of New Orleans, and strategic opportunities as immense as the one which Napoleon provided to Jefferson are exceedingly rare.

In retrospect, it may seem bizarre that there was any opposition whatsoever to the Louisiana Purchase—even in 1803 dollars, fifteen million was a modest price for a vast, resource-rich expense of territory—but, in the context of the politics of the time, it was understandable. There was a legitimate question as to whether the Constitution authorized the federal government to make such a purchase—and apparent hypocrisy on the part of Jefferson, who normally was given to a very limited view of federal power, but found himself defending the purchase's constitutionality.[21] (In addition, although of lesser importance, the acquisition of Louisiana also presented various practical legal and military problems, particularly concerning Spanish territorial claims, for the Jefferson administration.[22]) Federalist opposition to the Purchase is explicable when regional politics—and particularly the balance of the slave and non-slave states and the (entirely realistic) fear that new slave states would be carved out of Louisiana—is taken into account.

The first issue underscores Jefferson's intellectual courage in deciding to buy Louisiana. By nature more a *philosophe* given to abstractions than a practical politician, Jefferson placed a great value on ideology as a guide to action. To Jefferson's credit, he did not allow these issues to paralyze his decision making.[23] As he acknowledged, the Purchase was not within the bounds of his vision of the president's usual Constitutionally granted powers.[24] (Over time, the two elected branches have ceded constitutional interpretation to the Supreme Court, but it was not Jefferson's view that it was appropriate or healthy for the Court to have a monopoly in this area.) This highlights one of the most intellectually uncomfortable realities of leadership in a democracy—the frequent clash between legal, in this case constitutional, limits on leaders and the need to act in defense of state interests.

Inevitably, legal restrictions impose strategic costs—they, in effect, are a tax on foreign policy opportunities, as they limit the ability of leaders to pursue national gains. The obvious alternative is, however, not really acceptable in the American political system—allowing presidents to use *raison d'etat* as an all-purpose trump card that frees them to take any action they wish would destroy accountability, effectively releasing the Executive from the rule of law and investing it with unrestrained power.[25] A president enjoys near-complete control over the federal government's means of coercion—the military and intelligence services, the federal police apparatus, and so forth; therefore, the major external constraints on his or her power are law and custom (and the development of the latter is largely dependent on the former). Thus, there is a very strong case that respect for legal constraints on the president's power are vitally important.

Realistically, however, a president cannot always be limited in his or her actions to what a strict reading of the law would authorize, as he or she would be so tightly bound as to be enfeebled in the conduct of foreign policy. The cost of bypassing some strategic opportunities for the sake of legal rectitude is likely to be small, and in the great majority of matters it is entirely appropriate that presidents bow to law and custom. Yet, some opportunities are so rare (or some threats so great) that a president who would choose strict legality over action would be, at best, guilty of pharisaism—and such a leader would be dangerous to the polity, which would suffer for the sake of the president's ethical comfort. Thus, a responsible president is confronted with the problem of balancing law and executive duty, as Jefferson, in a famous letter to John B. Colvin, argues:

> The question you propose, whether circumstances do not sometimes occur, which make it a duty in officers of high trust, to assume authorities beyond the law, is easy of solution in principle, but sometimes embarrassing in practice. A strict observance of the written laws is doubtless *one* of the high duties of a good citizen, but it is not *the highest*. The laws of necessity, of self-preservation, of saving our country

> when in danger, are of higher obligation. To lose our country by a scrupulous adherence to the written law, would be to lose the law itself, with life, liberty, property and all those who are enjoying them with us; thus absurdly sacrificing the ends to the means.... [The examples cited by Jefferson in his letter] do not go to the case of persons charged with petty duties, where consequences are trifling, and time allowed for a legal course, nor to authorize them to take such cases out of the written law. In these, the example of overleaping the law is of greater evil than a strict adherence to its imperfect provisions. It is incumbent on those only who accept of great charges, to risk themselves on great occasions, when the safety of the nation, or some of its very high interests are at stake. An officer is bound to obey orders; yet he would be a bad one who should do it in cases for which they were not intended, and which involved the most important consequences. The line of discrimination between cases may be difficult; but the good officer is bound to draw it at his own peril, and throw himself on the justice of his country and the rectitude of his motives.[26]

Jefferson's principle is a practical and simple one: government's "officers of high trust" sometimes must make difficult decisions, but do so at their "own peril," albeit with the understanding that appropriate and public-spirited actions should not be penalized.[27]

This is an admirably Spartan point of view, placing responsibility with those who have accepted it while also recognizing that not every vigorous use of executive power is an assault on the Constitution. (The latter seems to be the perspective held by some would-be defenders of civil liberties who, lacking discernment, are inclined to see even the slightest evidence of presidential energy as evidence that the United States is transforming into an Orwellian police state.[28]) At the same time, it protects the citizenry from armies of overzealous minor officials who would present a much greater practical threat to civil liberty than could a small number of high Executive branch officials acting under the scrutiny of the Congress, judiciary, and media. Applying Jefferson's prudent rule to the "Louisiana question," it is clear that he made the right decision—whatever practical problems and constitutional hazards accompanied the acquisition of that territory were far outweighed by the opportunities presented.

Slavery, territorial consolidation, and external conquest

Clearly, the existence of slavery did much to drive a wedge between the northern and southern portions of the United States, even from an early point in the country's history. The politics of slavery shaped profoundly the domestic context in which all early US strategic decisions were made. Indeed, one even could argue that the failure to abolish slavery immediately upon independence was the first great strategic misstep of the United

States government—but, however tempting this judgment might be, it is not a reasonable one for the simple reason that strategic success must be judged in light of what is plausible, not what would occur in an idealized, "frictionless" strategic environment.

Clearly, it would have been enormously desirable both ethically and strategically if the United States had abolished slavery when independence was declared. It is, however, not possible to devise a realistic scenario in which this might have occurred in the context of a revolutionary separatist movement encompassing all thirteen of the original states. In the historical circumstances in which the Revolution occurred, a compromise on slavery was virtually inevitable. Many Americans thought slavery to be vile—even many slaveholders thought the institution to be an evil that eventually would pass away—but abolitionism was not yet a powerful movement that deeply moved millions, as it would become in the nineteenth century. (Indeed, US independence would do much to shape the American abolitionist movement—those who might once have merely had a distaste for chattel slavery but considered its existence outside their own colony a matter beyond their control were empowered by national democratic institutions to oppose slavery at the federal level.)

When confronted with the practical decision of whether to further the cause of independence by making concessions to colonies with slaveholding elites or stand on anti-slavery principle even at the price of (likely fatally) undermining the cause of independence, those among the Founders who might have favored complete abolition made the practical decision to appease slaveholders. This was an unsavory option, but the alternative would have sabotaged national independence while doing nothing directly to aid those held in slavery. Nevertheless, the tolerance of the institution of slavery *was* intellectually irreconcilable with a state based on an Enlightenment conception of liberty—though many thinkers tried to, somehow, fit the two pieces together. This inherent contradiction demanded eventual resolution: either American ideology would modify key founding principles to accept the permanent presence of slavery,[29] or the institution would have to be abolished.[30]

Two unpleasant realities that inevitably have accompanied the creation of great polities historically are violent consolidation of the state's territory and the assertive use of military power. In the American case, as in that of many other countries (Australia, Canada, Mexico, and Russia, for example),[31] the two processes are not altogether separable because political consolidation included the organization of territory that already contained indigenous populations who had de facto political control of the land on which they lived,[32] but did not have an internationally recognized legal right to possess that territory.[33] In essence, the United States conquered itself, with the internationally recognized government slowly eliminating independent tribal polities that existed on its territory. However, again as in numerous other countries, the government did not completely eradicate every vestige of tribal rule; in the American case, treaties were signed and reservations with quasi-sovereign tribal governments were created, although—as in the infamous events of the Trail of Tears—the federal government did not always respect the territorial and other rights conferred legally on tribal governments.

This process of internal consolidation involved a substantial use of violence over numerous decades (indeed, centuries, when one considers that it started long before US independence). Tribes often were unwilling to turn over land to the US federal government, which, quite understandably, they saw as a foreign entity intent on the theft of that which they valued most. The fact that these rival political claims resulted in warfare is both tragic and unsurprising.

Indeed, the internal conquest of the United States is simply a variation on a story that has played out thousands of times throughout the world, including in pre-Columbian North America: a militarily powerful political entity demanding that apparently weaker ones submit to its will; when full obedience is not forthcoming, the strong polity attempts (in the US case, very successfully) to use violence to enforce its will. However, the fact that the stronger political unit happened to be a modern state and the weaker ones were organized into tribes was highly significant in determining the military details of the conflict.

Contrary to popular mythology, modern archeology has made it increasingly clear that pre-Columbian North America was an arena of frequent military conflict—and there is mounting evidence that most tribal peoples worldwide frequently engaged in conflict, and that their wars sometimes even are, by any reasonable definition of the term, genocidal.[34] The United States government did not introduce conflict to previously peaceful soil; rather, it was uniquely effective militarily because it was a modern state. As such, it possessed a complex bureaucratic apparatus and the ability to marshal enormous resources for the attainment of long-term goals.

The fact that American forces employed higher technology than their foes occasionally is cited as the reason for US military success against the various tribes of North America, but this is oversimplified and broadly inaccurate. Because of their hunting and military value, firearms became increasingly common Native American possessions, particularly after assembly-line techniques were introduced that greatly decreased the cost of both rifle and pistol production; thus, tribes facing the US Army often were fairly well-armed. At the 1879 Battle of Little Bighorn, for example, some of Crazy Horse's men carried repeating rifles (although others had outmoded muzzle-loaders or bows); Custer's soldiers, in contrast, were issued single-shot Springfield carbines and Colt pistols.[35] The US Army did possess a permanent lead in some areas, such as the use of artillery, but given the tactics and terrain of the Indian Wars, this did not offer a decisive military edge.

In larger political-strategic terms, however, the US government enjoyed an incalculable advantage: the fact that the Native American tribes found it impossible politically to unite as one. Given that the US government presented an existential challenge to all the tribes, threatening not only to end their existence as fully independent political actors but to undermine their cultures, this failure to unify may seem odd. However, given the character of tribal politics, it is not only comprehensible, but unsurprising. The very notion that all the American Indian tribes formed part of a greater whole is a modern outsider's perspective, and it is as fundamentally misleading in many respects as the idea the Koreans, Turkmen, and Syrians are all a single people because they are all Asian. As one would expect, the tribes of North America—and, especially, bands within tribes—were relatively fluid: they would split, combine, be wiped out, and otherwise change, sometimes rapidly. This left some maneuver room for charismatic leaders who could create pan-tribal confederations—Tecumseh created perhaps the most important of these, and he made a serious effort to craft it into an independent and permanent state. However, as a practical matter it was difficult to keep many tribes united in a common cause, or even to keep individual tribes from ripping apart over questions of alliance and resistance. As Daniel Walker Howe notes,

> The call of the Shawnee brothers, Tecumseh and Tenskwatawa ("the Prophet"), for united Native resistance against the encroaching white settlers had been sufficiently successful to bring on widespread frontier race war beginning in 1811, but not successful enough to form durable pan-tribal cooperation. Tecumseh carried the message of militancy and traditionalism to the Southwest as well as the Northwest, and in both areas it divided tribes internally.[36]

By the time there was enough of a sense of shared common interest across tribes that a unified front focused on the settler menace was conceivable, effective resistance was very difficult—the process of internal political consolidation was well underway and the Indians formed only a modest percentage of the overall US population.

In essence, the disunited tribes simply lacked the ability to inflict sufficient military pain on the US government to coerce it to alter its policies greatly and grant a truly huge concession, such as recognizing the independence of a fully sovereign American Indian country consisting of much of the West. Tecumseh perhaps came closest to realizing this vision—the War of 1812 provided a favorable context, and his British ally was amenable to creation of such a buffer country, but he was killed in battle in 1813 and his confederation soon thereafter surrendered to the Americans. It is, however, probably unlikely that Tecumseh would have been able to craft an enduring state even if he had lived and the US government was willing to sign a peace treaty recognizing such an entity. An ephemeral triumph would not have altered underlying strategic conditions that were, from an Indian perspective, deeply inhospitable.

Even the larger individual tribes simply were far too small to compete militarily against the US government. The greatest disaster of the Indian Wars for the Army occurred at Little Bighorn, and its human cost on the US side was well under three hundred dead. Losing that number of warriors would have been devastating even for the largest tribes—and minor tribes simply did not have that many fighting-age males. By comparison, less than two decades earlier, the Union and Confederate Armies were conducting battles in which each suffered thousands of fatalities—and over the course of the conflict the two sides endured more than 600,000 military deaths (including both combat and disease) in total.

Given the structural advantages that the United States enjoyed, it is unsurprising that no president's Indian Wars policy stands out as being particularly key to eventual US consolidation of political control of its territory. Leaving all ethical considerations aside, it ultimately would probably have made little difference to the long-term strategic health of the United States if Andrew Jackson had not pressured the Cherokees into signing the Treaty of New Echota,[37] or if President Grant—a man who, unsurprisingly, possessed a good eye for military talent—had not placed General George Crook in various positions where his abilities as a skilled guerrilla fighter and diplomat were put to good use.[38] Instead, what is notable about the first 100 years and more of US policy toward the American Indians is its continuity. It perhaps is the clearest American example of a long-term US grand strategy in action.

Particularly from the Jacksonian era onward, the treatment of the Indians was perennially controversial, and many Americans, both in the elite and the general public, believed actions such as Cherokee removal and the launching of the Second Seminole War in 1835 to be immoral.[39] However, there were powerful forces, ideological, demographic, and financial, driving ongoing expansion into tribally controlled territory. Indeed, when it did try to prevent settlers from moving onto tribal territory, the government often was unsuccessful, and squatters in a given area could transform very quickly into a powerful interest group demanding both physical protection and legal recognition of their land claims. This, in turn proved to be a vital component in a potent, though always controversial, grand strategy: the US government, year by year, would extend its control over an ever-increasing amount of previously Indian-controlled land and consolidate that control over time, transforming peripheral frontier regions into full states within the Union. Sometimes it operationalized the first part of this strategy blatantly and violently, as in the Second Seminole War, but often it did so passively: light policing of the frontier and an unwillingness to disallow the claims of white settlers to Indian lands subtly extended the territory under full US government control. Both the active and passive measures pushed the Indians westward—often onto lands already occupied by tribes quite unwilling to consent to share them with newcomers. It of course was entirely predictable that many American Indian leaders would be unwilling to accept such treatment and instead would choose to protect their land claims through war.

Over the decades of internal consolidation, however, very few Americans actually analyzed US policy so straightforwardly—but a grand strategy can exist even if its underlying premises were rarely discussed. Critically, acceptance of the general goal of political consolidation of the national territory was deeply ingrained in the strategic culture. Indeed, even those leaders who abhorred the treatment of the Indians were entirely unwilling to do what would have been necessary to prevent the acquisition of Indian land: placing a heavy, permanent (and expensive) military presence on the frontier for the purpose of arresting, and when necessary fighting, white squatters, and levying a heavy judicial punishment on illegal settlement. Furthermore, the maintenance of *true* tribal political independence would have required recognition of the Indian nations as fully sovereign countries with complete legal control over their territories. Both of these steps were far beyond the realm of popular political acceptability for a myriad of reasons.

Effectively, the United States government and its citizens were in agreement that, using a mixture of active and passive measures, vast portions of the North American continent in due course would be conquered. While there was some flexibility as to precisely how this would come about and what concessions would be granted to the tribes, the grand strategy—pushing westward, establishing "civilized" settlements and restricting the aboriginal population to relatively small patches of territory over which the US government would exercise ultimate political control, was grindingly implacable and, ultimately, hugely successful.

US policy in regard to external expansion was far more dependent on contingency and individual presidential leadership. Although most of the US elite did maintain general expansionist goals—for instance, there was an oft-expressed desire to create a state of continental size stretching from the Atlantic to the Pacific Oceans—specifically how the United States would achieve its objectives was open. While the policy of internal consolidation made regular warfare with various tribes unavoidable, there was considerable disagreement over how belligerent the United States should be toward recognized states such as the British and Spanish Empires and, after its independence from Spain, Mexico. It is almost certain that, if different individuals had held office during the nineteenth century, the size and shape of the United States would today be profoundly different.

James K. Polk shaped the strategic geography of the United States more profoundly than any other president save Jefferson and Lincoln (the latter because he prevented the permanent division of the United States into two polities), yet his presidency is discussed relatively infrequently today.[40] Part of this no doubt stems from embarrassment: unlike Jefferson's peaceful real estate transaction with Napoleon or Lincoln's war against a slaveholding Confederacy, it is difficult to argue convincingly that Polk's conquest of Upper Mexico was anything short of predatory.

Yet, although the Mexican–American War often is oversimplified and treated as a straightforward, one-sided conflict, it actually was more nuanced—although it most certainly was, on the US side, an opportunistic war of conquest.[41] Critically, the Mexican government was extremely unstable, with a revolving cast of contenders for power vying against each other, a situation that encouraged reckless and nationalistic saber-rattling after the United States annexed the Republic of Texas. (Indeed, the conflict's first shots were fired by Mexican troops shooting at American soldiers who were attempting to enforce the highly questionable US claim that the Rio Grande was the border between the two countries.) Polk would have preferred simply to purchase vast tracts of Mexican territory, and he unsuccessfully attempted to do so, but he also was perfectly willing to go to war for Upper Mexico if it could not be acquired by purchase.

To Mexico's misfortune, many of its early post-independence leaders were self-interested schemers; General (and, on numerous occasions, President) Antonio López de Santa Anna is particularly notable for his unattractive combination of veniality and questionable military competence. Santa Anna actually was in exile in Cuba when the war with the United States began, but was allowed to return home and given command of an army by the Mexican government. Upon his return to Mexico, Santa Anna promptly, and illegally, declared himself president. He then proceeded to lose the Battle of Buena Vista to a much smaller force commanded by General Zachary Taylor—an event that likely was responsible for Taylor's later election to the US presidency—and, subsequently, organized a disastrously failed defense of Mexico City.

In terms of leadership, the United States of 1846 was considerably more fortunate than Mexico: President Polk was an icy strategist of considerable natural talent and General Winfield Scott, the conqueror of Mexico City, was one of the most impressive military figures of the nineteenth century.[42] However, Polk's adventure nevertheless could have been disastrous. The Mexican Army was a force of substantial size, though not particularly well-equipped—its deficiencies in regard to artillery would prove especially important. Nonetheless, it did have strengths: its cavalry was highly regarded,[43] and Mexican soldiers of course possessed an excellent knowledge of their country's geography and had good access to intelligence provided by friendly civilians. Bringing the war to an acceptable conclusion would require American forces to operate at the far extreme of their logistics capability, with units often marching through merciless and thinly inhabited enemy territory. Although the war proved that the Mexican Army had critical weaknesses, it probably was sufficiently competent and motivated that inspired leadership could have welded it into a highly effective defensive force: Mexican forces commanded by a figure comparable to Scott might have turned the desert into a graveyard for US units that were cut off logistically and herded into unfavorable terrain. As events actually transpired, however, the United States endured only a very moderate number of fatalities—about 13,000, a solid majority of these lost to disease, not enemy action.

Support for, and opposition to, the war largely was divided on a party-line basis. Democrats—with some exceptions, including John C. Calhoun—supported Polk's war, but most Whigs, including Illinois Representative Abraham Lincoln, were highly critical of the conflict. This opposition largely resulted from the perception that the war was aggressive in character, but perhaps an even more important issue was whether it might expedite the further extension of slavery (the radically pro-slavery Calhoun, unlike most of his contemporaries, both Northern and Southern, believed that the war was, over the long term, likely to endanger slavery). Both during and after the war that institution's proponents and opponents struggled fiercely over slavery's spread into newly acquired US territory.[44] Such questions were complicated by the fact that there were anti-slavery Democrats—such as the Barnburner wing of the New York Democratic Party—as well as pro-slavery Whigs.

The split over the war nonetheless was symptomatic of differences far deeper than mere partisan competition or even a philosophical disagreement over external military aggression. Rather, it was indicative of a growing sense that slavery was *the* defining issue in the United States—and this was making national unity increasingly uncertain. As noted above, from independence onward slavery had been a real (though, initially, largely dormant) strategic issue for the United States; over time it came to dominate American politics, including even discussions of foreign war.[45] In the years leading up to the Civil War, the controversy over slavery would fundamentally alter the political landscape, playing a key role in the implosion of the Whigs, the reshaping of the Democrats, and the rise of the new Republican Party.

In retrospect, it is clear that, despite the desperate efforts of both pro- and anti-slavery politicians, this issue was not one that forever could be contained by compromise. The growth of abolitionism into a potent movement that mainly was religious in its character and the increasingly shrill rhetoric of slavery's advocates, and their own appeal to religion, had created an ideological split as profound in its way as those which caused the Russian and Spanish Civil Wars.[46]

Events since the fall of the USSR have led many observers to associate civil conflict chiefly with ethnic and religious differences, and, certainly, one or both of these concerns have played a defining role in many of the world's civil wars; indeed, two quite divergent interpretations of Christianity's instructions to its followers were fundamental to the US Civil War.[47] However, ideological differences over slavery encompassed far more than questions of religious interpretation (and Caucasian Northerners and

Southerners did not quite see each other as belonging to different ethnicities, at least in any usual sense).[48] As time passed, the intellectual chasm grew progressively deeper—a common occurrence in ideological conflicts, as the theoreticians on each side define the differences between the two sides ever more finely. At the time of the Civil War, the abolitionist argument continued to have an essentially religious and (to use the modern terminology) human rights character. Defenses of slavery, however, over time increasingly had come to convey a civilizational perspective, with authors contending that slavery, or an institution quite akin to slavery, was necessary for the creation and maintenance of a good society.[49]

Examined in this light, it is clear that the United States faced an "existential decision" in the mid-nineteenth century—its Northern and Southern populations had rallied behind profoundly opposed visions of the character of a proper democratic polity. Although they shared many commonalities, and even mutually revered many of the same political heroes, this ideological split was profound. Opponents of slavery no longer would accept that which they had tolerated in the late eighteenth century,[50] while slaveholders—many of whom had, at the time of American independence, themselves been embarrassed by the institution and hoped that it would gradually fade away—had come to embrace human bondage as virtuous and natural. It is extremely difficult to see how these perspectives could have been reconciled through peaceful means.

"Normal" politics is predicated on the assumption that the parties involved are not so deeply opposed that cooperation is impractical. This model, however, breaks down when the factions in question are unwilling or unable to compromise. One of the most dangerous clichés relating to great controversies is that if opponents would only sit down and exchange views they would come to understand each other and choose to resolve their differences peacefully. In fact, many of history's most vicious conflicts have occurred between foes that were on quite familiar terms. The abolitionists and slavery defenders were metaphorically (and sometimes literally) kinsmen. They knew each other well and, increasingly, wished to kill each other. Finally, in Kansas in the 1850s, the two sides began to spill blood in earnest.[51]

A near-death experience: the Civil War

The survival of the United States as a single political entity was a close issue. This is not to say that Washington did not enjoy enormous advantages over Richmond; in most areas, the Northern edge over its foe was considerable, if not overwhelming. In terms of population, industrial capacity (including potential military production), miles of railroad track and amount of rolling stock, gold reserves and other financial resources, and even production of food (the South grew surprisingly little, as so much of its agricultural output was devoted to inedible products such as cotton, indigo, and tobacco), the government of the United States enjoyed major advantages.[52]

Even Southern generalship, often credited as largely making up for the Confederacy's deficiencies in other areas, arguably did not provide Richmond with any great advantage. Though there were some extraordinary general officers in the Confederate Army,[53] there also were some quite poor ones, a fact that had a major impact on the course of the war. The disastrous Confederate efforts in the West in 1862–63 largely can be attributed to uninspired generalship—and a commander-in-chief, President Jefferson Davis, who was unwilling or unable to force his subordinates to adopt a disciplined strategic vision.[54]

The South's "mission" in the Civil War was an essentially passive one—it merely needed to survive in order to triumph.[55] While, from the perspective of the Confederate States of America (CSA), an ideal outcome to the struggle would have included reparations for war damage and similar Northern concessions, as well as referenda or other measures which would give the Border States the option to "change their minds" and join the Confederacy, these were decidedly secondary issues. The first and most critical task of the CSA was to endure, and many in the North were willing to continence the South's independence. The reasons for this were eclectic, with individual motivations ranging from personal sympathy with the South, to the belief that any state had a right to withdraw from the United States and that using force to maintain the Union would be unconstitutional, to simple, sincere pacifism. Regardless of the reason why a given Northerner might accept Confederate independence, however, such an individual was furthering Richmond's interests, as the CSA would achieve its main policy objective if Washington stopped fighting the war.

Given the political conditions in which the secession crisis of 1860–61 occurred, it was entirely possible that poor presidential leadership ultimately would have resulted in Confederate independence. The closing months of the Buchanan presidency attest to this: as the United States was falling apart, Buchanan proved utterly incapable of effectively addressing the crisis; moreover, when Lincoln took office there was little reason for confidence in his strategic acumen. The new president was inexperienced in military matters—aside from, nearly thirty years earlier, briefly serving as a militia captain in the Black Hawk War, a conflict in which he had not seen combat. Moreover, he had very little national government experience of any kind. Lincoln only had served a single term in Congress and never had occupied an Executive branch position; in the main, his professional experience consisted of being an attorney and a state legislator. In résumé terms, Abraham Lincoln was one of the most ill-prepared presidents in American history. Fortunately, however, he possessed enormous natural strategic talent—though few had anticipated this, for the simple reason that he had never been called upon to exercise his abilities in a position of great responsibility.

Jefferson Davis, in contrast, hardly could have been better prepared for the presidency of the Confederacy; he had graduated from West Point, served with distinction under fire as a colonel in the Mexican-American War, held seats in both houses of Congress, and, perhaps most importantly, served four years as US secretary of war.[56] Moreover, Davis had been regarded as having been a very capable occupant of the latter post, and had only left the position in 1857, so his knowledge of military affairs was both deep and current. Davis, however, was an "anti-Lincoln"—though his past experience indicated that he would be a brilliant war leader, he proved both to be an inadequate grand strategist and a rather poor manager of his subordinate commanders.[57]

The juxtaposition of Lincoln and Davis illuminates one of the key truths of strategy, one that Carl von Clausewitz, among many others, attempts to grapple with: the role of strategic "genius" in determining the outcome of war.[58] Ultimately, it is impossible to predict how talented a commander-in-chief will prove to be. A sparkling résumé is a positive indicator, certainly, but past experience provides no ironclad assurances, especially as there is a very real difference between various levels of command, and the chasm between supreme command and any subordinate position is greatest of all.[59] On many occasions, officers who proved to be capable commanders at, say, the divisional level have failed when granted larger responsibilities; similarly, an excellent administrator of a peacetime Department of War might be an inadequate Confederate commander-in-chief. Genius—strategic or otherwise—is unpredictable.[60]

Lincoln's latent strategic genius is explainable at least in part by the power of his mind, which Eliot Cohen accurately describes as "subtle and cunning."[61] His intelligence is displayed clearly in his writings, which are the product of a man possessing both considerable practical insight and a philosophical inclination—a good combination for a president facing the dissolution of the Union, which was at its core a crisis of political philosophy, not a simple matter of military aggression. Lincoln's logical and literary skills are all the more impressive when one considers that he was almost entirely self-educated—lacking even a solid grammar school education, much less a university one, he nonetheless was capable of authoring the Gettysburg Address. Lincoln's intelligence alone does not, however, explain his strategic acumen—one can be both highly intelligent and strategically obtuse. Lincoln possessed, in addition to simple good judgment, which is a command attribute not to be despised, impressive clarity in his strategic vision; he had the ability to separate those factors which were critical to victory from those which were not.

As a grand strategist Lincoln possessed what Clausewitz calls *coup d'oeil*—in essence, the ability to examine a situation, understand its character, and see the way to victory. Clausewitz clarifies that the term is particularly useful in reference to tactical matters—such as Napoleon's ability to look at a battlefield and intuit how victory could be achieved[62]—the concept is applicable to strategy as well.[63] *Coup d'oeil* is an aspect of strategic genius, and the intellectual clarity that it gave Lincoln was of immeasurable value. Because Lincoln understood the nature of the problem that his administration faced, he was able to serve as a solid core to the war effort, and refused to deviate from his course despite the military and human costs: Lincoln's war policy, in its fundamentals, did not change from the beginning of the war to Lee's surrender. Unwillingness to deviate from one's course is not, in itself, proof of wisdom—indeed, persisting in folly would be quite the opposite. However, the fact that Lincoln was right so early, despite his almost complete inexperience, and then resisted constant, powerful temptations to alter his course (particularly those resulting from the human cost of the war, which clearly weighed on him) is deeply impressive.

After his election, Lincoln put his mental resources to the goal of understanding military matters, and he did so largely through the reading of books, as well as soliciting information from advisors and observing the evolving crisis with his characteristic thoughtfulness. He became conversant in military affairs generally, and penetrated to the heart of the strategic problem that his government faced—how to use its superior resources to compel Southern surrender as speedily as possible.

Much to his credit, Lincoln was not indecisive and did not seek compromise or mediation—throughout the war, he never signaled an interest in any outcome short of surrender by the rebellious states. This is largely taken for granted now, but it is important to understand that Lincoln had a range of options at his disposal, many of which—such as a call for a ceasefire and negotiations—would have squandered valuable time and called the US government's dedication to victory into question. Lincoln had an excellent intuitive understanding of strategy, one far superior to that of those international leaders who negotiate artful arrangements intended to resolve complex problems like the Israeli-Palestinian struggle and then are surprised when they discover that their diplomatic bandage has not resolved the underlying problem—and then repeat the entire process over again, seemingly learning nothing from repeated failure. Such actions are the product of an unwillingness to acknowledge that *some strategic problems cannot, as a practical matter, be resolved peacefully unless one side is willing to (formally or at least de facto) surrender.* In contrast, Lincoln correctly intuited that the choice that he faced was, in the end, simple: either he could fight to maintain a United States organized along the lines of his Constitutional vision (in which it was a perpetual Union from which no state could withdraw) or surrender to the Confederate desire for independence.

From a Lincolnian perspective, any outcome that substantially changed the character of the Union would have represented a catastrophic defeat for the US government, as it would have altered profoundly the constitutional order. Conversely, any acceptable outcome acceptable to the

Lincoln administration would result in the dissolution of the Confederacy. Such a gap in the interests was too wide to resolve peacefully, and any US government attempt to do so would have been a fool's errand.

Lincoln of course succeeded in preserving the Union, and as a result his country both survived its most dangerous nineteenth century crisis intact and settled a good deal of outstanding strategic business. Throughout its existence, the possibility of splintering always had presented a potentially fatal threat to the United States. Indeed, the Civil War was not even the first time that the United States seriously confronted the possibility of dissolution: in the War of 1812, notably, a reasonably serious secession movement had existed in the Northeast. However, the CSA's downfall settled decisively the question of whether states would be allowed to withdraw from the Union. Moreover, the contradiction between the Enlightenment principles central to American ideology and the existence of slavery was resolved (although racial injustice of course did not end).

The United States which emerged from the Civil War was markedly different from its antebellum predecessor. Post-Civil War America unquestionably possessed many of the attributes that one might associate with a great power to be reckoned with, including one of the world's most advanced industrial economies and an enormous, battle-tested Army. Washington did have some deficiencies—it needed a large and modern ocean-going Navy if it was to participate fully into political affairs in Eurasia, but these problems were correctable, given the size of both the US economy and population.

Nonetheless, during the mid-nineteenth century the United States did not choose to leverage its considerable assets so as to become an active great power. America returned to its traditional focus, continuing its internal consolidation, remaining generally aloof from European political affairs and choosing not to participate energetically in the global scramble for colonies. This reserve was prudent.

Holding fire: American reluctance to join the great powers

Because of its geographic position, the United States had the unusual luxury of facing relatively little threat from the great powers of the eighteenth century. Unlike a European state—particularly one facing a plausible threat of invasion—the United States could dare to spend relatively little on defense. Indeed, with the exception of a few periods of military emergency, particularly the Civil War itself, the degree to which the US government minimized defense expenditure is striking.

Although today reference to an American "national security state" is common, throughout most of its history the US government was far from militarized; even the Civil War did not mark a permanent break from that national habit. Because Reconstruction required substantial numbers of occupation troops, the US military was unusually large for several years following the Civil War, but as the Reconstruction process wound down, preexisting traits in American strategic culture were reasserted and the US military shrunk back to a size comparable to that of a third-tier European power.

Especially given the global role that the United States performs today, US strategic choices in the latter nineteenth century may appear odd to current observers. It is, after all, unusual for a state possessing the wherewithal to act as a great power simply to refuse to exercise that status, and for the Americans to continue to turn their backs on the politics of the "corrupt" Old World may seem provincial and unsophisticated—a crude assertion of American exceptionalism and a tribute to the continuing power of the seventeenth century conception of an America morally superior to the European world of squabbling princes; having cleansed themselves of the sin of slavery, the Americans could return to the righteous business of building the New Jerusalem. However, while there is perhaps a little truth in such an analysis—exceptionalism certainly did shape American intellectual life and behavior—it oversimplifies grossly US strategic culture and ignores the benefits of American reticence. Indeed, there is a compelling argument that "strategic precociousness"—particularly, seeking to become involved in great power controversies and influence European politics—would have been counterproductive to US interests over the long term.

Given the continuing American interest in obtaining territory and the character of the times, the most plausible way in which the United States might have entered the world of great power competition shortly after the Civil War would have been as a participant in the ongoing colonial free-for-all, even if, after the costly bloodletting of the early 1860s, there was little public demand for foreign military adventures. After all, it was assumed by many (though by no means all) French and British leaders that national health required constant overseas expansion. Statesmen from more landward-looking powers—such as Prussia/Germany's admirably level-headed Otto von Bismarck—tended to be somewhat less vulnerable to the mania for global acquisition. Given the geographic location of the United States, and its cultural affiliation with Britain, it would appear natural for the Americans to adopt a British viewpoint and join the Victorian imperial scramble; however, Washington was a relatively cautious and unenthusiastic imperial power. Nevertheless, some US leaders did nurse overseas colonial ambitions, and these were intertwined with the beginning of American engagement in great power politics.[64]

The Spanish–American War of 1898 often is treated as the beginning of American involvement in great power politics, and this essentially is accurate. Although there was a degree of ambiguity in the circumstances leading to the conflict—and the actual cause for the sinking of the battleship *Maine* remains a matter of debate—it was, in its essence, an imperial enterprise.[65] The conflict was a particularly interesting one in that it featured two states in very different stages in their "life cycles." Spain was a faded great power holding onto its few remaining overseas possessions in a foredoomed effort to maintain the pretense that it remained a global power. For the Americans, by contrast, defeating Spain both followed the general logic of the Monroe Doctrine and would constitute persuasive evidence of the great power status of the United States.[66]

The Monroe Doctrine had served the United States very well as a "strategic roadmap" since its enunciation in 1823. In its original iteration, the Doctrine declared that the American government would oppose any effort by a European power to recolonize countries in the Americas that had gained their independence. Spain very much was in mind when the Doctrine was promulgated. Madrid had only recently recognized the independence of states such as Argentina and Mexico, and the possibility of a Franco-Spanish effort—perhaps also supported by Austria, Prussia, and Russia—to recolonize Latin America was a matter of concern both to Washington and London. The British government approached the Americans about the possibility of jointly opposing any such effort. However, Monroe was convinced, largely by the arguments of Secretary of State (and future President) John Quincy Adams, that the United States should issue its own policy statement.

The United States of course had no real capability—or, in truth, inclination—to enforce the Doctrine militarily; the Royal Navy did far more than the US government to dissuade Franco-Spanish adventurism in the years immediately after the pronouncement of the Doctrine. Yet, over the long term, the Doctrine was much more critical to American than to British interests. As Britain increasingly withdrew militarily and politically from the New World—a development made possible by the declining significance of the Caribbean possessions to the overall British Empire and, particularly, Britain's success in essentially driving France, its great seapower rival, from the New World—the United States crept closer to attaining hegemony in the Americas.[67] In the latter eighteenth century, as competition for imperial acquisition became increasingly heated, the European states—including Britain, which wished to avoid any unnecessary confrontation with the United States—were fairly respectful of the Doctrine. The continuing independence of the former colonies of Latin America certainly should not be attributed solely, or even chiefly, to the Monroe Doctrine—Latin American state-building and, as time passed, an increasingly universal acceptance that the former colonies were fully legitimate states, were more important. However, the French effort to turn Mexico into a satellite state is instructive.

French intervention in Mexico began in January 1861 as a cooperative expedition with Spain and Britain to force the government of Benito Juárez to resume interest payments that the latter had suspended. Such vigorous debt collection by European powers was fairly common in the nineteenth century, but the British and Spanish withdrew from the effort in April, after it became clear that Napoleon III had much larger ambitions in Mexico. The French Army went on to fight a war of some size, eventually taking Mexico City in June 1863 and establishing a satellite regime that declared the country an empire and offered the crown to an Austrian Hapsburg, the Archduke Maximilian.

The timing of these events was hardly coincidental: a United States that was not utterly absorbed by the greatest political crisis in its history likely would not have tolerated the establishment of a French satellite—one with potential irredentist claims on American territory, no less[68]—on its southern border. Indeed, in April 1864, with the Civil War very much still ongoing, the US Congress unanimously passed a resolution condemning the creation of the new Mexican monarchy.[69] Soon after the Civil War—and, notably, with Reconstruction still in an early stage—Washington made its displeasure more concrete, authorizing a large occupation force under General Philip Sheridan for Texas. Sheridan both vigorously patrolled the Mexican border and surreptitiously supplied arms to the Juárez forces. In April of the following year, the United States set up a naval blockade, preventing France from further reinforcing or supplying its expeditionary force, moved forces to the Rio Grande, and demanded the withdrawal of French troops. France, confronted with the prospect of a costly and probably unwinnable conflict with the United States, soon complied with the American demands. The civil conflict in Mexico continued, but Maximilian's regime, unsurprisingly, did not long survive. The brave but imprudent Austrian puppet refused to flee the country; he died in front of a firing squad in June 1867.

The United States' vigorous reaction to the potential threat of a "French Mexico" is notable, especially given the time in which it occurred, with the bloodiest war in its history just concluded and Southerners under military occupation by their Northern cousins. This was not, in short, a time when most Americans easily could stomach a foreign war, much less a potentially very problematic tangle with a great power. The fact that the US government was willing to be so assertive says much about how seriously Washington took the prospect of further European colonialism in the Western Hemisphere (although, admittedly, the size and location of Mexico, as well as the recentness of the Mexican–American War, made control of that country a particularly sensitive issue). Furthermore, the reality that the Americans could rather easily compel Paris to back down from a very expensive enterprise to which Napoleon III had committed both blood and national prestige illuminates how rapidly American power had grown in recent years.[70]

Indeed, the post-Civil War United States differed deeply from the agrarian republic of the early nineteenth century. While the Civil War itself certainly assisted in making the United States a country to be reckoned with, it is easy to exaggerate the conflict's influence in this regard. Undoubtedly, the conflict encouraged the laying of railroad track, the building of factory infrastructure, and similar industrial development—though it also should be remembered that Gen. William T. Sherman, among others, vigorously *de*-industrialized a considerable chunk of the country[71]—but this all occurred in a polity that already was economically advanced, in any reasonable sense of the term. While the North clearly bettered the South in overall economic development, at the war's outbreak America as a whole was wealthy. This was reflected in how the Civil War was fought, with hundreds of thousands of men removed from economically productive activity for long periods, equipped with modern weaponry, moved by train for long distances, and so forth. Even the South did not fight a "poor man's war" by the standards of the mid-nineteenth century, and the North most certainly did not do so. In short, in 1861 the United States was a large, affluent society that possessed the economic and demographic characteristics necessary to bid for great power status by undertaking overseas adventures and vigorously involving itself in European affairs.

Of course, by undermining domestic unity the existence of slavery likely diminished the likelihood of foreign involvements. As noted above, many Americans opposed the war with Mexico;[72] even by the 1840s, slavery had corroded unity in foreign affairs radically. However, slavery alone does not adequately explain Washington's nineteenth century reticence. After all, the slavery question was resolved by the war (and the institution definitively was killed by the Fourteenth Amendment); in the latter decades of the century, slavery presented no barrier to American pugnacity in international matters.

The continued US reluctance to exercise its muscle in European affairs was largely, albeit indirectly, the product of the lingering influence of the leaders of the founding generation and their eminently sensible reluctance to interfere in the affairs of larger states. Washington himself famously warned of imprudent engagement in foreign, specifically European, affairs in his Farewell Address,[73] but it would be simplistic to reduce the views of all the Founders—or even just Washington himself—to the catchphrase "isolationism." Indeed, it is notable that both James Madison and Alexander Hamilton—two brilliant political thinkers very much at odds in their worldviews—played critical roles in the drafting of the Address. The former worked on a draft in 1792 (at the time, Washington intended not to seek a second presidential term), while the latter helped to shape the 1796 revised version that actually was published.

There was no unified "Founders' view" on foreign affairs, a quite obvious fact during the decades in which that generation served in office. It would, however, be fair to say that what one might call "realistic caution" was a legacy of the Founders.[74] Even by the standards of his contemporaries, Washington was notably pragmatic and his Farewell Address reflects that—its advice is general, but grounded in the specific conditions of the time. The Address never denies that the strategic challenges facing the United States may change, but it does not concern itself with the unpredictable distant future. The careful attitude characteristic of the founding generation toward foreign affairs—explicit in the Address, and implicit in most of the decisions of the US government during its first few decades—played a key role in shaping US strategic culture. By the time of the Civil War, wariness toward foreign entanglement was built into the American "strategic DNA"—it was a traditional part of the US way of state-craft. That country certainly had engaged in a variety of military struggles—indeed, had done so from its birth onward, and had fought substantial conflicts with great powers on several occasions (the Wars of Independence and of 1812, as well as the Quasi-War with France)—but the wariness toward *permanent* engagement in the political affairs of Europe remained.

This caution was, overall, highly beneficial to the United States—given the country's very limited human and financial assets (particularly during its early decades), the geographic distance between the United States and Europe, and the need to focus inward on the consolidation of the national territory, *maintaining a distance from great power politics was eminently sensible strategically*. Premature efforts to become a serious player in great power politics almost surely would have resulted in grief—especially given the American economy's reliance on international trade. That the United States *could* have swaggered onto the world stage immediately after the Civil War does not mean that it would have been wise to do so. The proper purpose of international engagement, after all, is not to provide leaders with an opportunity to prove themselves to be clever diplomats, much less great warlords. Rather, it is to advance national interests, and, simply stated, in the latter nineteenth century the United States did not have a pressing need to involve itself in European affairs. The great events of the time—such as the political and military conflicts relating to German unification and the Crimean War—only lightly impacted contemporary US interests and, potent though it was, the United States lacked the power to decisively influence these events; thus, it would merely have been meddling in foreign controversies, not balancing power in a useful way.

By the time that the United States did begin tentatively to step onto the global stage, it was a mature great power. The Spanish–American War was the first major American imperial enterprise focused outside of the North American continent. However, the conflict's imperial character is less intriguing than is the fact that it pitted the United States against a European one-time great power—with Washington in the role of predator. The United States willingly went to war with a state that, by virtue of its proud history, enjoyed considerable *dignitas*, even if its great power status had long since ceased to be a reality. Moreover, US forces won a speedy and inexpensive victory—promptly winning control not only of Cuba and Puerto Rico but also the Philippines—and initial US war goals were more than satisfied.

Spain proved unable to rally friends to protect itself from a strategic disaster. The genuine great powers of Europe thought it prudent to stand aside and let the Americans demolish the remnants of the Spanish Empire rather than, Madrid had hoped, defending the status quo by propping up their frail peer. This fact certainly does not indicate that the United States overawed the combined Old World powers—rather, it reflects the reality that none of these states were very deeply invested in the survival of the Spanish Empire, while, unlike in the decades when a robust Concert of Europe functioned, collective great power action was no longer diplomatically practical. Yet it still is noteworthy that, although few imagined in 1898 how great the influence of the United States over European affairs soon would be, the great powers already accepted the need to treat Washington with a degree of deference and caution.

Titan: the new world arbiter of European politics

The Spanish–American War was a "leading indicator," politically speaking; the United States did not immediately thereafter involve itself intensely in great power affairs (although it did arbitrate the Russo-Japanese War).[75] Of particular note, Washington played no major role in the diplomatic events immediately following the assassination of Archduke Franz Ferdinand by a Serbian terrorist, merely observing as European leaders progressively moved toward war. Further, it avoided direct entry into the conflict until May 1917—and even then, it was the German decision to resume unrestricted submarine warfare that provided President Woodrow Wilson with the catalyst that he needed to convince a reluctant public to go to war.

Whether American involvement in World War I ultimately served US national interests is debatable[76]—indeed, strictly speaking, unknowable. From a twenty-first century perspective, the formal grounds for American involvement appear rather thin, although it should be appreciated that, at the time, unrestricted submarine warfare was widely condemned. (Though, one notes, the British blockade of the Central Powers trampled the then-current understanding of international law[77]—and the blockade, which continued after the Armistice, caused an enormously greater number of civilian deaths than did German submarine warfare.) A complex mix of political, historical, and economic factors led Wilson to push for war in 1917, despite the fact that he had spurned American involvement early in the conflict, attempting to position the United States as a neutral broker of peace.

Critically, Wilson and the American policy making class in general saw the United States as being more akin to the Entente Powers (at least the Western European ones) than to Germany, a country easily caricatured as a bastion of reaction and Prussian militarism commanded by dyspeptic *junkers*, and Anglophilia certainly played a role in the US policy elite's view of the conflict. The Wilson administration's ideological motives for entering the war cannot, however, be reduced to a simple sense of fraternity with other democracies in general and the United Kingdom in particular. Rather, many Americans, most importantly Wilson himself, saw the war as a world-historical moment that offered an opportunity to change the future of mankind.

Wilson's general ideological preferences were reflected in the Fourteen Points, which were first announced in a speech to a joint session of Congress in January 1918. Wilson believed that he had provided a realistic blueprint for terminating the war and creating a permanent peace, but the Fourteen Points arguably was a deeply irresponsible document. Although some of the Points were entirely reasonable and necessary—such as the evacuation of Belgium and the restoration of that state's full sovereign rights—Wilson also made demands that could have destabilizing or otherwise deleterious effects. These included, among others, autonomy for the peoples of the Austrian and Ottoman Empires, adjustment of Italy's borders "along clearly recognizable lines of nationality" (which, given the entirely natural mixing of ethnic populations, did not exist), and that Russian territory be evacuated. This of course was only months after the October Revolution; perhaps Lenin smiled wryly when he learned that Wilson wanted to "assure [Russia] of a sincere welcome into the society of free nations under institutions of her own choosing."

That Wilson's intentions were noble is undoubted, but his idealistic manifesto might well have helped to create the conditions for the next act in "Western Civilization's Civil War."[78] The Fourteen Points immediately were supported by many Europeans, but the effect that the document had in Germany was especially significant; the Points convinced many Germans that their country would be dealt with fairly and that there would be a true "peace without victory." That of course did not occur, and thus the Points did much to breed German rage at the outcome of the war and create fertile conditions for the rise of hyper-nationalism and militarism.

It is conceivable that the war might have lasted a few months longer if the Points had never been issued, as they did ratchet up the pressure on governments that already were strained to breaking point by domestic unrest. Public knowledge of the Points made it all the more difficult for Germany to cope with the failure of Erich Ludendorff's desperate 1918 gamble, which committed the remnants of Germany's offensive fighting power in an effort to decisively breach the enemy's trench lines in France.[79] However, even if the Points did shorten the war (which is by no means certain), the price was the deepening of resentments that would undermine the legitimacy of the Weimar Republic; the latter emerged after the overthrow of the Imperial German government but was forced to sign a punitive Treaty of Versailles that did not reflect the spirit of the Points.

It is difficult to say whether Wilson's political intervention did any real harm in regard to the reshaping of the map of Central and Eastern Europe, but it certainly did not resolve any outstanding geopolitical problems. Absent a convincing victory for the Central Powers, the Austro-Hungarian Empire probably already was a "dead polity walking"; the US president merely added a bit of fuel to nationalist fires that already were burning high. Although it might have been very stabilizing and useful if the Empire could have been preserved in some form at least for a few more decades, this likely would have been impractical regardless of Wilson's actions—as with its Hohenzollern counterpart, the collapse of the Habsburg monarchy ultimately was an internal affair.[80] However, by licensing the view that national autonomy—rather than the strategic concerns of the victorious powers—should be the key organizing principle in the postwar division of European territory, Wilson inadvertently encouraged the division of the former Austro-Hungarian Empire into numerous small, weak states without any overarching structure that would bind them together and make them capable of functioning as a solid buffer between Germany and Russia/the Soviet Union. Thus, a reputable, if frail, great power was replaced by new polities which were doomed to serve as appetizers if either Berlin or Moscow should turn aggressive in the future.

Whatever the weaknesses in Wilson's idealist worldview, he was correct in believing both that the United States had a meaningful stake in the outcome of the ongoing Great War and that it could play a critical role in the conflict. There was a very real threat in 1917 that Germany would become the continental hegemon, and such a development would have been antithetical to US interests. As a matter of simple prudence, it was undesirable that a European hegemon exist, as such a state would then present a potential future threat to US hegemony in the Western Hemisphere and perhaps even the American homeland itself.

Nevertheless, Washington's intervention ultimately may not have served either American or European interests—if Berlin had emerged triumphant, the subsequent years of the twentieth century probably still would have been blood-soaked, but the fact that Nazism would never have arisen and the Bolshevik Revolution strangled in its cradle tempts one to believe that the following decades would not have been quite so grim. However, it also should be noted that, unbelievable as it may seem, the twentieth century could have been much worse—perhaps, to note one of the endless possibilities, the United States and the German Empire eventually would have fought a large-scale nuclear war. In any case, and regardless of whether its involvement was for good or ill, the United States clearly showed itself capable of profoundly shaping European affairs, even if the eventual Treaty of Versailles was not entirely to Wilson's liking.

It should be understood, however, that kinetic American military power was not necessarily critical to victory. US troops certainly played a useful role, and it is at least conceivable that Germany would have achieved a decisive breakthrough in 1918 if there were no American forces in France. Yet, it was the economic and military exhaustion of the Central Powers and public desperation to end the war, combined with the dispiriting *prospect* of ever-greater numbers of US troops entering Europe, that convinced the leaders and publics in those countries, correctly, that eventual military victory was implausible. Germany physically could have prolonged the conflict into 1919 if its civilian population had been willing to do so, but once Germans decided that further sacrifice was futile, the war effort collapsed. Impact on German morale—Wilson's release of the Fourteen Points and the certainty that the number of US troops would grow each month—was Washington's unique contribution to the war effort.

The Great War's end permitted one final bout of US disengagement from great power politics, although the degree to which the Americans removed themselves from European affairs often is exaggerated. The United States did not retreat into isolation—it remained an active power diplomatically. Indeed, the US government encouraged American bankers to provide loans that allowed the reparations scheme created under the Versailles Treaty to endure for as long it did. Without these loans, Germany quickly would have been forced into default: the latter's reparation payments, when combined with its domestic obligations, including the payment of benefits to millions of disabled veterans and dependants of the war dead,[81] and postwar economic troubles, were crushing. However, the United States continued to avoid formal alliances and did not join the League of Nations, while the risible belief that Washington's entry into World War I was the result of a conspiracy of arms merchants and similar malefactors gained surprising currency. The American public, having just lost more than one hundred thousand dead in a seemingly pointless European war, understandably desired a return to the policy of previous generations.

Of course, this was not practical, because of the rise of Imperial Japan and the Third Reich. Allowing the former to establish a vast empire in East Asia would have been highly imprudent, while the latter presented a potentially fatal threat to the United States. As noted above, US security would be endangered if any state had hegemony over Europe, but for Hitlerite Germany—a polity so aggressive that one might describe it as a psychotic empire—to be hegemon would have been especially hazardous.

Although President Franklin Roosevelt slowly maneuvered America toward belligerence, it was Japan's bombing of Pearl Harbor and, shortly thereafter, Hitler's gratuitous and deeply unwise decision to declare war against the United States, which dictated the precise timing of US entry into the conflict. Yet, unlike in World War I, where the United States joined the conflict very late, with its industry far from a full wartime footing and its military small and unready, by December 1941 the Roosevelt administration already had made significant progress in militarizing American industry and creating a large military force which could serve as the core for a truly enormous one.[82] As a result, the US ability to intervene militarily in Eurasia was far more impressive than was the case in the previous conflict.

The United States and Britain could not, however, plausibly have undertaken the Normandy landings, much less conquered Germany itself, if the fighting power of the *Wehrmacht* had not been depleted on the Eastern Front.[83] In that sense, it was the Eastern, not the Western, Front that was decisive in the war against Germany. However, on the other hand, the Soviet Union conceivably would not have survived if not for the combination of foreign military aid and the distraction of the Reich's military resources to cope with the bomber offensive over Germany and the Anglo-American efforts in North Africa, Italy, and, finally, Northwestern Europe. In a possibly even more impressive display of American power, the United States managed to be the decisive player in the destruction of the Japanese Empire.[84]

In the space of only half a century the United States moved from the margins of the great power system to being, in the wake of World War II, one of only two superpowers. Moreover, its willingness to remain politically committed to protecting its allies in Eurasia, would, as the next chapter discusses, be vital in determining the political destiny of the Old World—and, ultimately, the entire globe.

Conclusion

The rise of the United States is one of history's more impressive examples of a polity pursuing a grand strategy that ultimately allowed it to attain great power status. The rise of the United States was not especially rapid—many polities have risen from obscurity to greatness far more quickly—but this itself illustrates a virtue of American strategic culture. The United States made use of its robust political institutions to govern its growth rather than relying on military aggression followed by crude exploitation of the conquered territory. Military success against American Indian tribes (and, eventually, Mexico) obviously was a prerequisite to physical growth, but the policy of political integration of conquered territory into the polity was a sophisticated and highly successful one.

Critically, the United States proved capable of adjusting its grand strategy so as to account for changing international and domestic conditions. What one might call the "Farewell Address strategy" of relative disengagement from great power affairs was fundamental in guiding US foreign policy during the early decades of the republic, and continued to guide policy making even after the United States possessed sufficient raw power to act the part of a great power. For the reasons discussed above, the US reluctance to involve itself in great power affairs was prudent—indeed, invaluable, as this allowed it to remain focused on internal consolidation. However, once the United States grew powerful enough to intervene in great power politics in a decisive manner and came to believe (correctly) that the emergence of a European hegemon would present a critical threat to its interests, Washington abandoned its inward-looking strategy and adopted an active foreign policy posture.

It was only after the World War II, however, that the United States took the final step in replacing its policy of hemispheric isolation with one of permanent active involvement in great power politics, taking on the role of superpower protector of the non-communist states of Western and Central Europe. As the following chapter discusses, its performance in this role was adequate, and even exceptional in some respects, but over the course of the Cold War, it became increasingly clear that the US system for strategic decision making was far from perfectly matched to its superpower role. In particular, a notable gap emerged between the heavy strategic responsibilities placed on presidents—whose mandate included not only protecting straightforward US interests but shaping the worldwide security environment in ways that would be ultimately beneficial to the United States—and the strategic aptitude of many of the men who actually served in that office. In regard to *consistently* choosing presidents who were capable strategists, there was a discernable flaw in US strategic culture, and, as we shall see, this remains the case today, despite the United States' continuing key role in a complex global security environment that is developing into a multipolar global system.

2 Victory disease

Cold War triumph and its aftermath

> Great modern democracies are apparently incapable of dealing with the subtleties and contradictions of power relationships.
>
> George F. Kennan, 1947[1]

The Cold War was the struggle that defined the character of great power politics for nearly half a century. Kennan's pessimistic statement quoted above was not an unreasonable one to make in 1947—indeed, then-recent history had provided ample evidence that could be used to support it—but the United States nonetheless proved capable of maintaining long-term commitments to its NATO allies even at considerable cost and risk to itself. Indeed, once the Soviet nuclear arsenal was sufficient to permit Moscow to inflict state-shattering damage on its North American foe, the United States risked its own survival as a polity (and the lives of tens of millions of its citizens) in order to maintain its NATO commitments. Given the pre-1917 US tendency to hold European affairs at arm's length, its dedication in maintaining its NATO alliance commitments was especially notable. (The record of American fidelity to allies located in regions outside Europe was decidedly more mixed, as demonstrated in the cases of South Vietnam and—far less starkly—Taiwan.)

Whatever Washington's mistakes—and they were numerous, and occasionally, as in the war in Vietnam, appalling[2]—it achieved a stunningly impressive victory over the USSR. That the Soviet challenge was turned back—and without the necessity for World War III—was a strategic accomplishment of the first order. As Sun Tzu famously reminds his readers, "[A]ttaining one hundred victories in one hundred battles is not the pinnacle of excellence. Subjugating the enemy's army without fighting is the true pinnacle of excellence."[3] American leaders did not quite achieve Sun Tzu's "true pinnacle of excellence," as proxy wars with the Soviet Union did occur, but the non-occurrence of a NATO–Warsaw Pact war is impressive, especially as the USSR was both so ruthless and so exquisitely well-prepared for such an eventuality.[4]

The scale of the American triumph, however, was sufficiently great as to inspire a dangerous strategic arrogance. The dramatic 1991 victory over the Iraqi Army—which occurred shortly before the death of the USSR definitively brought the Cold War to a close—created a myth of American military omnipotence that was eventually to have very negative ramifications in, among other places, Iraq itself. Moreover, the fact that the Iraqis mostly were using Soviet equipment encouraged an unwarranted disdain for Soviet military competence; personnel quality and training rather than technology likely was the critical difference between Iraqi and US forces, although technological superiority certainly was important in minimizing the number of Coalition casualties.[5] Many observers came to presume that Cold War victory without war always was inevitable, rather than a lucky historical contingency, and, moreover, that the future would be shaped almost solely by Washington. When such egotism drives strategy, poor outcomes should be expected and that very much was the case during the decade between the Soviet Union's suicide and the 9/11 terrorist attacks.

The Soviet challenge: the United States as protecting power

In the phase immediately after the end of World War II, the United States demonstrated its ability to act as a decisive historical actor in European politics. By May 1945, with the Third Reich dead, France still in the early stage of recovering from occupation, and Britain having stretched its financial and human resources to their outer limits, there was no state or combination of states within Europe capable of effectively challenging Moscow. *Only* the Americans possessed the military power necessary to block the westward expansion of Soviet power. While we cannot know with certainty what a Stalin unhindered by American power might have done, there is little reason to suppose that the Soviet Union would not have been the hegemon, or even perhaps the outright conqueror, of all Continental Europe. In short, the USSR would have been presented with a sterling opportunity to achieve what Napoleonic France and Germany (twice) had failed to do, bringing under its direct or indirect control virtually all of Europe's human, industrial, and natural resources. For the United States—much less unlucky Britain, which would have been presented with the uncomfortable choice between submitting itself to Moscow's whims or confronting a Red Continent—this would have been a geopolitical nightmare.

Given the obvious unacceptability of Soviet hegemony over Eurasia, Washington was compelled to alter profoundly what had been its policy, as outlined in the previous chapter, of refusing to compete perennially against other great powers for global influence. Indeed, given the destruction of the old multipolar system, competition was especially focused: rather than many states jockeying for position, the reordered international system was centered on two superpowers with global perspectives and surgically sharp ideological differences.

The United States of 1945 was broadly, albeit somewhat lethargically, anti-colonialist, and invested relatively little effort in shaping the future of many parts of the world. Soon, however, the bipolar logic of the Cold War would lead Washington to invest itself deeply in the future of previously strategically marginal regions such as Southeast Asia. The Soviet Union needed even less prodding to see the Cold War in universal terms—as Marxist-Leninists, Soviet leaders were inclined to see the struggle against capitalism as worldwide in character. The Comintern was founded in 1919, even as the Russian Civil War was ongoing, and serious efforts at global proselytizing continued throughout the period of the USSR's existence.

By the latter years of the Cold War, the worldwide competition at times could take on a somewhat ludicrous air as the superpowers competed vigorously over countries, such as Angola, in which neither actually had a significant strategic interest. Such occasional excesses, however, do not alter the fact that the US-Soviet contest truly was a strategic competition of the most important kind,[6] and it is reasonable to assume that, had Moscow emerged triumphant, it would have endeavored to translate that victory into eternal global hegemony. An effort to create a stable, universal Soviet empire almost surely would have failed, and probably rather spectacularly—retaining command of the entire world is a difficult task under the best of circumstances. Nonetheless, the amount of blood spilled in the attempt could have been enormous. For instance, even the peaceful collapse of the capitalist economies and a Western willingness to adopt a communist form of government—the actual Cold War endgame in reverse—would not have solved the problem presented by the People's Republic of China, which, during the Maoist period, boldly had staked its own claim to lead the worldwide communist movement and even committed the unforgivable sin of accusing Soviet leaders of deviation from proper ideology. Absent the distraction provided by the United States and the West in general, Moscow might have been very tempted to militarily humble the PRC, decisively quashing heresy and ensuring Beijing's deference.

With the benefit of hindsight, it is clear that the Soviet Union was far from being the economically and politically vibrant entity that many Americans—including great numbers of influential ones—believed it to be. Rather, Moscow frantically was attempting to maintain both the reality of military might and the illusion of being a multifaceted superpower fully comparable to the United States[7]—and trading all prospect of sustainable long-term prosperity in order to do so.[8] It now is clear that straightforward economic realities ensured that the USSR could not both remain a garrison state and simultaneously remain competitive with the United States over the very long term.

One should, however, be cautious in applying "retroactive reasoning" to the Cold War. For years, it was *not* obvious to most Western observers that the Soviet system was so critically and systemically flawed as to ensure its downfall. Moreover, even those who believed that the Soviet experiment was doomed could not reliably predict whether the USSR would endure for a few decades or for a century or more. In the meantime, once Moscow had obtained a sufficiently large and deliverable nuclear arsenal, there was a very real and constant danger of an enormously destructive nuclear conflict which might destroy Western civilization entirely. Such a prospect would horrify even the most energetic anti-Bolshevik, and many Westerners (especially in the intelligentsia) did not belong in that category.[9] Thus, there were two key dangers, either of which conceivably could have come to pass: a cataclysmic war or a failure of will which would lead to a surrender to Soviet power.

Although—with the benefit of hindsight—Western surrender may appear to have been a highly unlikely outcome, when the Cold War actually was ongoing capitulation appeared entirely possible to many thoughtful commentators.[10] Particularly notable is the fact that in Europe—especially from the late 1960s onward—there was much doubt that the United States was a protecting power sufficiently prudent both to manage the difficult task of dissuading the USSR from aggression and preventing a war that, at a minimum and even if it remained conventional, could be expected to utterly devastate Germany. Given the possibilities of outright Soviet conquest and/or national devastation, a considerable number of Europeans were willing to consider creating arrangements likely to lead to Finlandization, a "soft surrender" that would permit domestic self-rule but tacitly acknowledge Moscow's hegemony. Of course, the Finlandization of much, or even all, of NATO-Europe would not have resulted in the immediate downfall of the United States—indeed, given the structural deficiencies in the Soviet economy, even a victory as great as severing the trans-Atlantic link might merely have been a fleeting accomplishment for Moscow. However, Europe's Finlandization would have demonstrated incontrovertibly that the United States had been incompetent in guarding its own national interests.

Given Washington's strategic errors—particularly its Vietnam misadventure—doubt concerning its skill as a protecting power was, at least partially, justified. However, taken as a whole, the US record in the Cold War was reasonably strong. As noted above, the gravest danger of the Cold War—a massive exchange of nuclear weapons—also was a disturbingly plausible one. Whether the world truly ever came fairly close to nuclear war still is very much a subject of debate.[11] However, it is quite imaginable that US mismanagement of the strategic relationship with the USSR could have resulted in a nuclear conflict. Obviously, even a conventional World War III did not occur—and, ultimately, the Soviet Bloc, and then the USSR itself, collapsed peacefully. The Cold War's outcome stands as strong circumstantial evidence that the United States was a reasonably competent protecting power overall—despite numerous, and sometimes egregious missteps, the final outcome of the superpower contest was, from a Western perspective, highly favorable. It is difficult to provide a simple, satisfactory answer as to why the United States was able to negotiate an acceptable outcome to the Cold War, and numerous interrelated factors surely played a significant role, but for the purpose at hand the relative stability of US policy is particularly interesting. The overarching structure provided by containment proved a formidable defense against the vices typically associated with foreign policy making in a democracy.

A general tendency toward moderation helped to "smooth out" grand strategy, preventing one or more key strategic errors from metastasizing and coming to play a dominant, even defining, role in US strategy. The open character of US society and political life no doubt largely was responsible for this phenomenon—criticism of US policy was continual, and came from many sources across the political spectrum. While much of this criticism was misguided, ill-informed, or even vapid, constant public discussion of government policy did encourage a healthy examination of received wisdom. Intellectual laziness certainly was not eliminated—notably, the degree to which the logic of Mutually Assured Destruction (MAD) discouraged serious thinking about nuclear conflict was astonishing—but in general it was difficult for policy makers to sustain policies based on strategic fantasy, no matter how badly they might have wished to do so. At times, unreasonable optimism did take temporary control of strategy—as in the Johnson administration, where the belief that the graduated use of force in Vietnam would provide for a quick, easy victory once the appropriate level of "pain" was inflicted on North Vietnam. In general, however, containment of the USSR was based on prudent calculations of long-term sustainability; the United States did not need to win the Cold War by a certain date, it merely needed to endure and prevent the catastrophic erosion of its position in the world. From this perspective, US policy was not particularly exciting, but it had the greater virtue of being realistic and, at least to a limited degree, self-correcting—highly desirable traits, given that its fundamental purpose was to prevent both great power war and Soviet domination of Eurasia.

In the Soviet Union, by contrast, the lack of public influence over policy restricted power to a relatively small group of high officials, civilian and military, most of whom were influenced heavily by the imperatives of their particular branch of the state bureaucracy. Given the extraordinary influence of the military and security services and the general Soviet obsession with global status and defense against potential aggressors, as well as the structural resistance to any change that threatened to undermine Marxist-Leninist dogma (and, thus, the legitimacy of the state itself), it is not surprising that the USSR developed a simplistic strategic vision. In the years between Stalin and Gorbachev, the USSR's leaders generally sought to avoid major war in the short term but sought continuously to increase Soviet military power and spread the state ideology worldwide, made cheap, dubious patches to serious economic and social problems, and hoped for a long-term victory that presumably would be the result of an ideological miracle of some sort. The latter was a crutch that allowed Soviet leaders to assume the inevitability of victory, and thus ignore the unsustainability of Moscow's military/security policy. In this regard, Soviet strategic logic was quasi-religious in character: the allegedly scientific laws of Marxist theory would provide, somehow, and to doubt this was merely to demonstrate that one lacked faith. By the time that healthy skepticism conquered fantasy in elite circles, the Soviet regime had damaged itself to a degree that would prove fatal.

What one might call the US "containment culture" was shaped by, and in turn encouraged the perpetuation of, a class of generally competent and realistic defense and intelligence officials. At least during the early decades of Cold War, this elite essentially was bipartisan in character. This group was most famously represented by figures such as Paul Nitze,[12] Dean Acheson,[13] and Alan Dulles, but within the national security bureaucracy there were many relatively obscure officials of a similar stamp. Often from affluent backgrounds and possessing a high-quality education—including, intriguingly, a sound knowledge of history and of the work of classical authors such as Thucydides and Julius Caesar—such individuals most often served in either a civilian governmental or military capacity during World War II and (at least off and on) remained in government thereafter; as a group, they formed the backbone of various agencies.[14] The existence of the "containment class" did not ensure intellectual stability—certainly, the details of US strategy changed in significant ways over time—but, when taking the long view, the degree of strategic continuity during the Cold War, particularly in the period before the Vietnam conflict became extremely controversial, is notable.

The cliché that "politics stops at the water's edge" was never especially accurate, but, compared to recent years, the degree of comity in the Cold War foreign policy elite is striking. Yet, as the discussion below indicates, there were very real tensions within the foreign policy community, and the centrifugal forces of the US domestic politics virtually ensured the eventual breakdown of the containment consensus. Indeed, the containment consensus itself was only made possible by the starkness of the threat facing Western Europe in the late 1940s and the clear, diametrical opposition of the Stalinist and democratic worldviews. What the intellectual focus on the concept of containment allowed, however, was America's transition from being a Western Hemisphere-oriented great power with a considerable uncertainty about its own global role to taking on the very different mission of being a protecting power in a bipolar order.

Erratic quality: the Cold War presidents and containment

One of the persistent myths of the US–Soviet competition—and one that most certainly has fed the notion that victory was near- (or even entirely) inevitable—is the belief that containment was consistently applied by both

Democrat and Republican presidents throughout the Cold War. It is true that no president abandoned containment altogether.[15] The Cold War presidents, however, varied enormously in their competence at applying effectively—and when necessary, adapting and reshaping—a grand strategy with Soviet containment as its central element. While none of the presidents did this flawlessly—it would be unreasonable to expect that of any leader—some of them clearly stand out as being superior to others.

Truman, who of course was the first Cold War president, deserves particular credit, as it was he who personally decided that the United States would pursue containment.[16] While the reasoning in pursuing this course may appear obvious in retrospect, it was not uncontroversial at the time; the role that the United States would play in postwar European, much less Middle or Far Eastern, politics very much was open to debate. Not only were many US leaders skeptical of direct military involvement in Eurasia—a viewpoint expressed, for instance, in Senator Robert Taft's opposition to the creation of NATO—but there even were some who favored "friendship" with the Soviet Union at virtually any price.[17]

It is clear that Truman was far from a flawless strategist. For instance, the US lacked any real strategy during the vital early months following the end of the war against Germany for preventing the consolidation of Soviet power in Central Europe. This failing can largely be attributed, though, to Roosevelt's own vague and idealistic policy, based on the erroneous notion that the USSR might be a long-term US "partner in peace," which Truman more-or-less continued for some time after his predecessor's death. Much less forgivable, however, was the fact that the administration utterly bungled its China policy. Mao's complete victory in the Chinese Civil War (i.e., the driving of the Nationalists from the Chinese mainland) may well have been preventable. However, American diplomacy—particularly the US demand in 1945 for an end to hostilities and a Communist/Nationalist coalition, which provided Mao a much-needed pause in fighting at a point when the final military defeat of the Chinese Communist Party (CCP) was plausible—unwittingly facilitated eventual Communist victory. Finally, even given a CCP victory in China, the Korean War might not have occurred if the United States had sent clearer signals concerning its willingness to defend South Korea against aggression from the North.[18]

Damning as Truman's failures may appear, however, it is important that a president's strategic record be judged against the difficulty of the challenges that he or she faces. Truman's period in office was one of geopolitical flux, with the old multipolar great power order collapsing, a high degree of uncertainty about the extent of Soviet ambitions, and domestic disagreement about what role Washington should have in global affairs. Given this, his overall record is more than defensible. Prudent decisions such as choosing to actively work to constrain Soviet power, undertake the Marshall Plan, and build NATO, indicate that Truman possessed a good intuitive grasp of strategy and an ability to implement it successfully.

In regard to the application of containment, historians generally have been kind both to Presidents Dwight Eisenhower and John F. Kennedy. This probably is justified in Eisenhower's case,[19] particularly as he made very serious efforts both to keep NATO robust and strengthen other US alliances, including through the creation of new regional alliances—the Central Treaty Organization (CENTO), a Middle East/South Asia alliance, and the Southeast Asia Treaty Organization (SEATO). While the record of neither of those newer alliances was impressive, and both eventually collapsed, they were indicative of the Eisenhower administration's earnestness in applying containment policy diplomatically. Also notable were Eisenhower's effort to secure the long-term sustainability of containment by ensuring that the United States could maintain the military power necessary to deter Soviet aggression while not doing so at a price so exorbitant as to damage US economic growth—which would, of course, then impact the US ability to maintain the Cold War struggle.[20]

The Kennedy administration record in regard to applying containment is somewhat more problematic. While, for instance, Kennedy's June 1963 speech in Berlin was a brilliant example of public diplomacy, the strategic disaster that was the administration's Cuba policy represented a failure to apply containment in a firm fashion. Even the Cuban Missile Crisis, commonly seen as the Kennedy administration's finest moment, was far from a total victory—in the secret US–Soviet understanding that ended the Crisis, Kennedy both agreed to the removal of nuclear missiles from Turkey and, more critically, that Cuba would not be invaded by the United States. The latter concession effectively signaled the demise of the Monroe Doctrine. Although Cuba of course was not Moscow's imperial possession in any formal sense, allowing the establishment of an outpost of a hostile great power less than 100 miles from the US Coast, and then agreeing that force would not be used to eliminate that military-strategic "colony," was utterly contrary to the Doctrine's spirit. (To be fair, the Eisenhower administration must share at least a portion of the blame in the death of the Doctrine, as it responded ineffectually as Castro took an increasingly anti-American stance and itself initiated the planning for the risible Bay of Pigs invasion.[21]) Yet, even if one does judge Kennedy's leadership harshly in some respects, his presidency was, strategically speaking, not an obvious failure. The same cannot be said of that of his successor.

The Johnson administration's Vietnam policy grew naturally out of the US containment policy, as well as Kennedy's Vietnam policy, the latter having enormously increased the commitment of American resources to that country during his time in office (although whether Kennedy ever would have committed US troops to a combat, rather than advisory, role in Vietnam very much remains a matter of debate[22]). However, containment did not mandate that South Vietnam had to be preserved at any price—the core purpose of the containment policy was to prevent the USSR from attaining an awesome geopolitical momentum that would allow it to become hegemon of Eurasia, not to prevent communist control of every piece of territory on the globe. While there certainly was a defensible case for "drawing a line" in Indochina, containment policy per se did not mandate the defense of the Republic of Vietnam (RVN).

Having decided to devote US prestige and resources to Saigon's defense, however, the Johnson administration spectacularly bungled the American effort in Vietnam. While the war was not lost during the Johnson years, the administration's errors created a difficult situation for its successor. Nixon's efforts to salvage a US victory were quite praiseworthy, and his administration came very close to ensuring the survival of the RVN—indeed, there is good reason to believe that, if not for Watergate, South Vietnam still would exist today (a point discussed in somewhat more detail in Chapter 6).[23] Moreover, his creation of a de facto alliance with China—though unquestionably awkward in certain respects—was a very sensible act in the context of the time.

During the immediate post-Watergate and post-Vietnam period, US foreign policy was in freefall, with Washington's reputation as a protecting power gravely damaged. Even at this point, however, containment did not collapse. Notably, the 1957 Eisenhower Doctrine had a logical successor in the 1980 Carter Doctrine; both addressed the possibility of Soviet power expanding in the Middle East, with the former a response to the Suez Crisis and the latter to the Soviet invasion of Afghanistan. Despite the very different circumstances surrounding their creation, both Doctrines reflected concern that Soviet influence might increase dramatically in the Middle East if the US commitment to containment were not reiterated. Although the Carter administration's foreign policy was disastrous overall, the fact that the president was willing to make an unambiguous—and, given the tenor of the immediate post-Vietnam years, very controversial—public recommitment to the principle of containment of Soviet power in a region vital to US interests illustrates containment's value as a "strategic organizing tool."

When confronted with the Iranian Revolution the Carter administration policy was aimless, and the response to the eventual taking of US hostages was incompetent. In regard to the Afghan situation, by contrast, the Carter record is far more defensible, even if the necessity of the US decision to boycott the 1980 Moscow-hosted Olympic Games is arguable. One suspects that much of the difference in that administration's response to those two problems resulted from the fact that Carter lacked a clear guiding principle in regard to the Iranian Revolution, which was primarily driven by forces internal to Iran and not chiefly communist-led or pro-Soviet in tone. (Marxists did play a significant role in the Shah's overthrow, but they were only a minority in the revolutionary movement; along with secular democrats and others, they soon were dealt with by Khomeini and his supporters.[24])

As noted above, the Reagan years saw a strong emphasis on containment and, further, the undermining of Soviet imperial power—indeed, collapse was closer at hand than even an optimist such as Reagan might have anticipated. Of course, the degree to which the Reagan administration's policies hastened the fall of the Soviet system remains debatable.[25] The US defense buildup and the initiation of the Strategic Defense Initiative often are cited as the factors that pushed Moscow into realizing its inability to permanently continue high-octane military competition with the much-wealthier United States. However, regardless of US actions, Soviet reformers might have undertaken economic and political reforms during the 1980s. Gorbachev and his circle clearly realized that the economic rot in the Soviet system was very deep, even if many Western analysts did not appreciate this fact.

Regardless of whether Reagan is given much or little credit for the events that came to pass shortly after he left office, his administration certainly did apply containment in an authoritative manner. Also, it should be noted that the reassertion of US power during the Reagan years likely encouraged reactionary elements in the Soviet government to remain sluggish in 1989 and not attempt to remove the Gorbachev clique and reverse the peaceful collapse of the Soviet imperium in Central Europe. Although Reagan was no longer in office, US boldness during the Reagan years gave the impression of the United States being a polity far different in character from the "feeble superpower" of the mid-1970s; reactionaries could not take it for granted, even if they overthrew Gorbachev and his associates, that the United States would stand by and allow the Eastern Europe revolutions to be crushed militarily. It is too-easily forgotten now, and was too little-appreciated at the time, but the period from 1989 to 1991 was an extraordinarily dangerous one. The death of a superpower is rarely a peaceful thing, and for a polity with a history as violent as that of the USSR to collapse without a great power war was extraordinary—and the reasons why this happened are worthy of careful consideration.[26] In any event, the G.H.W. Bush administration deserves credit for handling, with admirable competence, the events from the fall of the Berlin Wall onward, as containment policy transformed into the management of Soviet collapse.

Even from this very short sketch of how various presidents implemented containment, it is obvious that the existence of a clear fixed goal—the restraint of Soviet power—did not result in an entirely coherent US strategy over time and across administrations. Rather, significant discontinuities are clear, with US strategy developing in response both to discrete events such as Castro's takeover of Cuba or the American experience in Vietnam, as well as to the outlooks of both presidents and lesser policy makers. Even if it is acknowledged that containment was far from perfectly consistent throughout a Cold War lasting more than one half century, it still appears far more lucid and prudent than post-1991 US grand strategy.

The thriftiest explanation for this fact is probably also the best: the existence of the Soviet Union as a peer competitor and the resulting Cold War placed substantial practical constraints on US presidents: they could not decisively win but they were not willing to surrender the contest, leaving some form of containment as the only acceptable option. This strongly encouraged continuity over time. No one elected to the presidency during the Cold War did so on a platform demanding the overthrow of the containment paradigm and (a small and radical minority aside) there was little support in Congress for abandoning the core tenets of containment policy, such as maintaining a sizable nuclear arsenal, extending nuclear deterrence to NATO states and other key allies, and keeping a substantial US troop presence in Europe.

Arguments between mainstream "hawks" and "doves" thus took place in a context in which a radical reorientation of US policy was not considered seriously. Even Senators Ted Kennedy and George McGovern, for example, men who were dramatically dovish in their disposition, did not call for the elimination of NATO or entirely scrapping the US nuclear arsenal. Individuals who did support such policies automatically consigned themselves to the fringes; regardless of their private views, mainstream politicians dared not venture publicly too far beyond the conventional discourse. Of course, what constituted conventional discourse changed over time—for instance, by the late 1960s vitriolic criticism of US involvement in policy in Vietnam was the norm on the left, while such scathing denunciations would have been considered extreme only a few years earlier—but the containment paradigm remained in place.

The history of containment policy during the Cold War illustrates well the importance of continuity and coherence in grand strategy over time. Although US presidents varied greatly in quality as strategists, and some of them made grievous errors, the elegantly simple and straightforward strategic concept of containing Soviet power proved to be an excellent guidepost for US action. As later chapters discuss, the absence of a single superpower peer competitor—or a similar clearly defined threat—means that there is no overarching concurrence similar to the containment consensus currently existing that acts to discipline US policy making and encourage continuity in policy over time.[27] For reasons that will be explored subsequently, counterterrorism efforts do not provide a useful "policy core" around which US grand strategy can be ordered. Unless and until US grand strategy is reorganized mindfully, as it was in the Truman years, we should expect incoherence and drift, as changes in administration—and, particularly, when the White House moves from one party to another—result in a regular shuffling of priorities. Meanwhile, many of the more subtle security challenges of the twenty-first century largely will be ignored until they become altogether obvious—and deeply menacing.

Misadventures: Washington's Cold War errors considered

Washington's missteps during the Cold War period provide valuable insights into US strategic culture and vulnerabilities that endure to the present. In this regard, three factors stand out as being particularly notable: US difficulty in maintaining a strategy based on realpolitik, the tendency toward "mirror-imaging" that continued throughout the Cold War, and, particularly as the conflict continued, the difficulty that the United States had in applying military power and diplomatic pressure in an appropriate and consistent fashion so as to achieve US strategic goals at an acceptable price.

Containment's most important intellectual architect, George Kennan,[28] personally was averse to excessive idealism in policy making;[29] containment was, at its core, based on realpolitik—quite rightly, as confrontation with the USSR required a sophisticated long-term strategy that plausibly could lead to victory. However, the United States never was wholly comfortable with realpolitik and its practitioners. Gimlet-eyed policy was vulnerable to criticism from both left and right, the former recoiling at the willingness of the realpolitikers to cooperate with, and even put into power, all sorts of gangsters so long as they were reliably anti-communist, while the latter could not be entirely reconciled to a vision of the Cold War that did not place the moral aspect of the struggle at its center. The United States was never altogether comfortable with containment because such a policy was predicated on the notion that the Cold War ultimately was a great power competition not entirely different from past struggles for power, and that victory in such a contest would require no small measure of ruthlessness.

Most US conservatives (with the exception of tiny, and ever-dwindling, remnants of the "Old Right" who would not countenance a permanent US role in Europe) could, however, reconcile themselves to containment. This was largely because containment did not require outright rejection of the belief that the Cold War had a strong moral component, and thus those US conservatives who saw the US-Soviet struggle as essentially moral in character still could more-or-less reconcile containment's realpolitik with their own personal idealism. Practical politics and moral crusade were not altogether mutually exclusive, even if tensions existed between the two. Indeed, if the Cold War had a profound moral aspect—the defense of free and intellectually diverse societies against a grim totalitarian vision—that would serve to justify the human and financial sacrifices inherent to the confrontation. Containment did, however, require that the struggle's moral aspect be sublimated to some degree. First, it was necessary for the United States to accept that it could neither act immediately to liberate those living under communist regimes nor take other measures that carried an excessive risk of war. Moreover, measures that dampened tensions and reduced the immediate risk of military conflict were desirable, so long as they did not damage the long-term interests of the United States. Second, containment required that, at least to a limited extent, policy makers accept the Machiavellian dictum that "the ends justify the means" as a legitimate guide to action. Thus, however much supporting anti-communist dictators might discomfit US democrats, it was appropriate to do so if it was judged that such actions would serve broader US interests. In general, the right side of the American political spectrum—as well as a considerable number of anti-communist liberals and moderates—were willing to accept such trade-offs.

Some Americans, including a substantial element of the Left, however, never were willing to accept the moral price of effective implementation of containment. This is not to say that the concept of containment per se was rejected—there was a general belief that failure to resist the spread of Soviet power likely would result in Moscow's domination of Eurasia and that this was unacceptable. Nonetheless, even some policy makers tended to balk at the harsher side of containment policy.

The problem with such an attitude was, in essence, that of willing the ends but not the means. Containment simply could not be implemented effectively by a polity unwilling to "play hardball." Of course, the degree to which the United States should be willing to sully its hands was eminently debatable, and the argument that acting ruthlessly blurred the moral distinction between Washington and Moscow was, at least to a point, reasonable. However, the core problem that containment *required* actions that did not square comfortably with US ideals remained. This showed itself time and again, not only in opposition to support for dictators, but in skepticism about nuclear deterrence policy (the notion that keeping the peace required holding a sword to the throats of millions of innocent Soviet citizens understandably made many observers uncomfortable) and other areas. This included the attempt, spearheaded by the Senate's Church Committee in 1975, to rein in and tightly control the covert operations of an allegedly "rogue" CIA which, among other things, had been involved in assassinations and worked with individuals guilty of human rights abuses.[30]

Furthermore, though seemingly paradoxically, containment required that the keeping of the peace not be placed above all other critical national interests. Of course, containment was seen as an alternative to actual war, but the peace which it kept was also intended to be a satisfactory one insofar as US national interests were concerned. If the *overriding* goal were to ensure that US–Soviet war were to be prevented, this could—at least in the short term—best be achieved by voluntarily withdrawing from Eurasia. This, however, would be expected to be disastrous over the long term and therefore clearly was irresponsible. A grand strategy based on containment ultimately required a willingness to run the risk of, and if necessary fight, a war with the Soviet Union, and if Washington was not ready to accept this, containment would degenerate into an ever-more-obvious bluff.

A recurring problem throughout the Cold War was the tendency of many, perhaps most, major US policy makers to mirror-image their Soviet contemporaries. Mirror-imaging is a common—and, given human nature, understandable—foible, but one that can lead to catastrophic strategic errors. In essence, mirror-imaging is the tendency to assume that others share one's own general desires and goals, believing that they are like, rather than unlike, oneself. In an international relations context, whether the "mirror-imager" is defensively or offensively oriented of course would matter enormously in dictating behavior. Mirror-imagining should, logically, make a defensively inclined state more likely to "let its guard down," as it will assume that its counterparts are unlikely to attack. In contrast, an aggressive actor presumably will be highly suspicious of others and likely will see its peers' actions as threatening even when they are intended to be conciliatory.

Both Moscow and Washington mirror-imaged during the Cold War, and which did so more egregiously is debatable. However, for our purpose the important fact to note is that American policy makers displayed a decided tendency to presume that their Soviet opponents had similar goals, even when that belief was not remotely justified by available facts. One could cite myriad examples even from before the Cold War, such as Franklin Roosevelt's belief that the USSR could be persuaded to act as one of the "Four Policemen" (alongside Britain, China, and the United States) to maintain peace in the postwar world—a stunningly optimistic assumption, given Stalin's past record of behavior, which included aggression against several polities (including an invasion of Finland, absorption of the Baltic states, and cooperating with Nazi Germany in the partition of Poland) and an obviously grudging and suspicious attitude toward his Western allies.

During the Cold War itself, American mirror-imaging perhaps was displayed most clearly by the common US tendency, prominent within the State Department, to see negotiation with the USSR, especially in regard to nuclear arms control, as a search for common ground—a process of give and take whose purpose was as much to keep lines of communication open and build trust as it was to achieve tangible ends.[31] This attitude persisted even though Moscow displayed a very different attitude toward negotiations, treating them primarily as an opportunity for gaining advantage, and thus basically just another arena of competition.[32] The best evidence for the USSR's hard-nosed perspective on interstate negotiation was displayed by its standard modus operandi in regard to arms control,[33] which was to drive a very hard bargain, taking advantage of every concession offered by the United States, sign an agreement, and then act against the supposed spirit of the agreement or even cheat outright, as in the case of the building of the Krasnoyarsk radar, an egregious violation of the Anti-Ballistic Missile (ABM) Treaty.

Although it may be tempting to view mirror-imaging as essentially an excess of empathy, at least when an interlocutor's actions are seen in an excessively positive light, such a perspective is too generous. At its core, mirror-imaging is an act of cultural arrogance, reflecting a belief that other strategic cultures must be identical to one's own, because acting in a different fashion would be foolish or simply stupid. Such egotism certainly was displayed by the considerable number of US policy makers who believed that the Soviet Union needed to be "educated" on the realities of nuclear warfare, particularly the notion that mutually assured destruction (MAD) made victory in nuclear warfare impossible—and, thus, that further competition in nuclear arms was futile. The possibility that high-level Soviet policy makers might be intelligent folk who chose to devote resources to nuclear weapons because, after careful consideration and interagency discussion, they had reached very different conclusions—and, thus, that Soviet policy reflected educated contemplation rather than simple ignorance—appears not to have occurred to many US officials.

The challenge presented by mirror-imaging was not by any means limited to negotiation and similar routine matters. Rather, it impacted fundamentally how US leaders thought about the Cold War. Most importantly, a substantial number of American policy makers displayed an unwillingness to take Marxism-Leninism seriously, acting as though Soviet leaders had no intellectual investment in their state's declared ideology and that it did not shape their behavior and worldview. However, the evidence is overwhelming that (at least until the closing years of the Cold War, when increasing numbers of Soviet leaders became disillusioned because of the obvious failure of their regime to create a prosperous or intellectually vibrant society) Soviet leaders *did* take ideology seriously.[34]

As Kennan understood, the USSR's state ideology had been shaped profoundly by pre-Bolshevik Russian history, but this did not make Marxist thought irrelevant; the prevailing Soviet worldview was shaped by the interaction of history and ideology, as was the (profoundly different) American perspective. Partly because US strategic culture was, on the whole, uneasy with realpolitik for the reasons noted above, relatively few US policy makers were comfortable thinking of the Cold War as an intellectually arid contest between two competitors simply jockeying for power for its own sake. The problem, generally speaking, was not one of excessive cynicism but of reluctance to acknowledge that Soviet leaders might have a worldview that made it necessary for the United States simultaneously to be ruthless and cautious.

The difficulty that the United States had in applying military power appropriately during the Cold War is discussed above in the sketch of US presidents and the application of containment policy. When the decades of the Cold War are seen as a whole, it is striking how uncertain Washington was in its use (and nonuse) of military power, sometimes backing away from relatively low-risk, low-cost operations, such as using US forces to overthrow Fidel Castro in, say, 1960 and replace him with a government of pro-US exiles. In contrast, at other times, the US engaged in endeavors—most notably, the conflict in Vietnam—likely to be high both in risk and cost.

Similarly, US diplomacy reeled between forcefulness and timidity—and, often, those who experienced the former were US allies, while enemies encountered the latter. American leaders were fairly consistent in maintaining steady US relationships with the Western European countries and Japan, but maintaining fruitful interaction with stable democracies that relied on the US as their protecting power was a relatively unchallenging diplomatic task. US relationships with non- or semi-democratic states were, however, far more variable. Thus, the US sometimes would staunchly support an ally for decades—Ferdinand Marcos of the Philippines, for example—and then abruptly abandon that relationship. Similarly, at times Washington meddled unashamedly in local politics, as was the case in Iran in 1953 when it helped overthrow the sitting prime minister so as to allow Shah Mohammad Reza Pahlavi to maximize his personal power. Yet a quarter-century later, the shah's regime—arguably the most critical US ally in the Muslim world—slowly melted down while Washington looked on bewilderedly. Later, after the shah's fall, the United States proved unable even to muster the energy needed to undertake a serious attempt to prevent the deeply (and very publicly) anti-American Grand Ayatollah Khomeini from pushing aside other contenders and consolidating power.

From a rational cost-benefit perspective, many US military and diplomatic decisions are difficult to justify. Why, a coldly rational observer might ask, should the United States be so idle when faced with certain situations and so active (even, at times, overactive) in regard to others? The answer, of course, is that policy—particularly the policy of democratic states—is never made in a vacuum. Not only is every policy maker a unique personality, but the domestic political climate of the moment always intrudes in the policy making process. For instance, the United States of the late 1970s *was* a feeble superpower, plagued by poisonous domestic divisions which had emerged during the Vietnam War; in the post-Vietnam environment, many members of the elite (especially in academia and the media) tended to view US defense of its national interests in the Third World as immoral and unacceptable "neo-imperialism" rather than the normal, acceptable practice of great power politics.

The tendency of the United States to weave back and forth in its use and non-use of military power provides a stark illustration of the limits of any version of the Realist paradigm as it is applied to a modern democracy. It is reasonable enough to suppose that states generally act rationally to advance their interests; indeed, the evidence of history is utterly compelling in this regard. However, any attempt to apply this rule of thumb with excessive rigor—to treat it like a law of physics rather than a general guide for understanding human activity—is certain to confuse more than it illuminates. Importantly, states are corporate entities, not singular persons, though (as with certain other institutions, such as businesses and universities) it is usual to speak of them as though they possessed individual personalities. In a democracy that regularly switches out those at the top of the policy making pyramid, a high level of discontinuity is unsurprising: institutional memory is relatively low and individual leaders have an incentive to undertake abrupt policy changes that may create a personal legacy.

"Strategic culture" is a valid and useful concept, as continuing cultural traits are vital to understanding the behavior of states over the long term. States are not all identical in their behavior, a fact that is obscured if one focuses too obsessively on the Realist presumption that states are identical "billiard balls" that simply seek power or security; that useful fiction simplifies reality for purposes of analysis, but cannot explain all state behavior at all times (unless, of course, one chooses to expand the concept of "power" or "security" to the point where anything that humans might plausibly value is placed under its umbrella, thus effectively rendering such terms meaningless). However, even though strategic culture matters in state behavior, the precise composition of a country's leadership at any one time—as well as the overall international environment, the specific tensions shaping the domestic political scene, and myriad other factors—matter greatly. Politics, like any other creative human activity, is profoundly shaped by individual decisions. If the "great man" view of history is overly reductionist, paying insufficient attention to the long-term social, economic, and other trends that shape individual behavior and the ultimate fate of nations, the opposite perspective—viewing history as nothing more than the playing out of trends, with individual leaders consigned to the role of marionettes dancing to a tune played by impersonal forces—is at least as oversimplified, as it requires rejecting the contingent character of human events.[35]

The cultural characteristics that encouraged US missteps during the Cold War remain relevant. Indeed, removing the disciplining structure of containment likely allowed US weaknesses to become more prominent in the foreign policy decision making process. Notably, the American lack of comfort with realpolitik very much was on display when the Bush administration sought utterly improbable outcomes in both Iraq and Afghanistan—the creation of stable, democratic, and US-allied governments—while most of its critics offered a hazy vision of a worldwide anti-terror effort in which states and international organizations would agree to join hands and work together and previously intractable problems would be suddenly solvable. Recent US military action in Libya indicates that "fantasy policy making" continues to weave its spell over the unwary.

Similarly, mirror-imaging continues to plague US anti-terror efforts—and, given the enormously complex political environment of the Islamic world, and the vast cultural and political differences between the United States and states such as Saudi Arabia, Pakistan, and Indonesia, the narrow view provided by mirror-imaging is immensely distorting. For instance, President Bush's famous declaration that other states were "for us or against us" in the GWOT ignored, even denied, the more complex reality that a state like Saudi Arabia certainly would never be in favor of a US victory over Islamist ideology because it *is* an Islamist state that spends enormous amounts of money to propagate anti-Western Wahhabi Islam globally.[36] Some Saudi leaders truly do oppose *jihadi* violence (at least under most circumstances) and are glad to assist Washington in at least some of its anti-terror efforts—but, simultaneously, other Saudi decision makers silently cheer on *Al Qaeda* terrorists abroad while hunting them down at home.[37]

As the effort to cope with Islamist terrorism continues over coming decades—and there is every reason to believe that such terrorism presents a very long-term challenge—we can expect that US strategy, and particularly Washington's willingness to use military force, will vacillate wildly. This is because there is no overarching intellectual structure such as containment, or even a clear desired end state (after all, no serious person would believe all terrorism can be eliminated. Even given the recent, purportedly democratic revolutionary movements in Egypt, Tunisia, and elsewhere, there is no convincing evidence that Islamism is about to "play out" as an ideology and thus will not motivate future terrorists.). Therefore, it would be very surprising if US counterterrorism policy does not prove to be far less coherent than was the case in the Cold War.

Plinking rats: an unimpressive hegemony

The United States enjoyed a unique opportunity in the years immediately after the fall of the Soviet Union to shape the global security environment. For the only time in history, a single polity simultaneously both was vastly more powerful than any of its would-be competitors *and* capable of exerting influence worldwide. It always was inevitable that this period of unipolarity would not last forever—the United States lacked the military and financial resources to prevent the rise of other great powers and enforce permanent hegemony, and, more importantly, the utter ruthlessness required even to attempt to do so. The "post-Cold War period" (dated herein, with admitted excessive precision, as lasting from 25 December 1991, the date of the USSR's dissolution, to 11 September 2001) presented US leaders with a chance to shape the global security system far more profoundly than Washington had in the late 1940s.

During and after World War II, the United States undertook a variety of measures that shaped the security context in which the Cold War took place. Some critically important institutions—such as the United Nations and the institutions of the Bretton Woods system—were created before it became clear to Washington that there would be long-term Cold War between itself and Moscow. Other institutions—most critically, NATO—developed later, after the security landscape was better defined. The United States certainly made strategic errors during this period—most importantly, the United Nations never played the role of effective guarantor of global peace that Washington envisioned it would, and, indeed, in recent decades various UN entities, notably including the General Assembly and Secretariat, often have proven hostile to US foreign policy, and arguably to the United States itself.[38] However, it is clear that the United States made a serious effort in the mid-twentieth century to shape the global security environment to its benefit.

By contrast, US efforts to influence the security environment during the post-Cold War period were modest.[39] President G.H.W. Bush famously proclaimed, shortly before the Persian Gulf War, the creation of a "New World Order," but this never evolved into anything beyond a vague slogan. (Indeed, the phrase had been used by Gorbachev some time before, and its apparent meaning changed over time but never was altogether clear.)

There was some hope, especially in the period immediately before and after the Persian Gulf War, that the United Nations, and particularly the UN Security Council (UNSC), would come to play a newly important role in international security. Unfortunately, however, this notion—it was far too amorphous to merit being described as a "strategy"—was foredoomed. The UNSC was and is too public to address security issues in a timely and efficient manner: its deliberations provide a tempting stage for posturing to the global media, and this quality directly undermines its utility as a diplomatic forum. Also, the fact that any of the five permanent members of the Council may veto any action virtually ensures ineffectiveness, since the interests of those veto-holders often differ. After all, in a normal diplomatic context, a state may be persuaded to compromise in order to prevent other polities from pursuing a course of action that would harm its interests intensely. In the UNSC, by contrast, any of the veto-holders may forestall the taking of *any* meaningful action whatsoever, thus minimizing the incentive to comprise. Finally, and perhaps most importantly, the veto-holders represent 1945 frozen in amber—only three of the five might reasonably still be described as great powers, while Japan, India, and other major international players do not possess a veto. Thus, the UNSC, much less the UN in its entirety, was never going to serve as the core institution for great power diplomatic interaction.

During the post-Cold War period, serious US institution-building efforts were focused mainly on expansion of NATO and similar endeavors.[40] It is notable that, despite the lengthy debate that accompanied NATO's expansion into Eastern Europe, a clear vision of the role that NATO should play in the future never emerged.[41] Thus, that organization has never been reshaped fundamentally and given an obvious overall mission, though, on an ad hoc basis, it has been used for a variety of purposes, including state-building efforts in the Balkans and Afghanistan. Washington did play a key role in the initiation of NATO's Partnership for Peace project, but that effort was and is essentially focused on preparing potential new NATO states for membership and encouraging trust-building with polities (such as Russia and the Central

Asian countries) that likely never will become part of NATO. The Partnership for Peace itself is not a strong organization with a lucid mission.

Even more striking than the failure to reorient NATO and otherwise address the changed strategic environment in Europe was the absence of any clear strategy in regard to other regions, much less the globe as a whole. American efforts in East Asia largely focused on the intractable problem of preventing North Korean proliferation—and, given Pyongyang's apparent acquisition of nuclear arms, US policy was a failure—and managing the relationship with China. The latter was by far the more important of the two questions, even if it often received less public attention. However, a meaningful long-term "China strategy" did not develop during the post-Cold War period (and, indeed, has not since developed).

The G.H.W. Bush administration tried to maintain a strong Sino-American link and minimize the relationship damage caused by Beijing's crushing of the Tiananmen Square protests in 1989.[42] The Clinton administration came into office promising a much tougher stance toward the PRC—but then became generally conciliatory in tone,[43] although it did dispatch two carrier battle groups so as to show public support for Taipei in the 1995–96 Taiwan Strait Crisis, after Beijing attempted to intimidate Taiwan by firing missiles over its soil.[44] By far the most notable pre-9/11 G.W. Bush administration decisions concerning China related to the "Hainan Island incident," a diplomatic crisis that ended rather humiliatingly for Washington.[45] Looking at the history of the three administrations overall, one sees little in the way of a coherent policy toward China, much less a strategy for dealing with that country's (entirely predictable) ever-increasing wealth and status in the international system.[46]

In the Middle East, the triumph of the Persian Gulf War was followed by adequate "muddling through," though Washington eventually would suffer for its dereliction in shaping the international order. Hussein's regime never recovered financially or militarily from the Persian Gulf War, largely because of the UN sanctions that remained on Iraq after that conflict. In that regard, the Clinton administration's policy of Iraqi containment can be said to have been successful, since the apparent absence of a meaningful weapons of mass destruction (WMD) program after 1991 means that Hussein no longer presented a major threat either to regional order or as a possible user of WMD (or provider of such weapons to terrorists). Of course, those outside the Iraqi regime were not certain of the collapse of the Iraqi WMD program, and Iraq's behavior seemed to provide fairly compelling circumstantial evidence that WMD acquisition efforts continued;[47] it was only after his fall that it became clear that Hussein actually had been rendered toothless.

What is more striking than the success of Iraqi containment—perhaps a rather grand word to apply to constraining the behavior of a medium-income, California-sized regional actor—was that the dilapidated Ba'ath regime managed to survive for a dozen years and remain a thorn in the side of a unipolar superpower, even though it had no very close and powerful patrons and was a known "public nuisance" that had alienated most of its neighbors. If the United States truly had shaped the global security environment in a manner favorable to its interests, the 2003 US invasion should never have been necessary, as the world's significant states long before would have arranged for Hussein's replacement by a more pliable (though most likely Ba'athist and Sunni) dictator. After all, Iraq being ruled by an unpredictable autocrat was not in the global common interest, given the potential menace to the flow of reasonably priced Middle Eastern oil, as well as the possibility that Hussein would do something unwise and destabilizing, such as providing a terrorist group with WMD (again, the success of Iraq's WMD disarmament being unclear at the time).

Of course, oil exporters, most importantly Russia, may have seen Hussein's continued rule as helping to bid up oil costs by increasing the risk premium built into prices, and he had been a long-term, though occasionally difficult, client of Moscow; additionally, Hussein rented all the support that he could through personal bribes paid via the conduit of the astonishingly corrupt UN "Oil for Food" Program.[48] However, it nonetheless was in the interest of most major states that Iraq's trade be unrestricted, with the country therefore able to freely export oil and import goods from abroad, as well as finance its very substantial debts, and that Iraq be removed from the rogue state ranks, diminishing regional tensions while ensuring that Baghdad continued to play its longstanding role of balancing Tehran. Moreover, while allowing Iraq to come under the control of a new dictatorship might appear cynical, it is difficult to argue that Iraqis would not have benefited from an end of sanctions and Hussein's replacement by a dictatorial candidate picked with psychological stability and minimal human decency in mind.

The eventual US conquest of Iraq would prove, at least in the short to medium term, to be strategically disastrous for Washington. Moreover, it is notable that at no time during the post-Cold War period—nor, more damningly, even after 9/11—did the United States develop a meaningful long-term strategy to mitigate the risks that accompany global dependence on Middle Eastern energy and the very real prospect that a crisis, or even a single event such as a successful terrorist attack on Saudi Arabia's major oil processing facility at Abqaiq, might catastrophically disrupt energy supplies.[49]

Similarly, in other regions—Latin America, sub-Saharan Africa, and so forth—US policy also drifted, while there was little in the way of preparation for problems that Washington would face in the twenty-first century. In addition to energy-related issues, it was entirely predictable that during the post-Cold War period rapid technological development, changes in the global economy, the rise of Islamist terrorist movements, and other developments would present the United States with significant strategic challenges and opportunities. In some cases—especially those, like Islamist terrorism, that presented reasonably clear threats—Washington did take some desultory measures to address the issue. In terms of longer-term threats, particularly less-concrete ones such as the slow reemergence of multipolarity, there is little evidence that the US policy making establishment understood, first, that unipolarity was a *temporary* condition and, second, that Washington needed a strategy designed both to prolong the longevity of unipolarity and, even more importantly, ensure that the eventual corrosion of unipolarity would not be catastrophic for US interests and that a healthy multipolar system *in which the United States remained the leading power and the respected "arbiter" of global politics* developed.[50]

Conclusion

The beginning of the Cold War completed the US transition from introverted polity to global superpower, as the unique circumstances which marked the beginning of the US-Soviet standoff made it possible for the United States to accept the latter role. Given American history, there was shockingly little public and elite opposition to Washington becoming the protecting power to a great bloc of states and antagonist to a military peer which was, from 1948 onward, nuclear armed. As we have seen, despite numerous missteps the United States performed reasonably well in that task. As the country managed to navigate the treacherous currents of the Cold War without either losing Eurasia to Soviet domination or being forced to fight World War III which, even if non-nuclear and won by the democracies (both perhaps unlikely prospects), would have been a historical tragedy of the first magnitude, surely Washington deserves much praise for its handling of the long struggle.

The seeds for future failures, however, always were present. The containment policy provided a vitally needed common reference point for decision makers, but there was always considerable disagreement within the policy elite about how to implement containment, as well as much discomfort with the fact that Cold War exigencies often required the United States to act amorally, if not immorally. By the latter decades of the Cold War, the imperfect unity that once had prevailed in foreign policy making largely had broken down, with an increasingly sharp split between "hawks" and "doves." Though containment remained the general organizing principle for the conduct of the Cold War, how it would be implemented became ever more controversial; actions that decades earlier might have received little opposition—such as the Reagan administration's support for the *Contra* rebels in Nicaragua—resulted in fierce debate. Fortunately for the United States, however, even as its Cold War strategy was losing coherence and becoming increasingly erratic, the Soviet Union was facing a far more fundamental economic, military, and ideological challenge which it proved unable to address.

The end of the Cold War of course rendered Soviet containment irrelevant. Thus, the United States no longer possessed a general organizing principle for foreign policy. It has yet to find a satisfactory new one—after the 9/11 attacks, the unfocused policy of the decade from 1991 to 2001 was replaced by a new focus on counterterrorism. As we shall see, a grand strategy organized around counterterrorism proved to be entirely unsatisfactory—indeed, worse, in some important respects, than the policy drift that preceded it. Fundamental changes in the global distribution of power and the rise of new great powers were *noticed* by many observers, but US strategy was not revised accordingly. As a result, the United States still finds itself intellectually unprepared for key future strategic challenges.

3 The slow drift

Power without strategic clarity

For the reasons discussed in the previous chapter, the unipolar system was the consequence of a very particular set of historical circumstances that emerged with the collapse of the USSR and was not sustainable over the long term. The United States did not set out to conquer the world—global hegemony (or, more accurately, given the restraints under which Washington labored even in the 1990s, quasi-hegemony) merely was the result of a vacuum created by the absence of peer or near-peer competitors. However, the rise of various states and the enormous (and still-ongoing) social, economic, and technological changes that often are lumped together in the category of "globalization," ensured rapid change in the international security environment. Even in the heady early 1990s, it was foreseeable that Washington would not long maintain its position as the only giant in a world of gnomes. (The term "sole superpower" unfortunately confused matters, as the relevant question was not whether the United States could long maintain its position as the most powerful single state—an eminently achievable goal, if American policy and strategy was sound—but whether it would be *overwhelmingly* powerful compared to any other actor or plausible combination of actors.)

Historically, maintaining local hegemony for a long period has been difficult, but some powers have secured this (for instance, the Roman Republic/Empire over the Mediterranean). Notably, however, throughout the titanic great power struggles of the last half-millennium before 1991 no single power managed to establish a stable hegemony over Europe, much less the entire world. The American achievement literally was without precedent—no power previously had obtained even a quasi-hegemony over the entire globe. (While it was and is common for the United States to be spoken of as a global hegemon, this exaggerates the power that it enjoyed even at its height; quasi-hegemon is a more accurate, if clumsier, description of Washington's status in the aftermath of the Soviet Union's disintegration.) Ironically, for all their efforts at grave-filling, none of history's rapacious conquerors actually managed to equal the accomplishment of a commercial republic that several decades previous had given up outright territorial aggrandizement.

History, again: the return of great power military competition

As unipolarity continues to decay, an international system in which great powers compete vigorously—and perhaps violently—can be expected to develop, unless one presumes the occurrence of one of two alternatives. First, the use of military coercion could be prevented by some entity greater than any individual state, a "Super-Leviathan," so to speak, which did not consider great power violence permissible. Second, global politics could obey a new paradigm in which individual states volunteered to cease vigorously competing for power or, at least, would only do so in a peaceful fashion that no longer includes the threat of violence; the latter form of rivalry has been described by Edward Luttwak as "geo-economic."[1]

There is, however, little reason to presume that military violence has not become irrelevant to great power politics.[2] The first of the two aforementioned possibilities is readily dismissed; at this point there is no indication that some form of "super-sovereign" has emerged which compels submission and effectively can punish attempted great power disobedience. Liberal internationalists make a quite reasonable case that the rise of assorted international institutions and the deepening of international law has placed progressively larger constraints on great power action. However, the evidence that an international institution capable of actively commanding great powers to obey will come to exist at any time in the foreseeable future is negligible, especially given that such an institution likely would have to possess military capabilities sufficient to overawe any and all great powers.

The second possibility is somewhat more difficult to dismiss, as one cannot predict with any certainty the role which large-scale violence, or the threat thereof, will play in great power affairs. Any claim that the age of great power violence is past, however, has little evidentiary support. There indeed has been no open great power conflict since 1945, unless one counts the PRC of the Korean War era as a great power, which would move the relevant date up to 1953. However, the ability to predict the future on the basis of the period from 1945 to the present is questionable, particularly given that most of that era was dominated by two superpowers, and the remainder by one. The post-Stalin USSR was, in retrospect, a quite cautious entity, while the United States plainly was disinclined to start great power wars. This is a thin history on which to build a grand hypothesis that world war has become outmoded.

The prudent assumption is that history has not taken some unique turn that has rendered World War III, or a similarly cataclysmic event, impossible.[3] Certainly, several major states—including China, India, Russia, and the United States—have significantly enlarged their military spending over the last decade. This is not an action that would seem to indicate that those states believe major war to be impossible. Granted, in the US case increased military spending largely reflects post-9/11 circumstances, particularly the costs of the wars in Iraq and Afghanistan, and the US DoD budget is expected to spiral downward in coming years. Yet, the United States certainly still will procure equipment, such as the F-35 Lightning II fighter, built with highly capable opponents in mind. The spending of rising (or, in the Russian case, would-be recovering) powers is particularly intriguing. In many respects, these budding great powers are very unlike the immensely wealthy United States; in both China and India, hundreds of millions of citizens live in truly dire poverty, while improving the national physical infrastructure to a level comparable to the United States would require massive investment. Given such immense needs, the willingness to invest in long-term acquisition of very expensive military equipment such as fifth generation fighter aircraft and modern naval vessels—acquisitions which are not necessary to address "low-tech" problems such as, for instance, the insurgency in Kashmir—is telling. Certainly, it is indicative of a belief that great power status is, at least to some degree, a reflection of national military capability. Even so, it seems implausible that states would spend resources that could be used to address social needs *solely* to bolster their prestige. Thus, one may deduce that such spending reflects a belief that military conflict with a peer or near-peer could occur at some point in the future.

Today there certainly is no desperate rush to arm, such as was seen in the years immediately preceding World War I. Indeed, one major state, Japan, as well as the EU (a hybrid entity that possesses some of the characteristics that one would associate with great power status), have been notably reluctant to prepare for, or even consider the possibility of, future great power war.[4] No major power spends a strikingly large sum (the US defense budget is impressively large, but one must take into account, first, the global role that Washington plays and, second, that it is drawn from a fourteen-plus trillion dollar national economy). At the present, it appears that no major state senses an immediate and overwhelming threat from a peer or near-peer. Even in regard to conflict that many observers believe might occur (most notably, the United States versus China), it is difficult for policy makers even to guess very approximately when the military struggle will take place, if it happens at all. Since great power conflict does not appear imminent, major states are not desperately seeking to accentuate their military power as quickly as possible. However, several of them are progressively improving their military capabilities and appear to treat the possibility of eventual great power war as a serious one.

A too-narrow focus: the global war on terrorism in context

The rise of what has been referred to by various names as the "new terrorism" or "super terrorism" has been one of the most regrettable international developments of recent decades, and it certainly is appropriate that

US leaders treat organizations such as *Al Qaeda* as presenting a serious threat.[5] However, in the years since 9/11, Washington's attention to terrorism—and the related interventions in Afghanistan and Iraq—has discouraged serious discussion of longer-term, and ultimately more significant, security challenges facing the United States.

It is difficult to generalize about terrorism—a staggering number of groups with all manner of ideological and/or religious motives have resorted to terrorist tactics of one kind or another.[6] It is not possible to perfectly distinguish between the "old" and "new" terrorism. With that said, however, there is a meaningful general division between the terrorism of most of the twentieth century and the new terrorism that became increasingly prominent from the 1990s onward. In the decades immediately preceding the 1990s, terrorism generally was associated with nonstate entities which used violence in order to generate media publicity; however, the number of intended deaths in most terrorist acts was modest, or, in some cases, even zero. The wave of Palestinian aircraft hijackings in the 1970s, the 1984 Provisional Irish Republican Army (PIRA) attempt to assassinate Margaret Thatcher by planting a bomb in the Brighton hotel in which she was staying, and even the Symbionese Liberation Army's bizarre early 1970s "revolutionary" campaign in California all fit this general pattern. In most cases, the level of publicity and political pressure resulting from a terrorist act were the critical criteria in judging its success.

Some groups, particularly those occupying the gray area between small terrorist organizations and large-scale insurgencies—the PIRA, for instance—might seek to inflict high casualties on military or police forces if presented with the opportunity, but still recognized a distinction between such government forces and unarmed civilians. Although many terrorists would attack civilian (in the PIRA case, most often Ulster Protestant) targets, they usually did not seek to kill civilians in great numbers.[7] Indeed, from the perspective of many terrorists, high civilian death rates were undesirable, given the general revulsion for indiscriminate murder and resulting adverse political consequences.[8]

By contrast, several Islamist groups are remarkable for their efforts to maximize casualties as a goal in itself, with no meaningful distinction being made between security forces and civilians. Of course, large-scale casualties also result in increased media coverage of a given terrorist act, and this too is desired by terrorists, but the significant point is the shift in general attitude concerning civilian deaths. The 9/11 plot is the most notorious example of "fatality maximization" terrorism, but the recent record also includes thousands of other incidents, including the 2002 Bali bombings, the 2004 commuter train bombings in Spain, the 2005 public transport bombings in the United Kingdom, and an enormous number of strikes in India, Iraq, Israel, Pakistan, Russia, and elsewhere. Most such attacks inflict only a small number of fatalities, but that does not alter the fact that murdering as many perceived enemies as possible is an objective;

success is treated as synonymous with inflicting high number of causalities. The 9/11 attacks were merely a more effective use of human resources than a typical fatality maximizing attack; they differed in scale, not in fundamental character.[9]

The reasons for this increasing bloodthirstiness are complex; it has arisen as a result of, among other factors, the changing global media environment and the perceived ineffectiveness of the old terrorism in achieving political goals in many cases. In regard to Islamists and Palestinian nationalist terrorists (two groupings that sometimes are entangled, as in the case of Hamas) in particular, a radical rejection of any moral distinction between enemy civilians or non-civilians seems particularly important. A refusal to distinguish between civilian and non-civilian Israeli targets, treating all violent acts as legitimate "national resistance" and thus outside the realm of "terrorism," has long been used by Palestinian nationalists to justify attacks aimed at Israeli civilians. Somewhat similarly, but arguing from a religious rather than nationalist viewpoint, some Islamists claim that unbelievers living in the *Dar al-Harb* (the "House of War"—those areas of the world not under Muslim rule) are not protected by religious prohibitions against attacking innocents.[10]

Given the desire of many current terrorists to cause catastrophic harm,[11] concerns about terrorist use of weapons of mass destruction—particularly nuclear weapons—are much more compelling than was the case in previous years. During the Cold War, where few states possessed nuclear weapons and few terrorists showed much interest in WMD acquisition, much less use, WMD terrorism was more the stuff of novels than a serious possibility. More recently, however, the Japan-based *Aum Shinrikyo* cult both produced its own chemical weapons and used them in several attacks, including a major, though relatively unsuccessful, 1995 assault on the Tokyo subway system,[12] while a number of Islamist groups have attempted to acquire various forms of WMD.

Given the mentality of many terrorists, Islamist ones in particular, and the relative ease with which chemical, radiological, and (at least relatively crude) biological weapons can be created, it is highly likely that several, perhaps many, WMD attacks *of some kind* will occur in the next half century. While this is an unpleasant prospect, it should be remembered that most weapons of mass destruction are difficult to deliver effectively with the means that terrorists are likely to have available. Producing a quantity of botulinum toxin theoretically sufficient to kill millions is, as a matter of chemistry, a relatively simple task, but delivering the toxin in such a way as to effect that goal is, fortunately, extraordinarily difficult.[13] The same is true of most biological weapons that realistically might be produced by a terrorist group. Effective use of advanced chemical weapons, such as the sarin gas produced by *Aum Shinrikyo*, to produce mass casualties perhaps is more plausible, but production is problematic. (While the actual Tokyo subway attack killed only twelve people, this was the result of generally poor planning and execution—a better-conceived attack might have killed hundreds, or even thousands.) *Aum Shinrikyo* succeeded in producing sarin because it was a wealthy organization with numerous members who were qualified scientists and, perhaps most importantly, it was operating in a pre-9/11 environment in which most countries' counterterrorism efforts were relatively lax.

Radiological devices—conventional weapons containing some form of radioactive, but not necessarily fissile, material—present a different sort of challenge. There is an enormous amount of radioactive material available worldwide, being used for all manner of legitimate purposes ranging from medicine to irradiating meat. While terrorist groups, despite numerous attempts to acquire fissile materials, apparently have enjoyed little success in doing so, the security surrounding most radioactive material is relatively lax. In all likelihood, a "dirty bomb" would kill few, if any, people directly (though many individuals might face long-term health risks, such as an increased probability of developing cancer). However, the costs of cleaning radioactive debris might be exorbitant, perhaps even prohibitive—it is possible to imagine scenarios in which a portion of a major city was abandoned for decades, much like the "Zone of Alienation" near the Chernobyl nuclear plant. Thus, while terrorist use of radioactive weapons would be unlikely to inflict truly mass casualties, it could result in extreme expense, population dislocation, and social turmoil.[14] Fortunately, however, given the technical difficulties, particularly in crafting a device that would efficiently disperse radioactive materials over a wide area, the odds that a terrorist group will be able to catastrophically pollute a large urban area probably are small.

Nuclear weapons in terrorist hands present a unique threat, far greater than that presented by any other WMDs, combining relative ease of effective delivery with devastating consequences.[15] While it would be very difficult for terrorists to deploy a nuclear device in an optimal fashion—which, for purposes of maximizing casualties in an urban area, would require an airburst—a crude method like exploding it in a vehicle on a city street nonetheless would cause horrifying damage. The link between sophistication of delivery method (and general competence in undertaking delivery) and the creation of mass casualties is very close in regard to use of biological weapons and only somewhat less so in regard to chemical weapons; in regard to nuclear weapons, it is much weaker. Armed with a warhead of sufficient yield, even fools easily can kill tens of thousands of victims.

Given these factors, it is a rather simple matter to arrive at sensible *core* US strategic goals for the now-nameless conflict that formerly was called the Global War on Terrorism (GWOT): first, the prevention of mass casualty terrorist assaults similar to, or greater in scale than, the 9/11 attacks against the US homeland; and, second, the prevention of such attacks on US friends and allies. Terrorist use of WMD, particularly nuclear weapons, would be the most plausible fashion in which an attack on such a scale may successfully be undertaken. The (non-WMD) 9/11 attacks most likely were a singular event made possible by weak airport security, the employment of a new terrorist tactic (using a passenger airliner as a weapon aimed at a ground target), and simple luck on *Al Qaeda*'s part. It admittedly is not impossible that terrorists will be able to devise an equally devastating unorthodox attack in the future, but it is unlikely; it is far more plausible, however, that WMD would be the critical enabler for any future attack on a massive scale.

The fact that the United States does not even have a consistently used name for the struggle in which it is engaged is telling. As of this writing, it is approaching a decade since the 9/11 attacks—and the 1996 Khobar Towers bombing, the 1983 bombing of the US Marine barracks in Beirut, and the holding of US embassy personnel hostage in Iran from 1979 to 1981 all are even further in the past. Yet, the character of the war that Washington is fighting against Islamist extremists still is foggy. During World War II, Americans usually simply referred to the conflict in which they were engaged as "the war." In that context, this was an entirely adequate way to describe the struggle: except for marginal cases such as unlucky Finland, which landed on the Axis side because of Soviet aggression in the Winter War of 1939–40, it was clear which polities were enemies of the United States. These enemy states were treated harshly, as were their civilian populations, who found that non-combatant status did not offer reliable protection from what William Tecumseh Sherman had called "the hard hand of war." Washington's attitude toward the current struggle lacks such clarity and ruthlessness. What are its ultimate goals? What is the American theory of victory? What means of warfare are acceptable? The answers offered to such questions remain vague.[16]

During the period in which counterterrorist efforts were all placed under the umbrella of the GWOT, actor and director Terry Jones asked: "How do you wage war on an abstract noun? It's rather like bombing murder."[17] Although Jones' underlying argument—that NATO was wrong to conduct any form of war in Afghanistan—was strategically naïve, he was correct in his supposition that the concept of a GWOT was intellectually problematic. One of the most obvious problems with the notion of a GWOT was that the United States never pursued all terrorist groups with the same alacrity, for the simple reason that doing so would have been not just impractical, but outright demented.

Most of the world's terrorist groups posed only a limited direct risk to the US homeland—or, in the case of those organizations uninterested in, or even favorably disposed toward, the United States, none at all. The "limited risk" category surely even included many groups that overtly despised the United States but were focused on local matters, such as fighting Indian troops over Kashmir or, in the case of Hamas, attempting simultaneously to rule Gaza, fight Israel, and gain control over the West

Bank. The terrorists in which Washington had the greatest interest obviously were transnational Islamists focused on inflicting harm on US soil.

The Obama administration discarded the concept of a Global War on Terrorism, but even in this supposedly post-GWOT era, Islamist terrorists and insurgents remain the enemy against which the United States centers its counterterrorist efforts and, by default, its grand strategy. Yet, even in regard to counterterrorism, the United States will not necessarily forever remain focused mainly on Islamist terrorists. It is entirely possible that new ideologies antipathetic to the West in general, and perhaps the United States in particular, will develop and that these, in turn, will give rise to violent organizations. For the purpose of framing core long-term counterterrorism goals, the precise ideology of those threatening the United States is not the point, although understanding the nuances of a given terrorist group's worldview may be critical in determining how best to counter it operationally. The key objective is to prevent any non-state actor from inflicting catastrophic damage on the United States or its allies.

What is not realistic, however, is to expect that every single terrorist incident can be prevented. Simply put, the number of active terrorist groups—as well as freelance would-be terrorists who are not affiliated with any formal organization—is sufficiently great that *some* degree of damage to US targets both at home or abroad is inevitable. Thus, much of the rhetoric regarding terrorism that has emanated from both Democratic and Republican public figures is irrelevant and (intentionally or not) misleading, as it treats terrorism as a solvable problem rather than a strategic condition with which the United States permanently must cope. Terrorists always will be a part of the strategic landscape.

Importantly, however, the acuteness of the threat presented by catastrophic terrorism is variable; it has become particularly serious in recent years because of the sheer number of individuals globally who have adopted a radically anti-American/anti-Western worldview.[18] Violent Islamism appears still to be waxing, but it is entirely possible that, given time and the continuing development of global political conditions, it will fade as an ideology, and thus as a motivating factor for terrorism. How long this may take, however, is utterly unknowable—it could be a century or more and there is every reason, given the evidence of history, to assume that other pernicious ideological/religious movements will flower in the meantime. Moreover, it is possible, though perhaps unlikely, that one or more of these new movements will enjoy a considerable degree of support within the United States.

By contrast, Islamists almost surely never will enjoy much support in the United States itself. First, while dozens of US citizens and resident aliens indeed have been convicted for supporting Islamist terrorism in recent years,[19] this of course does not mean that most American Muslims either are, or in the future will be, amenable to Islamism, much less Islamist terrorism. Second, and even more fundamental to the question of Islamism's potential popularity, the Muslim percentage of the US population—including the entire spectrum from radicals to theological liberals—is small. Estimates of the US Muslim population vary, but a 2009 Pew Research Center report placed the number living in the United States at "about 2.5 million";[20] given a US population of over 300 million at the time, that would put Muslims under one percent of the overall population. (The Muslim population is expected to grow in coming years, both in absolute terms and as a percentage of the population, but how much it grows will depend on US immigration policy and other factors.) A mass movement, by definition, requires mass, and in the United States Islamists are greatly lacking in that regard.

American history provides a useful perspective on the inevitability of terrorism's resurgence. In the late nineteenth and early twentieth century, the chief terrorist threat to the US government was presented by anarchists; most famously, anarchist Leon Czolgosz assassinated President William McKinley. Over time, the popularity of anarchism faded, both in the United States and elsewhere, though its decline certainly did not end political violence, particularly in Europe—indeed, much of anarchism's political momentum flowed into various communist and fascist movements. (And, although generally not considered "terrorists" in the usual sense, fascist and communist street fighters certainly had a deeply corrosive effect on democracy in several European countries, with well-known results.[21]) During much of the twentieth century, the United States enjoyed a relative respite from terrorism and other internal political violence. However, terrorist incidents did occur; these included Ku Klux Klan violence,[22] as well as attacks by Puerto Rican nationalists—such as the attempted assassination of President Truman in 1950 and a 1954 attack during which five members of the House of Representatives were wounded by gunfire.[23] Also, particularly in the early 1970s, a number of terrorist attacks were undertaken by leftist groups such as the Weathermen and the aforementioned Symbionese Liberation Army;[24] however, this outbreak of domestic terrorism was a relatively minor phenomenon involving a small number of terrorists. There was little notable post-Vietnam domestic terrorism until 1995, when the deadliest twentieth century terrorist attack on US soil to that point—Timothy McVeigh's bombing of the Murrah Federal Building in Oklahoma City—occurred. However, there was virtually no public support for McVeigh's actions, including from the several million Americans who were to some degree ideologically sympathetic to the rightist militia movement with which McVeigh was associated.[25]

The absence of well-organized, large-scale terrorism aiming for the destruction of the US government or a similarly ambitious goal is notable, and may indicate—though it does not guarantee—that terrorist groups of any sort will find it difficult to recruit a substantial number of Americans in coming decades. It obviously is desirable that this be the case, as any violent movement garnering the active support of ten, or even five, percent of Americans could sustain terrorist groups sufficiently wealthy and with so many recruits as to present a critical security threat. Even the implementation of extreme measures that fundamentally undermined traditional civil liberties might not quash such a potent movement.

Several unpredictable factors will be significant in determining the acuteness of the terrorist threat which the United States confronts at any given time. We cannot know with certainty when Islamism will "peak" globally, much less anticipate what new ideologies—or violent permutations of existing ones—will arise.[26] (For instance, Italian fascism simply did not exist at the turn of the twentieth century, even if much of the socialist and other thought on which it was based did, yet Mussolini's March on Rome occurred in 1922.) Moreover, we cannot reliably predict the number of terrorists and terrorist groups which will operate domestically within the United States. Thus, it is impossible even to know the degree to which, at any given time, counterterrorism efforts will be focused abroad rather than internally.

This context both highlights the impossibility of ending the threat of terrorism on US soil and clarifies why it is necessary to focus particularly on the prevention of catastrophic attacks. Some terrorist groups—the Basque separatist *Euskadi Ta Askatasuna* (ETA), for instance—still continue to limit civilian casualties. Indeed a few organizations, such as the Corsican separatist *Fronte di Liberazione Naziunale Corsu* (FLNC), generally even try to avoid them altogether. However, Islamist terrorist groups have introduced new terror techniques (or, in the case of suicide bombing, regularized the use of a previously rare one) while rejecting the distinction between combatants and non-combatants. Even if Islamist terrorism itself fades over time, as anarchist terrorism did, there is no particular reason to presume that the Pandora's box opened by the likes of *Al Qaeda* can again be closed.

In the twentieth century, groups throughout the world practiced terrorism with widely varying success—most failing utterly, some (such as Peru's Maoist *Sendero Luminoso*) never attaining their goals but gravely damaging the society in which they operated, and a few (such as Michael Collins' IRA) largely attaining their objectives.[27] What Islamist groups, and *Al Qaeda* in particular, achieved was to make a terrorist campaign the subject of truly intense and sustained global interest. That, however, required a high-casualty, spectacular event and maintaining a credible threat that another such event could take place. To a limited degree, earlier terrorists—such as the Black September members who murdered eleven Israelis at the 1972 Munich Olympic Games—managed to achieve global notice, but the attention garnered was relatively brief; the fact that *Al Qaeda* (and international *jihadism* more generally) has remained the object of intense sustained media and political interest makes it unique. Any other terrorist leader with a universal ideology, or even one with a more limited orientation, if he or she is intensely narcissistic (not a rare trait for the elite members of violent groups),[28] would find this to be a very interesting achievement.

All of these factors provide a background not only for US policy, but for the politics of the twenty-first century in general. However, *the threat of mass casualty terrorism does not ensure that the strategic history of the century will be defined by terrorism.* Indeed, there is every reason to suppose that it will not be, even if one or more particularly horrible terrorist attacks occur. It is only if one assumes that great power politics as it has been known for centuries has ceased to function that terrorism likely becomes the defining "story" in international security, and that is a very large conjecture for which the evidence is minimal—*as a matter of prudence, US foreign and defense policy should not be based on that assumption.* Overall, the risks of reorienting US policy to make it permanently "terrorcentric" are greater than the risks of not doing so.

Risky inertia: the fixation on counterterrorism

A foreign and defense policy focused on counterterrorism—and that would be a reasonable description of the US stance since 9/11, if one treats the occupations of Iraq and Afghanistan chiefly as being counterterrorist efforts[29]—mandates a very different set of priorities than does one focused on great power politics. Such an orientation implies a foreign policy largely focused on the Muslim world and cultivation of whatever political conditions will minimize the Islamist threat to Western states.

The question of what measures will effectively combat Islamist ideology of course is itself controversial. During the G.W. Bush years, the US government essentially treated democratization as *the* key factor in addressing political-religious radicalization and terrorist recruitment over the long term—in both Afghanistan and Iraq, notably, the democratization of those countries was an overriding "theme" guiding US occupation strategy.[30] The Obama administration has been somewhat less concentrated in regard to what it believes most important in countering Islamist terrorism. At least rhetorically, the Obama team continues to place substantial value on the democratization of Muslim countries. Also, as Obama's June 2009 speech (rather ostentatiously titled "A New Beginning") in Cairo demonstrated—the current president appears to believe that US popularity abroad plays a critical role in counterterrorism. In any case, and whatever the differences their outlooks and strategies, in both the Bush and (at least to this point) Obama administrations, Islamist radicalism and terrorism have been treated as a key foreign policy concern.

A foreign policy focusing on terrorism also places a premium on successfully cooperating with other states, including other great powers, to infiltrate terrorist networks and otherwise undermine terror operations. When policy is focused on counterterrorism, damaging terrorist groups and preventing attacks by them are the obvious central strategic goals. Inevitably, the perceived relative importance of other policy goals declines, and they receive less high-level attention and funding. In any government, objectives that are seen as being in some way in conflict with more critical priorities can be expected to suffer neglect.[31]

An emphasis on counterterrorism also shapes military priorities in very distinct ways. Thus far, these effects have been somewhat muted because of the long-term nature of military planning, particularly in regard to procurement of major weapons systems—moving from initial conception to deployment of a weapons system can require decades, and procurement is a matter of intense industry lobbying and Congressional interest. Therefore, some systems that offer a questionable cost-to-benefit ratio in a counterterror context (such as the stunningly expensive F-22 Raptor) nonetheless survived in the immediate post-9/11 era. If US defense policy remains focused on terrorism, however, one would expect to see a shift away from high-cost, high-technology platforms designed for a conflict with a military peer. There indeed has been such a swing in recent years; during his time as Defense Secretary, Robert Gates encouraged the shifting of DoD resources toward programs such as the mine resistant armored protection vehicle (MRAP). The ungainly MRAP has no standard design—it is built by several different companies—but all versions of the MRAP are so fuel-inefficient as to make even the Humvee seem "green" by comparison. The MRAP's lack of standardization, hulking size, and fuel inefficiency present serious logistical problems. In the context of Iraq and Afghanistan, the MRAP's major advantage over Humvees—heavy protection against mines and improvised explosive devices (IEDs)—certainly merited its procurement and use; the vehicle has saved the lives of many US and allied troops. However, in almost any imaginable non-counterinsurgency conflict, the MRAP's logistical problems make it a poor option for transporting US forces. This is the terrible dilemma that leaders face when making acquisition decisions: the right vehicles and weapons for today's war might be completely inappropriate for tomorrow's war.

The recent US military focus—including on the continual improvement of relatively lightly armed ground forces capable of operating both in urban and rugged rural terrain, prioritizing local intelligence-gathering (particularly of the human sort), and reworking US Army counterinsurgency doctrine—very much has been what one would expect of a force whose central missions relate to counterterrorism and counterinsurgency. This orientation away from peer competitors and toward improving the capability to fight "small wars" is not inherently undesirable—indeed, it is eminently sensible *today*. Yet it should be understood as a trade-off in capabilities that could carry a high price at a later point.

No military can be expected to be equally good at conducting all forms of conflict—armies prioritize depending on perceived risks, not only in equipment acquisition, but in training and in the general "organizational orientation" that personnel acquire over their years of service. Of course, an entity as large as the US military will have many unique subcultures, but it also is hardly coincidental that the occupations of Iraq and Afghanistan exhibited so many failures in their early years. The US military had evinced relatively little interest in counterinsurgency since the Vietnam period (and, overall, the US counterinsurgency effort in Vietnam was poorly designed); once involvement in Vietnam ended, the Pentagon returned to its focus on large-scale, conventional (and presumably Central European) warfare.

The 1991 Persian Gulf War, though indicative of a changing threat environment, certainly did not discourage the emphasis of conventional warfare—rather, American success in using technology, especially air-delivered precision weapons, to inflict brutal losses on the Iraqi Army reinforced the tendency to see conventional war as the "correct" style of conflict for the United States. The unhappy attempt to practice counterinsurgency in Vietnam thus could be dismissed as a one-time deviation from usual, and correct, US military practice which emphasized firepower and maneuver warfare.[32] (The costliness of the Battle of Mogadishu, in turn, could be treated not as providing evidence of changing military requirements but as the result of the decision not to place heavy forces, including tanks, on the ground in Somalia.) Similarly, the new reorientation toward counterterrorist and counterinsurgency operations can be expected to carry a price in regard to conduct of other types of operations, such as many forms of naval warfare, air combat against highly capable opponents, the conduct of forced landings,[33] and so forth.

This returns one to the problem of perceived priorities. If the US foreign policy and military establishments continue to place counterterrorism at the center of policy making—a phenomenon made all the more likely by the rise of a large and inward-looking Department of Homeland Security—both US policy and defense capabilities will be different than if they were shaped primarily by US interaction with other great powers. The most important objective of the counterterrorism-centered grand strategy is minimizing the probability of a catastrophic terrorist attack on US soil.[34] The most critical undesirable side effect is a decrease in the US ability to fight and win a great power war. In turn, the latter can be expected to increase the danger of such a conflict occurring for the simple reason that the more plausible victory appears to a potentially belligerent great power (or, perhaps more likely, a great power coalition), the more likely that would-be aggressor is to launch a war.

It is impossible to predict with any degree of accuracy how likely either a catastrophic terrorist attack or a great power war will be in the next quarter century, much less beyond that timeframe. However, as the United States now has officially ended combat operations in Iraq, it would be desirable for the US military and policy making establishment to begin paying more attention to great power conflict and less to counter-*jihadism* while at the same time not *significantly* increasing the probability of a devastating terrorist incident within the United States. This is not an inherently contradictory pair of requirements. Importantly, a shift away from counterinsurgency operations would not mean that Washington would proceed to ignore *jihadi* groups. Counterterrorist efforts within the military and intelligence agencies—and the enormous Department of Homeland Security—would continue to exist. The most significant shift would be a change in orientation in military procurement and training, but even this will prove difficult so long as significant US combat operations continue in Afghanistan.

The United States will continue to gather intelligence on terrorist organizations, undertake counterproliferation programs aimed at terrorist acquisition of WMD, and provide military aid to foreign governments which are fighting terrorists. All of these activities were undertaken before 9/11, and the latter event caused a deep awareness of US vulnerability to terrorist actors which ensures that counterterrorism will continue to be perceived as important to national security for many years. Well-structured counterterrorism efforts—combined with the aforementioned challenges that terrorists have in obtaining WMD—make it quite difficult for a terrorist group successfully to perpetrate a devastating attack on US soil (a fact demonstrated by the absence of such attacks). However, *the marginal benefit of obsessively focusing US efforts on terrorism likely would be very small*; beyond a reasonable baseline, counterterrorism can be expected to offer steeply diminishing returns. "Good enough" counterterrorism can ensure that the likelihood of a successful mass casualty terrorist attack in any given year is tiny. It is, however, impossible to eliminate entirely the possibility of such an attack. This would be true even if all the defense and intelligence resources of the United States were used solely in pursuit of such a goal.

By contrast, shifting Washington's attention to great power politics plausibly could have a radically positive effect on US national security. At most, as noted above, it could prevent a great power war from occurring; this of course would be an extraordinarily desirable outcome, given the immense human and financial costs of such a conflict. However, even a far more modest result would significantly benefit the United States—if, for example, a great power-oriented grand strategy enabled Washington to better defend its interests and effectively shape the international security environment in a fashion that it found amenable, it would reap substantial benefits. The most important of these could be ensuring that the United States maintains its position as the world's greatest individual power.

While Washington should begin shifting much more of its energy to great power politics, it is, however, unlikely that this will soon occur. Certainly, the Obama administration thus far has shown little inclination to do so. As a result, the international position of the United States can be expected to deteriorate substantially in the meantime. This is unfortunate, but largely explainable by the fact that the US policy making elite is, appropriately, adverse to seemingly risky changes in strategic focus—a sentiment reinforced by the difficulties encountered in Iraq and Afghanistan. Now that (at least for the time being) the conflict in Iraq has been brought to a reasonably successful conclusion, it is natural for the policy establishment (and the press) to fixate on the war in Afghanistan and the "AfPak" theater more broadly. For the United States instead to deliberately and intentionally choose to reorient its policy goals toward the construction of a stable multipolar system would *appear* to be "taking the eye off the ball." The natural instinct is to assume that this therefore would be a dangerous example of strategic malpractice. Having previously underestimated the threat that *Al Qaeda* poses to the United States, there is a (quite proper) desire to ensure that such a mistake is not made again.

Unfortunately, however, this attitude can blind policy makers to the fact that the development of an unstable multipolar system presents a much greater challenge to the United States than terrorist groups do. The fact of the matter is that Afghanistan almost surely never will be a stable, prosperous country—and it is not vital to US interests that it be one (a theme discussed in further detail below). Pakistan's fate is a more significant question, given the country's population, deep cultural ties to Britain, and, most importantly, nuclear arsenal. That country may degenerate in major civil war, and it may even splinter—*but it is Pakistanis, not Americans, who will decide whether that occurs.* The notion that, say, Prussia could have manipulated Americans into not fighting each other in the 1860s would be regarded as bizarre by any student of the War Between the States. The notion that Americans can accomplish a similar feat in Pakistan in the 2010s is similarly unbelievable.

Whether the United States undertakes more or fewer drone strikes, what conditions it places on military and other aid, and similar issues of course do impact the domestic politics of Pakistan. American decisions thus may be helpful or unhelpful in regard to stabilizing Pakistan. Yet, it is often extremely difficult to determine precisely how particular American choices will affect the Pakistani scene—killing Pakistani Taliban leaders with drones, for instance, can be good for Islamabad insofar as it eliminates some troublemaking individuals, but the population at large hates the strikes and they have the indirect effect of creating public sympathy for the Taliban. More fundamentally, however, it is extremely unlikely that some American misstep will *cause* a horrible outcome in Pakistan and that this, in turn, will result in strategic disaster for the United States.

Because the United States is very powerful, many observers (both American and foreign) tend to assume that it constantly causes "butterfly effects" whereby some small US action causes a political hurricane on the other side of the world. Most likely, this has, on occasion, happened. However, it is probable that butterfly effects are quite rare—moreover, even with hindsight, it is almost impossible to determine with certainty when they actually have occurred. When the United States intentionally sets out to have a huge impact on a country's future and uses blunt force to do so—by invading it, for instance—this will have major consequences for the future of the polity in question. However, that is not a butterfly effect—it is more akin to Washington turning the gears of its hurricane-generating machine.

Both Pakistan and Afghanistan were deeply troubled states well before the 9/11 attacks were perpetrated. A sledgehammer use of American power changed who held power in Afghanistan, but even after nearly a decade of effort, the country has not been stabilized. If the United States and NATO had better handled the occupation of Afghanistan, would that country today be a peaceable, stable democracy? In all likelihood, the answer is no. Benevolent occupiers often are little more than tourists, when one takes the long view. (Malevolent occupiers, by contrast, usually find it easy to fundamentally alter the future of a conquered people—building mountains of skulls is not difficult for those who have the means and mindset required to do so.) When, as in regard to Pakistan, the foreigners are not even occupiers, their influence can be expected to be even more modest.

Further complicating the US response to changes in the international system is the fact that there is no straightforward solution to the problem of how best to guide the development of multipolarity. The rise of new great powers realistically cannot be prohibited by Washington, and preventive war against plausible future antagonists such as China and Russia is (rightly) considered utterly unacceptable. Raising the defense budget—particularly for research and development programs, which would allow the United States to retain a qualitative edge in weapons systems for as long as possible—would provide something of a hedge, but would not fundamentally alter the international security environment. Additionally, given the size of the US national debt, among other concerns, it is most unlikely that the US Congress will soon throw mountains of additional money at the DoD; it is far more likely that the US military faces lean years ahead.

There is not a simple answer to how the United States should adapt to the ending of US unipolarity—focusing on great power affairs is a question of perspective, not of implementing a highly specific plan of action. In an American strategic culture dominated by the belief that problems are fixable, warnings about the inevitability of relative decline are most unwelcome. Moreover, the policy elite clearly is most comfortable when a defining strategic "mission"—such as containing the USSR or destroying *Al Qaeda*—exists; the multipolar vision described herein does not offer a theory of victory.[35] Indeed, the very notion of "victory" would be inapplicable. Rather, Washington's intent would be to manage the international security environment in such a manner as to minimize the probability of great power conflict while ensuring that its interests are protected and, critically, preventing the emergence of a great power hegemon (or hegemonic coalition) that would dominate Eurasia. Multipolarity could endure for many decades—and during that period the United States essentially would be attempting to prevent disastrous outcomes while guarding its own prosperity and interests.

Cautious manipulation of the international security environment is not a world-saving project, and thus is rather alien to US strategic culture as it has developed in the century since Wilson issued his Fourteen Points. As previously noted, the United States always has nurtured exceptionalist impulses, but since World War I it has come to see itself as playing a unique (even quasi-mystical) role: the polity that will lead other polities to a democratic, peaceful future. This rarely is stated bluntly, but it has become ingrained into US strategic culture and grand strategy. Thus, the assumption of a multipolar environment that will be very much like its predecessors—potentially violent and, in all probability, containing one or more great powers that are ideologically illiberal and bluntly unwilling to "reform" themselves—cuts against the grain of US strategic culture.

Given these various factors, there is every reason to suppose that the United States will avoid focusing on the reality of future multipolarity for as long as possible; rather, the Middle East and the AfPak region will continue to be the main focus of US strategic planning and intellectual energy.[36] A very bold president could effect a major course correction in US policy, but thus far there is very little evidence that President Obama is inclined to do this. Certainly, if the administration has some grand scheme to fundamentally transform the American relationship with China, India, Japan, and other major states, it so far has kept it well-hidden.

The current president has demonstrated a commitment to US–Russian nuclear arms control, but his concern over this issue actually harkens back to a bipolar world that no longer exists. Efforts to diminish the size of the Russian and American nuclear arsenal will not necessarily damage US interests, so long as numbers do not drop so low that an actor such as China decides to *increase* the size of its arsenal so that it is comparable to or larger than the ones controlled by Washington and Moscow. However, it is unlikely that such negotiations much enhance US security by bettering relations with Moscow—Russian leaders are deeply distrustful of the United States, and this has remained the case despite a battery of arms control treaties drawing nuclear numbers ever-downward. Moreover, the notion that decreasing Russian and American arsenals somehow will convince proliferators such as Iran and North Korea to disarm is fanciful; there's no logical reason why decision makers in Tehran and Pyongyang should decide to abandon their nuclear ambitions because great powers are trimming their own arsenals. Bilateral arms control negotiation is merely a "Cold War retro" pastime, not a foundation stone for the management of a multipolar international environment.

Conclusion: crafting a grand strategy for a multipolar world

It is impossible reliably to predict the long-term future, but grand strategy—if it is practiced in any form worthy of the name—requires placing intelligent wagers on how history's arc will bend. There was every reason to believe that unipolarity could not be sustained permanently; this, in turn, would mean that the international system would face new stresses and possible undesirable developments, including the possibility of great power war at some unknown future point. The United States not only did very little over the last two decades to address this potentially survival-level threat, but did not even pay it much attention. Instead, a decade of intellectually stultifying triumphalism was followed, after 9/11, by excessive attention to the limited threat presented by relatively weak Islamist terrorists (who could not, in any event, be completely nullified as a potential threat).

The 9/11 attacks placed counterterrorism at the center of US grand strategy and set in motion a series of foreign policy choices, some of which were deeply damaging to American power, consuming vast financial resources and speeding the collapse of a unipolar system in which Washington was overwhelmingly powerful. Monstrous though the attacks were, counterterrorism always was an overly narrow focus for a superpower with global interests and which historical circumstance had burdened with the thankless task of trying to maintain some reasonable degree of peace and good order in the global system. Now that Bin Laden is dead, the US has ceased to play an active combat role in Iraq, and the withdrawal from Afghanistan is underway, it would be wise for the United States to close the book definitively on the "GWOT era" and clearly move beyond the myopic grand strategy of the past decade, instead adopting one that is focused mainly on the future of the international system and, particularly, the relationship among the great powers. Unfortunately, there is little evidence that the United States—or, more particularly, the incumbent president—is ready to make this decisive shift.

4 The decider

The importance of presidential greatness

I'm the decider, and I decide what's best.

George W. Bush[1]

While many critics responded derisively when then-President Bush uttered the above statement, he actually stated a critical strategic truth with admirable economy. The sitting president *is* "the decider" in regard to foreign and defense policy; even the most embattled and unpopular president dwarfs all other figures in the US government in these areas, partly, but not solely, because of the president's unique constitutional role. Over the course of history—particularly from World War II onward—US strategic culture progressively, and despite the disapproval of many,[2] has come to accept that the presidency should be "imperial." While the power of the presidency did experience a radical decline in the wake of the Watergate scandal, this was a temporary occurrence, and the Oval Office soon recaptured its standing.[3]

It is notable that much (though not all) of the opposition to the enormous power of the presidency in foreign and defense matters essentially is special pleading based less on principle than on objections to how the sitting president wields his authority. One notices a curious tendency of many political observers to find very similar behavior by two presidents of different parties to be, in one instance, a perfectly acceptable exercise of power and, in the other, a shocking outrage. Overall, however, it is clear that in American strategic culture the imperial presidency is regarded as an essentially legitimate institution. This is demonstrated powerfully by the simple fact that it continues to exist, despite the reality that Congress and the courts could, if they wished, gravely undermine the president's power over foreign affairs. That these two branches do not continuously lay siege to the Oval Office, but instead usually just quibble over particular controversies that do not threaten the core powers of the presidency—such as the status of prisoners at Guantanamo Bay, for instance—is telling.

Term-limited emperors: the presidency and foreign policy

The centripetal historical forces that have led the presidency to play a supreme role in certain policy areas, and to marginalize Congress far more than most of the Founders likely would have thought desirable, are complex. However, as the Introduction to this work notes, one of the critical reasons for the waxing of presidential power is simple: neither the Judicial or Legislative branches of the US government could manage foreign and defense policy effectively, and the Executive branch is inherently pyramidical—with the exception of the Vice-President, its high officials are appointed by and serve at the pleasure of the president.[4]

In addition to controlling the machinery of the Executive branch, presidents are free to alter foreign and defense policy as they see fit, although Congressional control over the federal budget does constrain presidential power in critical respects. This particularly is the case in regard to security-related matters, as Congress decides both the general level of funding (the budget of the Defense Department itself being the most important, but far from the only factor) and whether specific programs are funded. Thus, an especially controversial program may be curtailed, or eliminated altogether. Moreover, because the length of time that a president may serve is restricted by the Twenty-Second Amendment to the Constitution, his or her ability to shape the general structure of the military establishment is constrained; given long procurement times and other issues, even vigorous efforts like the defense buildup of the early 1980s show their greatest impact only after the administration of the president who initiated them has left office.

Even granting such constraints, however, presidents have enormous power over how the United States acts in the world. Most strikingly, even if presidents formally lack the power to declare war they possess it de facto, a fact which has been demonstrated many times. Yet even this is not the only tool they possess for crafting the international security environment. Although all presidents make high-minded statements that reflect the values of American civic religion—endlessly praising the virtues of democracy, for example[5]—the degree to which they try to implement such oratory, and how they attempt to do so, can vary enormously. Thus, as previous chapters explored, there is little that assures continuity in foreign policy, especially when there is no overarching intellectual structure, such as containment, that is accepted by the policy making elite and broad public.

The freedom that presidents enjoy to shape policy should not, however, be seen as necessarily negative. Indeed, arguably a powerful presidency can be an excellent solution to a critical strategic problem that afflicts virtually every modern democracy: acting effectively in a world in which authoritarian governments suffer much less from the constraints imposed by mass media and public opinion than do their democratic peers. In this regard, non-democratic governments enjoy a certain structural advantage, as the ability to respond dexterously to the flow of international events—and to make unpopular decisions—is maximized. Of course, this does not ensure that they will use their freedom of action wisely, as the history of the twentieth century demonstrates.[6] However, if wielded properly, such plasticity potentially can be a powerful asset in the conduct of foreign policy.

The presidency can offer an excellent compromise between complete independence from public and media pressure—which obviously is inherently unacceptable in an electoral democracy—and unashamedly yielding to whatever opinion polls indicate that the public favors at a specific moment. If they are willing to surrender sufficient political capital, presidents can dare to take very unpopular actions, and have the power to do so, but the relatively short period between presidential elections ensures that within a reasonable period of time the electorate can reject the executive's action and demand a change in course. Thus, democratic accountability remains in place, but the potentially corrosive effects that "24/7" media and related swings in public opinion can have on policy coherence are somewhat tempered. Yet, of course, presidents can only be expected to leverage their opportunities well if they have reasonably sound strategic judgment—placing extraordinary decision making power in the hands of one individual can be disastrous if he or she is not up to the task.

Moreover, over the long term consistency in strategic performance is very important. If a polity is generally mediocre in strategic performance, its power potential will corrode and it will become increasingly difficult to prevent a catastrophic strategic setback. A strategic mastermind who happens to hold office at the right time might be able to rescue it from a particular disaster, but *past failures make success more difficult to obtain.*

There is a compelling case to be made that the importance of obvious crises—particularly great power war—in determining the long-term fate of states can be overemphasized. There of course have been numerous cases in which a catastrophic military defeat dramatically damaged a previously healthy great power, or even resulted in its total collapse. It is, however, worth remembering that many political entities have died slow deaths,[7] with military defeat, revolution, or a similar crisis only delivering the *coup de grâce* to a regime that had strategically underperformed for decades, or even centuries.

This famously was the case with the Ottoman Empire, but there are many similar examples. The Mughul Empire, for instance, was explosively successful in the mid-sixteenth century, began to decline by the early eighteenth century, and a century later was reduced to being a mere British tool. Finally, after the Sepoy Rebellion (also known, among other names, as the Indian Rebellion of 1857),[8] the British decided to do away with it altogether. In the quite different geostrategic circumstances of Central Europe, the Polish–Lithuanian Commonwealth also burst forth in the sixteenth century and then proceeded slowly to decline. It was a powerful, populous, and geographically huge entity when it was formed in 1569, but had a rather unhappy seventeenth century (with some exceptions, the most enduringly famous being John III Sobieski's crushing of the Ottomans at the Battle of Vienna in 1683). Beginning in the reign of Peter the Great, the Commonwealth was dominated by Moscow, and finally it disappeared altogether in a series of partitions that ended in 1795.[9]

The United States does face any grave and ongoing foreign policy crisis, and certainly is not threatened by foreign conquest. Rather, the danger is that Washington's national position may progressively decline to the point that its ability to decisively influence great power competition in Eurasia—the landmass on which, by a considerable margin, the majority of the world's people live and where most human economic activity occurs—is critically diminished. If the US is unable to guide great power competition—and, if necessary, successfully win a great power war—it will not be capable of guarding its own interests efficiently. The grand strategic imperative is straightforward: guide great power competition in such a manner as to prevent the occurrence of great power warfare; if this effort is unsuccessful, ensure that the United States will emerge victorious from such a war at a non-ruinous price.

For good or ill: the presidency and American strategic culture

Given the degree to which their folk history emphasizes personal independence and distrust of authority, the emphasis that Americans place upon "great men" is incongruous, but this contradiction itself is telling. The US tendency to celebrate national heroes with perennial public holidays, for example, is alien to the British political tradition, even though the latter laid the foundation for its American counterpart. Most Britons would find the notion of annually celebrating the birth of a long-deceased public figure such as Elizabeth I or Pitt the Elder, or even a relatively recent one such as Winston Churchill, to be peculiar. Even when a British national hero is celebrated architecturally, it is in a rather more modest fashion than Americans favor: Nelson may have a column, but Washington has a giant obelisk, while Lincoln and Jefferson have temples worthy of Roman gods.

Hero-worship has been a powerful force in the political life of the United States since its foundation, but it is critical to see this tendency in the proper perspective: in part, it simply reflects the need and desire of a young country without a clear ethnic identity and history to construct a national mythology. All nations build national mythologies that reflect what the members of the nation value and what they believe makes their group distinct and admirable, but perhaps a young—and in some respects "artificial"—nation like the American one can be expected to have a particularly powerful hunger for stories that bind countrymen together and give them a sense of common history and culture. Used in this sense, "mythology" is not pejorative, though, at least on some delicate points, national mythologies invariably tend to be at odds with objective historical truth.

American national myth building was intense in the early decades of US history, with some of the Founders being deployed as living demonstrations of patriotism and other virtues. Washington, unsurprisingly, was the most critical figure in American mythology during the early period of US history, and the legend built around him as the Father of the Country was of a figure of such unwavering character as to make the average saint seem slightly naughty by comparison.[10] Later, Lincoln would be catapulted to a similarly lofty position in the American pantheon almost immediately after his death. This reflected both his historical role and his personal martyrdom in the cause of restoring the Union. In a nineteenth century America in which the vast majority of the population were at least nominally Christian, and in which Christian themes played a key role in the shaping of public discourse, the story of Lincoln's death resonated powerfully. Moreover, unlike Washington—an aristocrat by birth, a conspicuously wealthy landowner thanks to wise investment and marriage to an affluent widow, and a man who carefully maintained a degree of aloofness in his relationships throughout his adult life—Lincoln's modest origins and folksy manner (the latter, ironically, probably was as carefully calculated as Washington's remoteness) made him a bit more accessible and archetypally "American."

The US national pantheon has never been restricted to presidents. Benjamin Franklin was regarded as a major figure for most of the country's history, for instance, though his fame seems to have faded a bit in recent decades. Today, Martin Luther King looms large as, essentially, a personification of the civil rights movement. (As with Lincoln, the fact of his assassination added a powerful mythic element to his biography.)

It is, however, clear that presidents have played a particularly strong role in American mythology. Partly, this simply is the result of the political prominence that presidents have always enjoyed, but which became much more pronounced in the twentieth century.[11] Ironically, the proliferation of media appears to have redoubled the focus on the president and his cabinet and advisors—and, of course, generals tasked with command of combat operations. King is unusual insofar as he attracted attention precisely because he did not hold office, instead leading dramatic protests and risking physical assault and arrest; not unlike Lincoln, his mythos has a strong religious flavor—in his case, that of a prophetic dissident standing outside the elected political elite who ultimately is martyred.

The fact that the president serves as both head of state and government also is significant in relation to the role of presidents in US mythmaking.

Many democracies assign the position of head of state to publicly nonpartisan, and otherwise redundant, monarchs or otherwise try to ensure that the head of state is politically uncontroversial and possesses little actual power. The United States, by contrast, comingles ceremonial and governmental duties, and the president has no plausible near-equal in status, unlike, for instance, the relationship between the French prime minister, the formal head of government, and France's president. American pundits commonly speak of their worry that the presidency itself may be damaged by the actions of the incumbent, whoever that happens to be at a given moment, and that this will have an undesirable impact on US national power. Such concerns no doubt often are sincere, but appear misplaced; as noted previously, the presidency as an institution seems to be quite healthy, regardless of the Watergate burglary, allegations about the embarrassing personal lives of several presidents, and assorted other scandals and follies over recent decades that may temporarily have damaged it. How much the position of head of state actually enhances the power of the presidency as an institution is debatable, but it certainly is important to myth building, as it removes any question concerning whether the head of state or government is the "real" embodiment of the nation as a whole.[12]

The discussion of presidential myth building is relevant to strategic culture because the former has played, and continues to play, a major role in shaping the latter. American strategic culture places the president at the core of the foreign and defense policy process. Formally speaking, the Constitution grants the president relatively modest powers, including the right to: perform as the commander-in-chief, a vaguely defined status that grants authority over "the Army and Navy of the United States, and of the Militia of the several States, when called into the actual Service of the United States";[13] negotiate treaties "by and with the Advice and Consent of the Senate" (a power greatly constrained by the requirement for two-thirds approval in that body); and appoint various officials, including ambassadors, subject to Senate approval.[14] In terms of strategic decision making, the most important of these powers is the president's role as commander-in-chief.

As the Constitution does not detail precisely what the limits are to a commander-in-chief's power, presidents frequently have used this role to expand the boundaries of their legal authority. This process has not resulted in a linear history of ever-expanding presidential power; the president who made the most assertive use of his role as commander-in-chief was Lincoln. However, as discussed previously, in general the Executive branch has marginalized Congress in regard to strategic decision making (with, it again should be noted, the latter's implicit consent—Congress is not without resources that would allow it to contest presidential control far more effectively than has been the case historically). Most notable is the fact that, the basically ineffectual War Powers Act aside, presidents have taken total control over decisions regarding US entry into war—although, during prolonged conflicts, Congressional influence seems to increase in tandem with public war-weariness. There has not been a formal Congressional declaration of war since 1941. Yet, post-1945 the United States has fought—depending on whether one counts the invasion and occupation of Iraq and Afghanistan as separate wars rather than merely two theaters in a single GWOT—either four or five major conflicts and engaged in a multitude of lesser military operations. The president has taken on a role not unlike that of a monarch who can make war at will but lacks control over the means by which his adventures are funded.

Many of the Founders no doubt would be uncomfortable with how the presidency developed as an institution, but it was their choices that made today's presidency possible. The Constitutional Convention was not simply remiss when it failed to define the presidency precisely; its vagueness essentially was a compromise between those who wanted a vigorous executive and those who preferred a weak one. The task of defining the character of the presidency was left to Washington, who, it was universally, and correctly, presumed, would become the first president. Washington, in turn, governed with moderation and refused to use his control of the military and personal *dignitas* as Augustus had, to subtly make himself the permanent center of political authority.[15] He remained in office for two terms and then left office willingly and without looting the treasury—an admirable example which all too many postcolonial leaders in Africa, Latin America, and elsewhere have chosen not to follow.

Nonetheless, the fact that it was Washington who defined the presidency combined with the generality of Article II of the Constitution made it, in retrospect, very likely indeed that the presidency progressively would push Congress aside in the making of foreign policy and strategy. This returns one to the issue of mythology in the shaping of US strategic culture: when a living legend defines an office, his or her personal status has a formative influence on it. At its inception, the presidency was imbued with enormous prestige by virtue of the fact that Washington held the office; he gave it greater standing. From the first president onward, US strategic culture has treated the presidency as fundamentally different from seemingly similar positions such as the Chief Justice of the Supreme Court or the Speaker of the House. In turn, the pre-existing prestige of the presidency assisted subsequent presidents in their effort to exercise power (and some presidents, like Jackson, Lincoln, and the two Roosevelts, helped to create—from the perspective of the person sitting in the Oval Office—a virtuous cycle, as strength built on strength).

The combination of Washington's definition of the presidency, the president's dual position as head of state and of government, the vagueness of the powers of the commander-in-chief, and the American strategic cultural assumptions that flowed from the preceding factors created a continuing momentum that allowed the presidency to dominate the other branches of government in regard to foreign and security policy. One should be cautious to avoid the claim the presidential supremacy in this area was inevitable; contingency shapes historical events, and a string of notoriously incompetent presidents early in US history might have allowed the supporters of legislative supremacy to "fight back" effectively, perhaps by way of Constitutional amendments that would erode presidential powers by more precisely defining them. Nevertheless, the presidency clearly did enjoy the equivalent of a five mile head start in a marathon—the historical outcome was not surprising.

US strategic culture treats presidential dominance in strategic decision making as natural, and thus possible alternative arrangements are regarded with suspicion. Historically, the degree to which the Executive branch dominates strategic decision making has varied somewhat—the years immediately following Watergate represented the greatest crash in presidential power in the twentieth century—but presidential supremacy in this area is long-standing and obvious. In general, Americans see presidential control over strategic decision making as customary and sensible; their entire history (both mythic and actual) has conditioned them to accept this state of affairs. Few Americans—including those in the policy making elite—even much ponder the question of whether presidential supremacy in strategic decision making is objectively desirable; they do not question it because they see it as inevitable. This of course does not mean that individually they approve of every presidential action. They do, however, consider the control that the institution of the presidency exerts in foreign and defense affairs to be legitimate, even if they regard the actions of a specific president as foolish, or even illegal. Absent a series of obvious catastrophes over several administrations, which might eventually convince public and elite opinion that a restructuring of the defense and foreign policy apparatus was necessary, the president will remain *the* US strategic decision maker.

In strategy, as in many other areas, practices which bring about success are likely to be repeated. For instance, if a strategic community's past experience has been that "war works," that community is likely to rely on war frequently to achieve its policy goals. Conversely, a series of shattering defeats (or even a single, particularly calamitous, one) may shape a strategic culture so that it is deeply adverse to the use of organized violence and will seek to avoid war even if it must pay significant costs financially and/or in terms of prestige and reputation. The experience of the United States has been that presidential dominance of foreign and security policy works reasonably well. After all, illustrated previously, American strategy has been highly successful overall. Such a record of success itself has a powerful effect on strategic culture that should be kept in mind. Unfortunately, it also makes it all the more difficult for Americans to recognize the ways in which the presidency appears to be increasingly dysfunctional as a "strategic institution."

Failure within the policy elite: the NSS example

The National Security Strategy of the United States (*NSS*) is the most prominent and comprehensive public statement on grand strategy that currently is issued by the US government. The *NSS*, new editions of which are issued on an irregular basis, essentially is the declaratory grand strategy of a democratic superpower, and, as such, one might expect them to be impressive, even majestic. That is not, however, the case. In actuality, these documents tend to consist mostly of bland truisms and wishful thinking; they are a lowest common denominator product of the interagency process. For example, the 2002 version of the *NSS* makes the claim that:

> For most of the twentieth century, the world was divided by a great struggle over ideas: destructive totalitarian visions versus freedom and equality. That great struggle is over. The militant visions of class, nation, and race which promised utopia and delivered misery have been defeated and discredited. America is now threatened less by conquering states than we are by failing ones. We are menaced less by fleets and armies than by catastrophic technologies in the hands of the embittered few.[16]

The history of the twentieth century indeed was defined largely by ideological struggle, and some very nasty ideologies (such as Nazism and the Stalinist variant of communism) have been brought into such disrepute that they probably are safely dead and buried. However, the notion that "militant visions of class, nation, and race" will never again trouble humanity—which would appear to be the implication of the above quotation—is a stunning assumption that, notably, ignores the ongoing occurrence of ethnic violence. There would appear to be quite a few people in the world who do not believe that militant visions relating to *their* nation are discredited. Perhaps even more oddly, the above statement would appear to place the struggle against Islamist terrorists outside the "totalitarian vs. democratic paradigm."

The above paragraph was rewritten considerably in the 2006 version of the National Security Strategy, and became more specific, asserting that:

> The United States is in the early years of a long struggle, similar to what our country faced in the early years of the Cold War. The 20th century witnessed the triumph of freedom over the threats of fascism and communism. Yet a new totalitarian ideology now threatens, an ideology grounded not in secular philosophy but in the perversion of a proud religion. Its content may be different from the ideologies of the last century, but its means are similar: intolerance, murder, terror, enslavement, and repression.[17]

This version of the statement is much improved, as the possibility of future conflict occurring along lines of class, nationalism, or race no longer is denied. It perhaps is a bit optimistic to claim that "freedom" has triumphed over fascism and communism, given that China, among other places, still is formally communist, while Marxists from Venezuela to India soldier on in their war against the bourgeoisie. As a brand, fascism probably has been irrevocably damaged, but it is noteworthy that there are plenty of non-communist countries that are not any freer than, say, Mussolini's Italy or Franco's Spain. However, the general thrust of the sentence is basically reasonable.

More importantly, Islamism—which obviously is the unnamed totalitarian ideology mentioned above—is implicitly acknowledged to be a movement that presents a global threat to the United States. Also, the removal of the reference to an "embittered few" terrorists was prudent, given the fact that there are tens of millions of individuals who participate in Islamist movements of some kind—whether openly violent, like *Hezbollah*, or at least professedly non-violent, such as the Egyptian Muslim Brotherhood and *Hizb Ut-Tahrir*—and untold hundreds of millions more who are at least vaguely sympathetic toward particular Islamist groups. Of course, many thinkers are inclined to deny that Islamism inherently is totalitarian in character,[18] and there certainly are major differences between Islamist groups and movements; as with communism and fascism, there is not one single definitive variant of the ideology. Clearly, however, some Islamist movements—such as the Taliban—are totalitarian to the point of psychosis, even if others are more ambiguous. Given that Islamists tend to have theocratic goals and a deeply suspicious attitude toward Western notions of liberty, with women's rights and freedom of conscience (including the right to change one's religion or reject all religious belief) being areas of particular concern, as well as the record of Islamist governance in Afghanistan and Iran, it would seem entirely reasonable to treat Islamism as being an ideology with an inherent totalitarian tendency. One can be a non-totalitarian Islamist, but a totalitarian Islamist perhaps holds a more intellectually coherent position.

The purpose of analyzing these two snippets from the 2002 and 2006 versions of the NSS is not only to illustrate how hazy strategic thinking in Washington can be. Perhaps even more important is that it shows how over the course of only about three-and one-half years, from September 2002 to March 2006—a period of time in which the global security environment was not altered radically (unlike, say, in the years between 1913 and 1917)—conventional wisdom about the long-term strategic challenges facing the United States underwent a substantial change. In 2002, totalitarian "militant visions" had been conquered, never to trouble us again; by 2006, a purportedly new one was menacing humanity. Similarly, in 2002 a few angry terrorist renegades provided the chief threat to global security and great power war (i.e., war against "conquering states") was dismissible out of hand; by 2006, the terrorists represented only the vanguard of a powerful totalitarian movement. (The latter change, one might speculate, likely reflects the fact that Washington found it considerably more difficult to destroy Islamist-inspired insurgencies than it expected. Not for the first time, Americans were surprised to discover that, in fact, more than a few human beings do not aspire to be governed by democratic institutions built on Western notions of liberty.[19])

This is all the more striking when one considers that the same administration issued both the 2002 and 2006 documents. In the "big picture" very little changed over the time separating the two versions of the NSS; this illustrates clearly that *the United States is a polity that does not possess a clear long-term strategic vision.* Indeed, it has become extremely myopic; in 2002, it was utterly obvious that China was on the long-term ascent[20] and that Russia remained dangerous even if (indeed, partly because) it had declined enormously since Soviet times. A state that cannot think beyond the very short term cannot, in any meaningful sense, think strategically; it is strategically reactive, and does not know how to shape the security environment in a logical fashion.

Of course, as a public document, it would be surprising, and no doubt diplomatically unhelpful, if the *National Security Strategy* were entirely blunt in its discussion of US security policy. However, while much is omitted from discussion in such texts—there is, for instance, suspiciously little reference to the ambivalent relationship between the United States and Saudi Arabia in either the 2002 or 2006 versions of the *NSS*—these reports are not exercises in *dezinformasia* intended to obscure the real goals and attitudes of the US foreign policy establishment. (Indeed, this would be a quite counterproductive tactic, given that the chief user of the *NSS* is the US government itself, which treats it as an authoritative statement of its grand strategy.)

The instability and shallowness of US grand strategy are harshly demonstrated by the ever-morphing *NSS*. The 2006 version of the *National Security Strategy* now is considered inoperative, superseded by the Obama administration's first *National Security Strategy*, which was issued in May 2010. The paragraph discussed above appears now to have been removed entirely; the *2010 NSS* was completely restructured and rewritten, as though the world was born anew in the four years that had passed since the *2006 NSS* was issued.

The shyness in discussing the motivations of Islamist terrorists evident in the two previous versions of the *NSS* remains in the 2010 version. The *2010 NSS* states that "this is not a war against a tactic—terrorism or [*sic*] a religion—Islam. We are at war with a specific network, al-Qa'ida and its terrorist affiliates who support efforts to attack the United States, our allies, and partners."[21] This statement indirectly rejects the GWOT language used by the Bush administration—an unsurprising development, as the Obama team already had rejected the GWOT formulation well before the *2010 NSS* was issued. However, the fact that the US government had been vigorously prosecuting a conflict for, at that point, nearly nine years but had not yet definitively determined precisely who or what is the enemy is telling.

The fact that the *2010 NSS* focuses on the prevention of terror attacks against the United States and its allies rather than on the (literally impossible) notion of "defeating terrorism" is helpful, but in many respects the document represents a step backward. The struggle which has been the focus of US grand strategy since 9/11 does have a reasonably clear main objective—preventing Islamist terrorist attacks on the soil of the United States and its allies—but beyond that the discussion in the *2010 NSS* is unfocused.

In regard to the motives of Islamist terrorists—and the term Islamist, notably, appears nowhere in the document, nor did it appear in the two preceding versions of the *NSS*—only the most opaque of statements appears. In the course of a discussion on US-Muslim engagement, it is noted that, "we reject the notion that al-Qa'ida represents any religious authority. They are not religious leaders, they are killers; and neither Islam nor any other religion condones the slaughter of innocents." The intent is obvious, and generally laudable: to religiously delegitimize *Al Qaeda* leaders and differentiate them from the millions of Muslims who do not agree with the organization's goals and methods. The statement, however, is galactically pompous. What imaginable authority does a secular government have to arbitrarily decide who is or is not an Islamic religious figure? What is the evidence that "religious leader" and "killer" always are exclusive job categories, and that no religion condones the slaughter of innocents? The children who were immolated by Aztec priests in ceremonies to appease the god Tláloc might well have had a different view.

As with the two immediately preceding versions of the *National Security Strategy*, difficult tasks—such as defining precisely who, aside from card-carrying members of *Al Qaeda*, the enemy actually is—are avoided. This is not merely a matter of political correctness: there really is no consensus in the US policy making class on the ideological and intellectual boundaries of the conflict. After all, the Saudi proselytizing of Salafist Islam has been the main force for the spread of such thought globally, while Saudi money has provided the resources for the creation of Sunni Islamist terror networks.[22] The question of how the United States should respond to the ideological challenge presented by the Saudis rarely is even asked, much less answered thoughtfully. (Saudi Arabia explicitly appears only twice in the *2010 NSS*, once in a list of US partners in the Gulf region, the other time in a neutral mention of the fact that it is one of the G-20 states.[23])

In a complicated international environment, if the United States is to achieve its policy goals, it is vital that it be able to apply its "comparative advantages," particularly its military ones, in an appropriate way, and that requires (or at least is enormously aided by) a cogent grand strategy. It is a very reliable rule of thumb that, if it is to be used effectively, power—be it military, economic, diplomatic, or otherwise, must be employed in a purposeful fashion with consideration for how a polity wishes to shape the security environment over the long term. The absence of a definitive formal document does not mean that a state lacks a grand strategy—the issuing of a document such as the *NSS* of course is a relatively recent innovation; in the seventeenth century, Philip V of Spain had a grand strategy, but he did not issue public documents outlining it in detail.[24] However, conversely, the existence of such a document does not prove that a meaningful grand strategy exists.

Clearly, a meaningful grand strategy has not spontaneously emerged through the consensus of the policy making elite as a whole. The US strategic community has not responded to the information available about the international security environment by coming together to share a common view of how the United States should attempt to cope with that environment. This is not surprising, both because of longstanding trends—as noted above, even during the Cold War consensus in the policy elite was never complete and harmony within the policy elite diminished over time—and because no president has put forward a strategic vision sufficiently compelling to aid the creation of a new consensus (as Truman once did). These problems obviously are interlinked: the ever-sharpening distinction between self-identified "hawks" and "doves"—and, relatedly, between the Republican and Democratic Parties, which respectively are dominated by these factions—makes the creation of a new consensus difficult. In turn, the absence of presidential strategic vision reinforces the tendency for the policy making elite to splinter. Under any circumstances, it would be difficult to resolve this quandary, and only a very strategically capable president might be able to do so. It is not impossible that this will occur, but there are good reasons to be skeptical about the likelihood of such an eventuality, at least before great damage is done to the US position in the world.

The United States has ceased to have a grand strategy worthy of the name; its actions have been unfocused. Enduring problems, such as North Korean nuclear proliferation and the Israeli/Palestinian conflict are subjected to occasional diplomatic interventions that create an appearance of progress but does not actually resolve them. That would not necessarily be objectionable—after all, some unpleasant strategic conditions are not subject to resolution, and states simply must cope with them as best they can. The worrying aspect is the apparent delusion on the part of American leaders, including presidents, that such measures actually *will* lead to the resolution of the problems to which they were addressed. Such fantasy-based action is the opposite of strategically informed policy making. (Of course, the United States at times has been assertive in using its power but the results have often been unsatisfactory—the invasion and occupation of Iraq being a preeminent example of this problem.)

Warlords: presidents as military leaders

As noted above, the powers of the commander-in-chief are somewhat vague, which has been advantageous to the presidency insofar as it has allowed the Oval Office to use the "commander-in-chief card" to acquire and retain dominance in foreign and defense policy making. Even in time of war the president does not possess untrammeled power—notably, there is no constitutional provision explicitly allowing the declaration of a state of emergency, the suspension of Congress and the courts, or similar practices—but clearly the commander-in-chief does have a unique strategic role that is especially evident during international conflicts.

In part, this role reflects the mythic role of the presidency discussed above. The president serves as a modernized version of the heroic king[25]—a war chief whose moral and military leadership is critical to victory. Of course, unlike the heroic king, the president does not—or at least should not—exercise operational command. Instead, he or she represents both the coercive power of the US government and civilian control over the military—the latter a significant point to the Framers, given their not-unreasonable fear of a military coup overthrowing the republic.

The image of the national leader as warlord is political symbolism in a very raw and intoxicating form—justifiably, it has always served as a source of discomfort for those concerned about the corrosive effects of hero worship on democratic government. The Founders were quite aware of this danger, no doubt in large part because Roman history was a common intellectual reference point for them (as it was for other educated folk in the English-speaking countries in an era that produced Edward Gibbon). In placing the position of commander-in-chief in civilian hands, the Constitution created an institutional structure that, in key respects, was quite different from that which prevailed during the Revolution: Washington was, formally speaking, inherently subordinate to the Second Continental Congress, a position which he acknowledged as legitimate, if often irritating. There is every reason to believe that if the Congress had chosen to exercise its right to relieve the commander of the Continental Army of duty, a not-unimaginable proposition (as the Conway Cabal demonstrated), he willingly would have complied with its will. By contrast, the president is not subject to Congressional authority, except insofar as he or she is vulnerable to impeachment and removal. However, it would be difficult to argue convincingly that placing final command authority in the hands of the president—rather than Congress itself or (to the Founders, unthinkably) a uniformed military leader—failed to enhance political stability. Although numerous presidents, most notably Lincoln, have exercised their power as commander-in-chief so vigorously as to be accused of being tyrants,[26] the United States has never undergone an "executive coup"—no president has attempted to cancel elections so as to remain in power, or taken a comparable action. At the same time, the US military has demonstrated great scrupulousness in respecting civilian control.[27]

Nevertheless, there is an unavoidable tension that is created by ultimate civilian control over military operations. While there have been several US presidents who were long-serving professional officers, they were unusual; most presidents only briefly served in the military or did not do so at all. Thus, the supreme warlord of the United States usually has not been a military professional, and it is very easy to bring the judgment of non-professionals into question when difficult decisions are made concerning the conduct of war. This issue has recurred repeatedly throughout US history—Lincoln's warmaking, for instance, was brutally criticized throughout the Civil War, while Truman's decision to remove Douglas MacArthur from command of UN forces in Korea was one of the most controversial of his presidency.[28]

Save for the atypical Grants and Eisenhowers, presidents do not possess the personal credentials convincingly to make the argument that their operational and tactical judgment simply should be accepted by Congress and the public as superior to that of their uniformed advisors, and only a politically foolish president would attempt to do so, as it would appear extraordinarily arrogant. The president's broader strategic viewpoint is, however, another matter. As the preeminent US grand strategist, the president is expected to lay down national objectives and structure how military force shall be used to attain them; thus, the setting of war goals and the consideration of what the limitations shall be in the use of force are among the myriad matters that fall into the president's zone of responsibility. For a president to refuse to provide guidance in these areas it would constitute negligence in office. However, these proper presidential areas of responsibility are inextricably tied to operational and even tactical questions; a president cannot structure strategy without impacting operations. For example, whether one is speaking of Truman's refusal to conduct operations against Chinese soil during the Korean War—arguably the most critical issue in the clash between the president and MacArthur—or Clinton's readiness to conduct air, but not ground, operations against Serbia in 1999, presidents make political/strategic decisions that have a major operational impact. Perhaps the most extreme example of presidential prerogative in the military area is that ever since the invention of nuclear devices the US arsenal has been under the control of the president, who, quite appropriately, is expected to make detailed decisions about nuclear use.

The difficulty in separating the political from the operational complicates the question of what the proper role of the president is in warfighting. Criticism of presidential meddling in operational and tactical matters often is valid; presidents should, for instance, provide general guidance concerning limitations on the use of force, but, with rare exception, should not take it upon themselves to act as targeteers who dictate conventional bombing missions in detail.[29] Presidential interventions in low-level tactical issues are entirely legal, but unwise—partly because they are deeply demoralizing to the military professionals who should be making such decisions, and also because civilians in Washington inevitably do not have a solid command of relevant "facts on the ground" in a dynamic tactical environment. (Indeed, even high-level field commanders may have a relatively weak understanding of many of the tactical details that are relevant to their area of responsibility, which can be a source of much frustration for lower-level officers who have a better comprehension of local conditions.)

At the same time, however, the duties of the commander-in-chief do require presidents to intervene in military matters, and, if need be, to make what normally are considered professional military decisions; there is no clear line between wise intervention and foolish meddling. Eliot Cohen has made the argument—using the experiences of figures as varied in time and circumstances as Lincoln and David Ben-Gurion—for a strong civilian hand,[30] and there is much to be said for his perspective. Cohen acknowledges that even great civilian leaders make military mistakes—but he additionally makes the unarguably correct observation that military professionals also do so. Ultimately, he attributes much of the success of the four civilian statesmen whom he discusses to intuition or, in Clausewitzian terminology, genius.[31] This is an important point—and discussions of strategic ability unavoidably return to this slippery quality, which exists but is unquantifiable. However, of course, this does not solve the problem of when it is appropriate for presidents to intervene in military matters, and at what level of detail it is appropriate that they do so; one cannot reliably separate the genius from the goat until after the end of a conflict.

In short, the president holds, as in other areas related to foreign and security policy, an irreplaceable position in regard to the conduct of armed conflict. The importance of the president's military role is, however, especially striking, because it is by action in this area that a chief executive most directly and immediately may impact the fortunes of the United States. The consequences of presidential failure can be staggering—at the extreme, in the case of large-scale nuclear conflict, potentially leading to the destruction of the polity and the deaths of tens of millions of citizens. However problematic it is to vest one civilian with such responsibility, there unfortunately is no alternative that would be both practical and fitting with US strategic culture.

Warning the warlord: public criticism as counsel

Perhaps the best potential check on presidential error in wartime—and it admittedly is a very imperfect one—is public criticism and audit of the sitting administration.[32] It is tempting to see criticism of wartime presidents as intrinsically unhelpful; after all, the unavoidable reality is that heated debate over military decision making does encourage dissention and undermine national "moral solidarity," thus indirectly inflicting some degree of damage to a war effort. However, the benefits of such criticism may well—given the overall cultural context in which presidents operate—outweigh the cost incurred in diminished national unity.

As discussed previously, presidents have displayed radical variation in their overall strategic aptitude. A figure such as Lincoln is an extreme outlier—an unquestionable amateur who happened to possess an extraordinary strategic mind; the odds that such an individual would take office in 1861 were slim. A president such as Lyndon Johnson might represent the other extreme: an intelligent, seemingly capable figure who nevertheless proved, over the course of the Vietnam War, essentially to be immune to strategic learning. Neither had demonstrated particular interest in or knowledge of military affairs at the time he was elected president (though Johnson, given his many years in the House and Senate, including on the Senate Armed Services Committee, probably had a better familiarity with the details of then-current defense issues), but one proved highly competent while the other did not.

In Johnson's case, public criticism seems to have been of little advantage—indeed, it placed enormous mental stress on a man with a deeply troubled inner life,[33] and thus perhaps drove him to make even poorer decisions. However, a strategically educable man might have benefited from such input. In any bureaucratic hierarchy, subordinates tend to be reluctant to be forthright with their superiors when they believe that the latter are making errors. The mythology surrounding the presidency further discourages frankness, as does the "tribal" nature of US politics; dissent is likely to be interpreted as disloyalty by some of those surrounding the commander-in-chief, even if not by the president him- or herself. It is especially difficult for subordinates to be blunt with presidents who have volatile tempers and/or are likely to take constructive criticism personally (common leadership flaws which several modern presidents have demonstrated). In such circumstances, criticism by members of Congress and the public potentially *can* play an invaluable role, serving as an intellectual corrective for a chief executive who might otherwise be insulated from contrary opinions.

Reliance on outside critics to correct policy error by sitting presidents is, again, a deeply flawed and inconsistent mechanism. There is never any guarantee that it will be helpful and, as noted, in some cases criticism may even inadvertently drive a president to make poorer decisions than might otherwise have been the case. The latter is a non-negligible risk and cost accompanying open public criticism—but the price of openness in strategic decision making must be considered in comparison to that of a closed system in which the head of government is insulated from conflicting viewpoints and bad news. (Whatever the flaws in the US conduct in the 2003 invasion of Iraq, for instance, Bush's strategic performance at least compares favorably with that of Hussein, who was hopelessly disconnected from political and military reality.)

Moreover, while the United States occasionally has practiced some degree of active censorship of strategic debate during wartime, government censorship of public debate does not fit comfortably into US political and strategic culture. The use of the word "active" in this context is meant to denote government efforts to control debate in the press and in other public forums and to threaten dissenters with legal sanctions. This is quite distinct from limiting the release of war-related information, controlling the movement of reporters in war zones by refusing to provide them with protection except in authorized areas, political spinning (or even unarguable mendaciousness), and similar actions that may distort public debate but do not attempt to prevent it. These activities are controversial, at least in the view of professional journalists—with the exception of outright lying to the press and public, the broader electorate generally appears to be somewhat apathetic about such practices—but they do not constitute true censorship.

Interestingly, given that it was not a conflict in which US defeat was likely, or even would have an immediate and terrible impact if it did occur, government censorship perhaps was most intense during World War I, with the Wilson administration displaying a disturbingly authoritarian attitude regarding constitutional freedoms. There is every reason to believe that past government censorship is more of historical interest than a reliable guide to future government behavior. After World War II, efforts to limit strategic debate during wartime broke down almost completely, and the Supreme Court decision permitting the *New York Times* to publish the Pentagon Papers set a strong precedent limiting even the US government's ability to control public dissemination of pilfered classified documents. In recent years, the environment has only become more amenable to dissent during wartime, be it responsible, reckless, or even, by the standards used during the two World Wars, potentially treasonous—at this point, even US citizens who publicly endorse *Al Qaeda* and Taliban efforts to kill Americans probably need not fear prosecution, so long as they confine their activities to verbal and/or written support. Moreover, the US government's response to the disclosure of thousands of classified documents in recent years—most notably, in a succession of disclosures by the WikiLeaks organization—has been cautious, legally speaking. Effectively, the US government has—probably wisely, given technological realities—given up trying to limit public dissemination of documents once they have leaked.

Given legal precedent and prevailing attitudes concerning freedom of speech, it is extremely unlikely that strong wartime censorship will return, at least absent an enormous and obvious threat. Therefore, criticism during wartime should be considered a permanent feature of the US political environment and a useful one insofar as it compels presidents to consider and engage with perspectives significantly different from their own.

An issue related to criticism of presidential warmaking is the impact of conflict on public approval of presidents. Both during and after their time in office, the reputation of presidents is intimately tied to the conflicts which they wage, and, unsurprisingly, their popularity tends to vary with public perceptions regarding military success. This is not to say that the electorate's perception of most presidencies is defined almost entirely by conflict, perhaps excepting those rare times in which virtually the entire resources of the federal government (along with public attention) is given over to warfighting—such as nearly the entirety of Lincoln's time in office, the brief American involvement in World War I, and the period from the bombing of Pearl Harbor to Japan's surrender.

Nevertheless, warfare sometimes does deeply impact a president's popularity. Two Cold War-era presidents, Truman and Johnson, declined to run for reelection (in 1952 and 1968, respectively) largely because public frustration over a prolonged conflict with a seemingly second-rate opponent had made them unpopular. More recently, G.W. Bush won reelection in a close race approximately a year and half after the beginning of the US invasion and occupation of Iraq. Ironically, if the war had been launched earlier, as many in the Bush administration wished, the outcome of the 2004 election likely would have been quite different.

Bush's approval rating began a long-term downward drift after hitting an extraordinary high shortly after 11 September 2001;[34] his stunning popularity clearly had resulted from the US public "rallying around the president" after the terrorist attacks on New York and Washington, and this broad trend continued after his reelection. The administration did enjoy a spike in popularity during the early period of the Iraq War,[35] unsurprising given the aforementioned wartime rallying phenomenon and the success of the US military in effecting the overthrow of the Iraqi government quickly and with (to that point) little human cost. Over time, the citizenry increasingly came to see the Iraq War as overly costly in both human and financial terms, which encouraged the long-term degeneration of Bush's approval rating. While continuing combat in Iraq and Afghanistan certainly was not the only reason for Bush's low approval ratings, the GWOT obviously played a role in driving his approval down; this, in turn, surely undermined presidential effectiveness in other policy areas.

The latter point is a significant one: most presidents regard their popularity as valuable political currency and do not wish to undermine public esteem except in the service of significant goals.[36] A president sometimes can carry on doing important work despite personal disapproval—Truman, for example, continued to construct the solid foundation of US containment policy even as his personal approval disintegrated—but the widely held perception that an unpopular president is politically ineffectual is self-fulfilling: Congress often is unlikely to compromise with, much less defer to, unpopular presidents in regard to the latter's legislative agenda, while the press's focus on a president's low approval rating can cause further erosion in the public's view of that individual. The result is a political death spiral that can prevent an administration from achieving any of its key domestic goals and undermine (though, given the president's previously discussed supremacy in regard to defense matters and foreign relations, not completely eliminate) its ability to achieve its foreign policy objectives.

These above factors make public criticism and perception influential restraints on presidential warmaking. Moreover, Congressional action during wartime tends to be highly dependent on public mood; a president who is overwhelmingly popular generally has little to fear from Congress, while one who has lost public confidence should expect a parade of hearings, intense critiques, and, perhaps—as Nixon faced when his presidency was disintegrating—even successful efforts to use control over appropriations to trump the president's authority as commander-in-chief.

As noted above, public strategic debate carries a non-negligible cost in terms of national unity, and its actual impact on the conduct of a war can be either positive or negative—indeed, given the fickleness of public opinion, its net effect probably most commonly is mildly negative. However, the alternative is both unappetizing in the context of US political and strategic culture and, critically, likely would carry a higher price. Beleaguered and publicly reviled leaders tend to make poor warlords, but ones divorced from strategic reality, ranting and moving non-existent divisions around on sand tables, are almost invariably worse, and in modern times polities which do not allow open strategic debate have displayed a decided tendency to create the latter.

Thus, the unsolicited "advice" that public strategic debate provides to presidents can play a critical role. This probably would not be the case if most presidents were possessed of strategic genius—though even a genius sometimes benefits from the perspective of his or her critics—but that has not been the case in the past and certainly should not be expected in the future. The market in public strategic debate is not an efficient one, in an economist's sense of the term, even if it is open insofar as anyone and everyone (especially in the age of the blog, a remarkably low-cost way to broadcast globally) can supply an opinion; the sheer mass of contributors to US strategic debate does not mean that the prevailing view will not be harebrained. However, the alternative is an unaudited reliance on (unlikely) individual genius.

Conclusion

As this work emphasizes throughout, the US system of strategic decision making is notable for the degree to which power is vested in a single man or woman whose authority has (by democratic standards) few checks. This is both potentially its greatest vulnerability *and* greatest strength—the placement of awesome power in a single pair of hands is a wager on individual excellence.

The slow collapse of the Cold War consensus has left the policy elite without a clear vision of what the United States is attempting to accomplish over the long term. Realistically, only an exceptional president could craft a new consensus that would encourage coherence in US strategic activity and minimize the confused staggering that has come to be characteristic of American foreign policy. Even a president who saw the global security situation very clearly, however, would not find it easy to build a new consensus: the policy elite now is splintered to the point that most of its members share few common assumptions about the world, except perhaps for unhelpful ones that undermine clarity in strategic thinking—such as the belief in democratization as a panacea for all manner of social and political problems in any given society.

If, nonetheless, a president did prove capable of imposing a unifying strategic vision, the United States would benefit enormously. However, unless such an exceptional figure emerges, it is probable that US power will continue to corrode until the damage has become strikingly obvious. If the latter occurs, public and elite opinion likely will "self-correct," with a consensus emerging regarding the necessity for a fundamental reconsideration of the premises on which US foreign and defense policy is constructed. However, if the damage to US power is deep enough, Washington might well be unable to maintain its position as the greatest of the world's powers.

5 Feet of clay

Making inadequate strategists and war leaders

Previous chapters in this work addressed failures of presidential leadership, particularly from the Cold War period onward. If several recent presidents proved to be unimpressive strategists, it of course does not necessarily follow logically that future ones also will be mediocre. However, the evidence that this problem will continue is compelling. The American political system increasingly has moved away from selecting (in a quasi-Darwinian sense of the word) presidents for the experience and mindset likely to lead to strategic success in a challenging multipolar environment. This is not to say that Americans are isolationist, much less that they do not want their country to be successful in foreign affairs. Rather, broadly speaking, both the American public *and even policy elites* know relatively little about strategic history and practice; they simply lack the tools necessary to hold a national discussion in which the likely strategic acumen of potential presidents is assessed in a sophisticated manner.

Shutting the school: the decline of strategic education

Shortly after graduating with his undergraduate degree from Harvard, Theodore Roosevelt published *The Naval War of 1812*,[1] a work that was to be highly influential in shaping the military historiography of the second war between Britain and the United States. That a young member of the American upper class—which Roosevelt definitely was, being, in terms of family background, one of the most privileged men to become president—would write a work of military history despite the fact that he was not pursuing a formal academic career was not, in the late nineteenth century United States, particularly surprising.

Roosevelt's literary endeavors (he produced an impressively large number of historical, autobiographical, and other works over the course of his life) provide an insight into the sort of environment from which many American presidents—as well as lesser members of the policy making elite—were drawn. Many US presidents since childhood were exposed to the sort of material which serves as the foundation for a sound strategic education, receiving formal and informal instruction in history, classics, philosophy, and other material which contributes to a refined worldview and an appreciation of enduring realities, such as the continuing validity of Thucydides' observation that human beings fight wars for fear, honor, and interest.[2]

This is, it should be understood, quite different from the sort of narrow education that most undergraduate students of foreign and defense policy are offered, at least in the United States. The study of foreign policy is treated as a subcategory of political science, and the bulk of a student's effort is dedicated to understanding bureaucratic processes, highly abstract international relations theory, and similar material. This is worthy subject matter, but the salient fact for the purpose at hand is that an intelligent, thoughtful student can easily emerge from such an education with very little feel for the "texture" of strategy—the solidity of judgment about the character of humanity and the ways in which power is exercised that is the prerequisite for strategic genius.

There is no formula for cultivating strategic talent; indeed, the very notion of a formula misses the point entirely.[3] There is an artistic character to political practice in general, most definitely including international power politics; genius can only be cultivated, not imposed by fiat.[4] Moreover, every individual will have unique psychological and intellectual strengths and weaknesses—for instance, the same Lyndon Johnson who was a majority leader capable of masterfully manipulating his colleagues in the "micro-diplomatic" environment of the US Senate was utterly at a loss when dealing with Vietnamese communists whose worldview was profoundly alien to his own. On the Senate floor he was master of using his ability to understand, and ruthlessly control, other men who themselves were practiced politicians,[5] but his failure to comprehend his Vietnamese foes was so total that the latter might as well have belonged to a different species. A better strategic education might have made Johnson a leader capable of dealing craftily with Hanoi—or perhaps not, as it could be the case that he was psychologically incapable of addressing his failings. In any event, however, it is unlikely that a good strategic education would have made him a poorer strategist.

It is partly because strategic genius is artistic that it is a topic generally avoided in US public discourse. The absence of a reliable solution to the problem of ensuring presidential talent in the making of foreign and security policy encourages fatalism—since it is impossible to ensure that presidents will be good strategists, the temptation is to ignore the issue altogether and assume that a good group of advisors will "make up for" any personal deficiencies of the commander-in-chief.[6] Insofar as attention does focus on personal strategic talent, professional experience and similar factors are used as a (very weak) proxy for a high score on the nonexistent "strategic IQ" test.

Some fields of knowledge relevant to good strategic judgment have developed greatly in recent decades; this is especially notable in regard to some of the social sciences. Psychology, for example, is immensely more advanced as a field of study than it was a century ago, and an understanding of individual motivations and group behavior in decision making is an invaluable resource in policy making. (In regard to strategic studies, advancing psychological understanding has been particularly influential in shaping deterrence theory.[7]) The understanding of economics, similarly, has advanced considerably. Although there are leaders worldwide, Hugo Chávez being a notable example, who still use obviously flawed economic theory as a keystone block for policy, they do so despite a mountain of evidence that their programs are ill-conceived and will not accomplish stated goals. Thus, in some respects potential future leaders today enjoy advantages that entirely were beyond the reach of their predecessors.

Nevertheless, in some respects the environment for strategic education has become far less salubrious than it was a century ago, at least in the United States. First, bright students are less likely to be exposed to some kinds of potentially useful knowledge, particularly of the literary or historical sort. An educated American of the eighteenth or nineteenth century almost invariably had some grounding in the history and literature of the classical world, for example—it could be taken for granted that a conversational reference to Scipio Africanus or Agamemnon would be understood—and a reasonable knowledge of European philosophy and British history also was common in elite American circles.

Familiarity with *The Iliad* of course is not a prerequisite to be a successful strategist. However, contrary to the perception that now reigns in American (and also European) policy making circles, seemingly impractical literary and historical knowledge can prove far more vital than would a command of whatever transient data is presently considered to be of importance. Nuanced strategic thinking cannot be reduced to a set of PowerPoint briefing slides, much less to a wire diagram describing the interagency policy process. As Christopher Coker skillfully demonstrates, there is much in *The Iliad* that is entirely relevant today in thinking about warfare in general—and that epic provides insights into honor-based strategic cultures that an American conducting a campaign against Afghan or Iraqi tribesmen might find most useful.[8] Knowledge of literature and history can encourage a flexibility and realism of thought that is vital to thinking seriously about warfare and the use of power.[9]

Perhaps the greatest failure of current American strategic culture is the degree to which culturally comfortable assumptions—many of which are the sort of beliefs that often are described derisively as being politically correct but that nonetheless continue to reign over public discourse—substitute for serious consideration of what motivates leaders with whom the United States is interacting. There is a tendency to replace complex, and, from an American perspective, culturally uncomfortable narratives with simple ones that are culturally amenable.

When the United States involved itself in the conflicts in the Balkans during the 1990s such tendencies very much were on display. Most of the US government's highest officials evinced little interest in the long history that had led to the fighting over control of former Yugoslav territory. All which had passed before the present was treated as a nuisance, a distraction from the pressing problem of ending the ongoing fighting.[10] This was a strikingly narrow way to perceive the struggle—and, in contrast, those doing the fighting believed the past and present to be deeply interwoven. Indeed, the US (and, it should be noted, EU) attitude was narrow even by the standards of the modern Western policy elite—it hardly would have required a great leap of imagination for Americans to imagine that many of them would find secession to be a matter worth killing over. (The constitutionality of Confederate succession, after all, is rather dry stuff compared to the bloodsoaked national myths of the various ethnicities of former Yugoslavia.) The willingness to shrug off the complications of history in turn allowed the construction of a simple tale of victims and victimizers, with Slobodan Milošević used as the chief representative for the latter. The American/EU narrative was not, it should be emphasized, entirely without foundation—Milošević was a nasty cutthroat and large numbers of innocents were the victims of war crimes committed by Serbs—but it ignored every nuance, underplaying both the historical complexity of the issues at hand and the reality that many Serbs were the victims of war crimes committed by members of other ethnic groups.[11]

Unsurprisingly, this simplified narrative encouraged the crafting of a policy that lacked sophistication. The United States, along with its European partners, did achieve the goal of ensuring the survival of Bosnia-Herzegovina and, later, the ousting of Serb forces from Kosovo and that entity's de facto separation from Serbia. However, there is no reason to believe that the US government intended to create a ramshackle Bosnian state perennially on the verge of violent disintegration and an independent Kosovo whose local power structure is largely dominated by Mafiosi and similarly unpleasant characters, or that such outcomes have served US interests.[12] Yet the logic of the US policy was such that there was no other plausible "victorious" outcome. The United States would have been defeated if Serbia had somehow managed to stymie Washington and compel it to accept political humiliation rather than pay the military price necessary to overpower Serbia; instead, the United States achieved approximately the best outcome that it could reasonably hope for—and yet it was not an especially desirable one.[13]

Of course, few American leaders of previous generations had much knowledge of the intricacies of Balkan history; the point is less the lack of specific historical knowledge than it is the lack of appreciation for the scope of human experience and culture—and the resulting misguided belief that nearly every human being has "an inner American" waiting to emerge if given the opportunity to do so. The historical examples on which the American policy elite—including presidents—*as a group* can knowledgably draw are few; thus, the same few examples reemerge time and again in internal government discussion and public statements of policy. August 1914, the Munich Agreement,[14] the Cuban Missile Crisis,[15] the supposed lessons of Vietnam and the fall of the Soviet Union,[16] and a handful of other references comprised the common historical vocabulary of US policy discourse. The situation in the Balkans in the 1990s often was compared to the Balkans in 1914, however implausible the possibility of wider, much less great power, warfare.

The poverty of the American policy making establishment's historical vocabulary has an indirect, but powerful, effect on the quality of US policy. Reasoning by historical analogy always is a hazardous enterprise, as no two events are precisely alike in detail. However, the possession of a greater quantity of analogies can have enormous value—attempting to drive a square peg into a round hole is unlikely to have a good outcome, but driving an octagonal peg through the hole might be possible, even if the fit will be imperfect. Even more importantly, richness of historical understanding provides a better general perspective on current—and possible future—events. This enhances the likelihood that leaders will be able to prevent problems from developing into serious threats, or, at least, that they will cope successfully with crises when they do emerge.

It again should be emphasized that an education overflowing in material that can be strategically instructive does not guarantee that the student will develop into a master, or even a competent journeyman, strategist. There is no way to ensure that a given individual will perform well in high office. Some policy makers who are brilliant in subordinate roles are unsuited for supreme command, and even those leaders who have the right stuff may be erratic in the quality of their leadership. (The seemingly innumerable successes and failures of Churchill's career illustrate the latter point vividly.[17]) Nevertheless, the fact that most future presidents (as well as other senior civilian policy makers) receive little education in strategy during their younger years surely has tangible, if indirect, effects.

A shallow pool: the strategic knowledge of potential presidents

As discussed above, in recent decades the US electoral system has served as an exceedingly weak control mechanism for ensuring the "strategic quality" of US presidents. Most presidents from during and after the Cold War have taken office with little previous experience in foreign and/or defense policy. Certainly, this indicates that the voting public does not place an extremely high value on such experience. If voter demand for seasoned foreign and defense professionals was high, then every four years the states of Iowa and New Hampshire would be filled to overflowing with retired generals and diplomats, former cabinet officials, and similar contenders.

This lack of emphasis on relevant experience in foreign and defense matters, however, does not necessarily mean that voters do not place any value on strategic competence—that certainly does not appear to be case, and it would be most surprising if it were. Very likely, American voters are somewhat naïve in assessing previous experience: perhaps, for instance, voters tend not to appreciate how little knowledge many governors, and even members of Congress, actually have about foreign and defense policy. Moreover, given the difficulty of predicting what (if any) negative consequences would flow from the placement of a strategic incompetent in the Oval Office—as president, such a person *might* make decisions that would result in some sort of disaster at an undetermined time in the future—many voters choose to concentrate on seemingly more concrete issues like unemployment, taxation, and regulation.

Efforts by journalists and campaign professionals to use the career patterns of previous presidents to predict forthcoming presidential elections tend to be constructed on the questionable assumption that the last few elections have created powerful and discernable historical trends. However, given the tiny number of elections being discussed, it is easy to exaggerate the power of perceived trends. For some time, particularly following the Bush victories in 2000 and 2004, it was popular among pundits to reiterate the supposed advantages that Southern and Western governors have in presidential contests and the difficulty that vice-presidents and senators allegedly have in being elected to the highest office. However, in the 2008 election both the Democratic and Republican nominees were US senators; moreover, the victorious candidate was a Midwesterner with Hawaiian roots. (Also, one might note that in 1960, 1968, and 2000 sitting vice-presidents did come extremely close to winning the presidency—and many argue that Nixon and Gore were the "real" winners in, respectively, 1960 and 2000.)

The general background of presidents varies considerably—individual charisma, intraparty struggles, vagaries in the public mood, unpredictable global events, and other factors contrive to make it impossible to draw up a method for reliably predicting future presidents on the basis of previous professional experience. In speaking of the elections from 1948 onward, the general guidelines that one might extract are unimpressively vague: politicians from states with large populations enjoy an advantage over their small-state counterparts; individuals tend to have served as a state governor, US senator, and/or as vice-president before becoming president; future presidents sometimes serve in the House of Representatives, but they do not ascend directly from that body to the presidency; and—most importantly for the discussion herein—individuals who become president will *not* have spent much of their careers serving in the unelected policy bureaucracy. Yet, even these very general rules are highly unreliable; Eisenhower broke three of the four guidelines, if his military career is counted as service in the policy bureaucracy. The only one of the four that has consistently remained unbroken over the last six decades is the third one—bad news perhaps for ambitious House members, though in every election cycle several confident and optimistic (or, in some cases, outright deluded) Representatives nonetheless brave the cruel Iowa winter.

The fact that so few recent presidents have served in high-level unelected positions is rarely remarked upon, but very instructive. Intuitively, one would assume that presidents previously would have occupied one or more senior offices in the Executive branch. After all, if voters place at least *some* value on strategic acumen, then experience in foreign and defense policy—most likely with the Departments of Defense, State, Homeland Security, and/or at the National Security Council or in the Intelligence apparatus[18]—presumably would be electorally valuable. (Similarly, serving as Treasury Secretary or Director of the Office of Management and Budget would inspire voter confidence in a candidate's economic knowledge.) Nonetheless, very few Cold War or post-Cold War US politics presidents have previously occupied *any* appointed position in the Executive branch, much less have done so repeatedly throughout their career.

There of course are a great many men and women who do spend large portions of their career in appointed Executive branch positions, and many of them cycle through several departments during their time in government. A handful of them—such as Paul Wolfowitz and the late Richard Holbrooke—even become very well-known public figures despite never holding a Cabinet position. However, the career track of such policy professionals is quite distinct from the one that is likely to lead to the presidency.

This was not always the case. During the nineteenth century, it was not uncommon for presidents previously to have served as Secretary of State; indeed, Thomas Jefferson was the first individual to hold the latter office. Future presidents were less likely to have occupied other high federal offices—curiously, no Secretary of the Treasury has ascended to the presidency—but during the early decades of the Republic, national politicians often cycled through the upper echelons of the Executive branch and/or held foreign ambassadorships. James Monroe provides an extraordinary example of this: while serving as a US Senator from Virginia, he resigned his seat to become US Ambassador to France; he subsequently returned to Virginia politics, but then again became a diplomat, participating in the negotiation of the Louisiana Purchase and serving as Ambassador to Britain. He even de facto served simultaneously as Secretary of State and Secretary of War during the War of 1812. In October 1814, Monroe resigned as Secretary of State so as to take up a position in the War Department. However, President Madison did not name a replacement at the State Department, thus effectively making Monroe the holder of two Cabinet portfolios for the remainder of the War of 1812. After the end of that conflict, Monroe left the War Department and continued serving as

Secretary of State until taking office as president in 1817. During the Monroe administration, in turn, the cabinet was dominated by some of the most significant US politicians of the era: for the entirety of his two terms, the Secretaries of State, Treasury, and War were, respectively, (future president) John Quincy Adams, William H. Crawford, and John C. Calhoun.

After the early decades of US history, there was a trend away from former civilian Executive branch officials ascending the presidency. Most of the presidents of the mid-to-late nineteenth century (from the 1828 election of Andrew Jackson onward) seem not too dissimilar to their late-twentieth century counterparts: the highlights of their civilian careers tended to be serving as governors and/or members of the US Senate. The major difference is that most of them had served as general officers during wartime (though it should be noted that most of them were not career military personnel in the modern sense). This trend was particularly prominent in the later decades of the nineteenth century, when former Union officers dominated the presidency. Until the last Civil War veteran/president, William McKinley, died in office in 1901, every president after Andrew Johnson was a Republican Union veteran except for Democrat Grover Cleveland, a Northerner who had purchased the military service of a substitute during the conflict. Save for McKinley, who was very young even at the war's end, they all had attained general officer rank. (Although it perhaps should be noted that while Chester A. Arthur was a brigadier general in the New York militia, his military service was in a logistical capacity and relatively brief—the latter not by choice, as his position was a patronage appointment and the election of a new governor resulted in the loss of his commission.)

As recently as the early twentieth century it was not uncommon for presidents previously to have held cabinet, sub-cabinet, or other Executive branch positions: both Theodore and Franklin Roosevelt served as Assistant Secretary of the Navy; William Howard Taft held various posts, including Governor-General of the Philippines and Secretary of War; and Herbert Hoover served as head of the Food Administration during World War I and later was Secretary of Commerce. In the period since Franklin Roosevelt's death, however, it has been unusual for presidents previously to have held either a high military rank or occupied a senior position in the Executive branch. Most presidents after Roosevelt have been veterans, but only Eisenhower was a general officer. G.H.W. Bush is the only recent president with previous senior civilian Executive branch experience other than (though, in his case, also including) serving as vice-president; Bush had been the US Ambassador to the UN, Chief of the US Liaison Office in Beijing (the de facto Ambassador to the PRC at that time), and Director of the CIA.

Examining the historical evidence of the last half-century and more, it appears clear that, in regard to presidential politics, the electoral value of senior civilian Executive branch experience is unimposing. Even good generalship tends to pay modest political dividends—World War II produced only one US general/president; World War I,[19] Korea, Vietnam, and the 1991 Persian Gulf War created none. Voters might in principle approve of candidates having "hands-on" experience in areas related to foreign and defense policy-related decision making, but this factor clearly is not overwhelmingly important to them.[20]

Partly, no doubt, this is explainable as a matter of simple chance—some plausible presidential candidates with such qualifications choose not to run: Colin Powell, both a longtime general officer and (while still in uniform) National Security Advisor, very likely could have taken the Republican nomination in 1996, but he did not seek it. Similarly, there was much speculation that former National Security Advisor and Secretary of State Condoleezza Rice might run for president in 2008, but she did not do so.[21] Yet, some candidates with an impressive résumé regarding defense and/or foreign policy matters have put themselves forward, but gained little traction; notable examples include Henry Cabot Lodge, Jr. in 1964, Alexander Haig and (very briefly, as he withdrew before the primaries began) Donald Rumsfeld in 1988,[22] as well as Wesley Clark in 2004. None of these candidates even secured their party's nomination, much less won the presidency.

Perhaps the most likely plausible explanation for recent lack of foreign and defense policy experience among recent presidents is that talented politicians tend to be drawn to opportunities to run for Senate seats and governorships. This is largely because such positions in themselves are prestigious and powerful, but also many ambitious politicians have an eye on the White House even as they seek election to a lesser office. This of course creates a self-fulfilling prophecy, encouraging the media to focus on senators and governors as potential presidential candidates, and thus making it easier for those in such offices to raise money than otherwise would be the case, and so forth. (The advantage of large-state over small-state governors and senators in presidential primaries partly, if not mainly, stems from their opportunity to build strong state-wide donor networks, a potentially critical advantage, as it allows the creation of a large campaign fund months before the party primaries actually begin.)

At the same time, the professionalization of the military has discouraged would-be office-holders from remaining in uniform for a long period—many American voters admire veterans, but spending a large chunk of one's career in the military in the hope of gaining promotions that then *perhaps* could be translated into an electoral advantage obviously is not a reasonable political strategy in today's US political context. Young Americans with deep political ambitions usually serve only briefly, if at all, as full-time military officers. Though a handful of officeholders remain in the Active Reserves for a long period of time and some officers do allow previously suppressed political ambitions to flower after they retire, it is deeply unlikely that we again will see a long string of general-presidents:

the occasional Eisenhower perhaps will appear, but "starred presidents" will remain uncommon.

At this point in history, appointed positions in the Executive branch appear to be a political dead-end, if one aspires to be President. (Although the current Secretary of State likely hopes that this rule is not ironclad.) From a cost/benefit perspective, it appears that individuals whose career goal is to be president are acting rationally when they avoid the Cabinet, as well as when they choose not to become career officers.

In terms of its impact on US foreign and security policy, however, the move away from civilian Executive branch service by future presidents probably has been unfortunate. While there is no reliable link between "strategic experience" and competence as commander-in-chief—a point illustrated by the dramatic contrast in the careers of Abraham Lincoln and Jefferson Davis—it would be difficult to believe that such an association is altogether specious. There is every reason to believe that, as a general principle, individuals who have grappled with the realities of foreign and security policy throughout their career are *more likely* than untested beginners to serve competently as supreme commanders. If inexperience were the key to strategic excellence that fact would have become obvious centuries ago—because history then largely would have been a story of how no professional could hope to survive against sufficiently amateurish novices.

Moreover, given the absence of sound strategic education noted previously, hands-on experience is the most likely way in which future presidents will be challenged to think about foreign and defense matters strategically. Theodore Roosevelt did not necessarily gain much intellectually by serving as an Assistant Secretary of the Navy because he already had a well-developed strategic vision before taking up that office (indeed, he was so confident in his views that he was not at all reticent about agitating for a war with Spain, even when that required gross insubordination). It is unlikely, however, that most future presidents will receive the sort of education that encourages depth in strategic thinking. (The most probable exceptions to this would be former generals—the US military makes strategic education a requirement for career progression.)

There is, however, admittedly something of a Catch-22 in regard to the value of Executive branch service in the current day. The degree to which culturally comfortable assumptions reign over the strategic thinking of the policy elite calls into question whether a long period of mentoring will hone an individual's strategic instincts or dull them to the point that he or she will treat flawed conventional wisdom uncritically. One could make the argument that a complete novice at least has not imbued bad strategic ideas. One should remember, though, that an inexperienced and unknowledgeable president is likely to lack the confidence to challenge the conventional wisdom repeated by his or her advisors. In general, it is safer to wager on knowledge than on ignorance. There is a reasonable chance that a strategically experienced president will display an independence of mind and refuse to accept bad conventional wisdom uncritically; an uninformed president is much more likely to prove malleable.

Only a president can override the desires of the various agencies of the US government and impose a strategy by fiat and regardless of whether his or her subordinates approve of it—the ultimate exercise of presidential leadership, and one of the most hazardous politically, as displeased advisors often are not above stealthy retaliation in the press. A president with little knowledge of foreign and defense affairs is unlikely to be inclined to such boldness, and probably should not be—the US interagency process does result in the occasional Vietnam but (at least so far) has never caused a Sicilian Expedition or Battle of Manzikert, the sort of strategic miscalculations so profound as to directly or indirectly result in crippling national damage from which timely recovery is impossible. However, over a long period of time, the fruits of a bureaucratically led process should be expected to taste mediocre, especially when the policy elite lacks a clear unifying vision and is beholden to many strategically dubious notions.

For the United States, at least occasional excellence in presidential leadership is prerequisite to excellence in grand strategy. Moreover, at certain critical historical junctures, strategic excellence is required of *any* great power if it is to thrive over the long term. The individuals most likely to exhibit brilliance as supreme commanders are those with expertise in foreign and defense matters, but, unfortunately, at this point and for the foreseeable future few presidents will in fact have the sort of background conducive to excellence of performance in the making of strategy.

Conclusion: the wrong questions

Currently, the US electoral system is not at all an effective filter for presidential strategic talent. Partly, this is the result of the fact that US media reports on elections encourage a public focus on qualities that have little to do with strategic genius, such as felicity of public expression, general charisma, ability to raise money, and strong debating skills. (Even the latter is a bit generous, as it would be more accurate to say that the emphasis is on a candidate's ability to deliver prepackaged talking points during a quasi-debate; the Lincoln–Douglas senatorial debates demanded qualities of mind that are little exercised in today's bland televised exhibitions.) Most current American journalists have no discernable understanding of strategy as an art; they literally do not know the right questions to ask so as to separate Clausewitzian geniuses from strategic dunces whose heads are crammed with dangerously misguided notions.

It would, however, be facile simply to blame the media for mediocrity in presidential strategy. "The media" is not an outside force imposed on the public—market forces are the main shaper of the US media landscape, which, in any case, has opened up greatly in recent years, as the Internet has weakened once-potent gatekeepers like the news divisions of the major television networks. The more fundamental problem is that voters effectively *choose* not to put a higher premium on strategic competence. In almost all cases this is surely not a conscious choice—voters do not perceive that they are trading strategic artfulness for something else, such as rhetorical smoothness or "likability." This absence of awareness represents the failings of many institutions—media, governmental, and educational.

In any case, however, the fact is that the presidential electoral system presently does a poor job of filtering out the strategically naïve and/or inexperienced. This would not be a critical problem if most presidents had an appropriate education and a wealth of hands-on foreign and security policy making experience on which to draw. However, it would be very surprising if many future presidents break this pattern—indeed, at this point, the electoral system effectively discourages long service in the military and civilian policy bureaucracy, while the sort of broad and deep humanistic and historical education enjoyed by many past presidents has become so unfashionable as to be nearly extinct. The predictable result is that many future presidents who are not competent grand strategists will occupy the Oval Office.

There is no simple solution for this problem, as it reflects a largely unrecognized, but nonetheless dangerous, weakness in the US political system. The United States has created a system that demands, if not quite demigods, at least consistent presidential competence in the making of grand strategy. If most presidents do not meet this standard, it follows that American power *will* diminish, with whatever negative consequences might then follow. However, the failing is correctable, though first it must be acknowledged. Recognition of the problem—and ruthless, but constructive, examination of it—may, given time, make it possible for the broad electorate to understand better how to select for good presidential strategic judgment.

6 Lost wars, bleak peace

The tragedy of presidential weakness

Especially capable military forces have, on rare occasion, been known to rescue their own government from the consequences of the latter's strategic ineptitude. However, it is very imprudent indeed to rely upon any military force—no matter how capable—to do this consistently.

Repeating errors: Vietnam, Iraq, Afghanistan, and beyond

Even today, the American effort in Vietnam is poorly understood. The received wisdom regarding Vietnam is flawed in many respects, but one of the most notable is the image—reinforced by countless academic and popular books—of a superpower that foolishly stumbled into a war that it did not understand to defend an illegitimate government against dedicated guerrillas who, armed with nationalist fervor, constituted a tide that could not be held back forever. In this vision, the American failure in Vietnam was the inevitable result of ignorance and hubris—the "arrogance of power," in Senator J. William Fulbright's memorable expression. Of course, once the imprudent but well-armed Americans ceased actively resisting the revolutionaries, the inevitable occurred and the government of South Vietnam collapsed.

As careful students of the Vietnam War know, this vision is deeply flawed; among other things, it greatly oversimplifies the character of the conflict, the question of South Vietnam's long-term viability, and the nuances of both Vietnamese nationalism and Communism. It is, however, unsurprising that so many former Johnson administration policy makers and other one-time supporters of US intervention in Vietnam have been inclined to reinforce this conventional wisdom, as it effectively minimizes their responsibility for American failure in the conflict. If the struggle truly was unwinnable, the war's supporters made only one truly meaningful error: initially supporting intervention in Vietnam. Any other errors which they made thus would be moot; questions regarding whether the United States was too restrictive in its bombing policy, should have operated in Laos, or whatnot would be purely abstract, without any meaning to the final outcome of the conflict.

For many of the former policy makers who presided over the Vietnam debacle, this perspective surely is comforting; it seems far less damning to have, in good conscience, made one important mistake rather than erred again and again. The alternative outlook, after all, implies that policy makers instead committed a long run of errors that ultimately resulted in an unnecessary defeat for the United States and damned millions of South Vietnamese, Laotians, and (especially) Cambodians to death, prison camp "reeducation," or other terrible fates. The latter viewpoint is, however, the more accurate one. The conventional wisdom of Vietnam may, in due course, crumble[1]—indeed, it likely will, as time cools the passions aroused by the war and those invested in the prevailing narrative pass from the scene. However, a process very similar to the one that created the "Legend of Vietnam" is now ongoing, and it would be most unfortunate if that catastrophically flawed mythology—which has done much damage to clarity of strategic thought in the United States and worldwide—is replaced by Legends of Iraq and Afghanistan.

It should be stated, first, that what the United States attempted in Iraq was not merely equal in difficulty to its enterprise in Vietnam—it was, in actuality, *more* difficult in certain critical respects,[2] given that the announced American goal was the creation of a stable, unified, and democratic Iraq. Ethnic, religious, and tribal/familial divisions in Iraq are far more problematic than was the case in the Republic of Vietnam; in particular, the political significance of the religious divisions in the latter country was exaggerated by outsiders (especially foreign reporters). In contrast, the ethno-religious fault lines in Iraq are very deep and work against the creation of a democracy that can take root and thrive over the long term. These problems are exacerbated by the fact that Iraqi society was deeply damaged by the reign of Saddam Hussein, both socially and economically—notably, the regime's steady use of terror normalized brutality and sharpened preexisting ethnic/religious grievances.

Hussein's Iraq was a curious state. Iraq's "hard authoritarian government" was not at all reluctant to use terror to ensure obedience,[3] but traditional, local sources of authority—tribal sheikhs, religious leaders, and so on—were not entirely eliminated; they continued to exist and (at least to a limited degree) function as an alternative power structure. Iraq's government clearly was modeled on the example of previous twentieth century authoritarian and totalitarian regimes—Hussein himself had a particular admiration for Stalin, and some of his actions, such as the cruel displacement of the Shia "Marsh Arabs," were reminiscent of Stalin's ethnic policies. However, there was no real effort to create a "New Iraqi Man" and sweep away old religious, ethnic, and tribal loyalties altogether; indeed, such distinctions were critical in how Hussein's regime was constructed. By making Sunni Arabs, and particularly his relatives, the core of the regime and enthusiastically stomping on Shia Arab and Kurdish throats with the state's boot heel, Hussein made clear that Ba'athist ideology did not actually trump other loyalties. Although there were Shia and Kurds, as well as members of smaller ethnic and religious groups, in the Ba'ath Party, Iraq's regime clearly was not a truly a "diverse" one, whatever its alleged socialist ideals.

The same of course could be said of any number of similar regimes; given the demographics of the Soviet Union, for instance, there was a noticeable shortage of Central Asians in Moscow's highest leadership positions. However, most self-declared socialist governments at least attempt to make a convincing show of ethnic equality and similar societal virtues. By contrast, anyone could see that Hussein's government clearly was, first, a personal, family (including tribal) operation; second, a Sunni one; and only lastly a Ba'athist regime. Iraq thus was a strange amalgam of ancient and (very brutal) modern government.

Destroying the modern aspect of Iraq's government structure proved extraordinarily easy for the Americans and their allies, which is unsurprising: in the "March to Baghdad" Washington could leverage its military advantages over Iraq to the maximum.[4] However, when the modern edifice of Iraq's government was smashed, what remained was, in its fashion, enormously more complex: a network of religious, tribal, ethnic, and other loyalties and many thousands of leaders whose authority was respected by some specific group of Iraqis. These leaders ranged enormously in influence—Iraq had thousands of minor sheikhs and similar local notables, but also men such as Grand Ayatollah Sistani, who was and is respected (though not necessarily always obeyed) by many millions of Iraqi Shia. Indeed, in some respects it was and is deceptive even to speak of "Iraqi society" in the singular, as this phrasing reinforces an unhelpfully state-centric view; in regard to who is considered a respected leader in, say, a rural village in Kurdistan or Baghdad's Sadr City or the richest neighborhood in Tikrit, there likely is little overlap. As the Americans quickly discovered, the rules governing a decentralized tribal society are quite different from those prevailing in a modern democracy based on abstract concepts such as citizen equality and the rule of law.

Tribal societies are notoriously challenging to govern even under the best of circumstances because societies constructed along these lines are, to use contemporary jargon, "networked," while modern ones tend to be far more pyramidical in structure. In a diagram, a tribal society may appear pyramidical, with a king or similar figure at the top, but this tends to be deceptive, as it eliminates the nuances stemming from interpersonal relationships. A king's personal power may depend largely on his own charisma, his relationships with various tribal and clan leaders, and similar factors. Modern governments, by contrast, generally try to substitute the rule of law (or, in despotic regimes, the illusion of the rule of law) for such subjective factors: if the president of the United States orders the Seventh Fleet to deploy, his or her personal popularity does not determine whether American admirals will obey the order.

In addition to the difficulties of governing a tribal society, there also were decidedly larger problems related to reshaping Iraq. While Iraqi society was tribal, it nevertheless was influenced by global forces and that country's internal struggles had very serious international implications. Most notably, the violence between Iraqi Shia and Sunnis and, especially, the "resistance" against US forces had implications well beyond Iraq, with many actors outside that country having a deep interest in what happened there. Moreover, technology, particularly the creation of a truly global media, created an odd loop: something that happened in Iraq in turn influenced the larger international scene, which in turn fed back into the situation in Iraq. The Abu Ghraib scandal was a prime example of this phenomenon; the atrocities occurred in Iraq, but it was mainly international media outlets such as *Al Jazerra* that made Iraqis aware of the abuses, thus feeding rage within Iraq itself.

In assessing the virtues and vices of American strategy in regard to Iraq, it is critical to take account of the fact that *all of the aforementioned factors and problems were known to, or predictable by, US policy makers.* Beginning a few months after the invasion, many policy makers and supporters of the war expressed surprise in regard to various problems in Iraq such as the stubborn unwillingness of the Sunnis to accept the end of the Ba'athist regime and the seriousness of the trouble caused by Muqtada al-Sadr. Often, their astonishment was sincere, but it was the result of a decided tendency to discount the difficulties that would accompany the rebuilding of Iraq, and this was a strategic error of great significance. That discounting of foreseeable problems by policy makers was quite similar to what had occurred during the Vietnam War.

Like the Johnson administration, the G.W. Bush administration showed (both in the era leading up to the 2003 invasion and afterward) a tendency to ignore hard questions that could not be answered readily. In the case of Vietnam, few decision makers had the wisdom to ask what the American theory of victory was if North Vietnam simply refused to bow to US bombing and other pressure and continued the war year after year. Even long after it became obvious that that was in fact precisely what was occurring, not many of them had the boldness to argue for controversial measures such as tearing up the 1954 Laos Accords—Laotian neutrality already was blatantly being violated by North Vietnam—and placing a permanent US military presence on the ground in Laos whose task would be to cut the Ho Chi Minh Trail.[5] In essence, having been denied the easy war for which they had hoped, Johnson administration policy makers refused to adapt the measures necessary to win the difficult war which they actually faced. Similarly, numerous senior Bush administration officials had believed (given the historical record, imprudently)[6] that the occupation of Iraq would be short and undertaken by a minimal number of troops; a stable and democratic Iraqi government quickly would be established, with the latter rapidly taking over most security duties.[7] As it soon became clear that this in fact was not what would occur and that the occupation would be a difficult one, most Bush administration policy makers—much like their Vietnam-era predecessors—did not argue for a rapid and fundamental shift in how the United States was conducting the war. Instead, again like their predecessors, they incrementally modified US strategy rather than reexamining its very premises.

Why, in both of these cases, did American leaders prove incapable of quickly assessing the flaws in their initial strategy and then adapting accordingly? There is no simple answer to this question, but it is clear that it is not simple incompetence—whatever their failings, high-level policy makers in both the Johnson and G.W. Bush administrations overall were highly capable and intelligent *individually*; indeed, many of them enjoyed a very strong reputation until they presided over military disaster.[8] Certainly, "group-think" played a negative role in decision making—constant reinforcement of prevailing views encourages members of a group to ignore contrary evidence.[9] If a member does decide to reject the group's accepted position, there is a tendency to see that individual as a crank, if not a turncoat. Again, however, this does not provide a fully satisfactory explanation for strategic errors in Vietnam or Iraq, particularly the latter, which was very sharply debated both inside and outside government well before troops ever set foot in Iraq. Even after the country was occupied, internal debate about how to handle the insurgency was heated.

In war, there is a constant "dialogue" between foes: strategies will evolve as each opponent attempts to exploit the enemy's weaknesses. Adaptation is—or at least should be—constant in war, a fact attested to again and again. In short, conflict is an evolutionary process; Clausewitz's comparison of war to a wrestling match is an astute illustration—like wrestlers, the foes constantly seek even the tiniest advantage that then, in turn, can be leveraged to provide even greater advantage. All the major Bush administration officials surely understood this, and this is attested to, for example, by the constant questioning and probing within the Department of Defense, with Secretary Rumsfeld demanding a constant stream of information, studies, and updates. Indeed, the hard questions in a leaked October 2003 memorandum by Rumsfeld embarrassed the Bush administration; among other queries, Rumsfeld asked, "Are the changes we have made and are making too incremental?"[10] The administration's embarrassment was misplaced: these are precisely the sort of questions that a Secretary of Defense should be asking key subordinates in wartime, and the fact that this was not obvious to most observers is a testament to the deficiencies in the American public discussion of strategy. However, even a willingness to ask difficult questions did not save the administration from floundering for many months in Iraq, until finally finding an operational strategy that in turn allowed progress toward US political goals in that country.[11]

In general, it is best to describe the failures of US policy makers in regard to both Vietnam and Iraq as resulting from an excessive disregard for military history and a failure of strategic imagination. In both cases, key policy makers, such as Secretaries of Defense McNamara and Rumsfeld, entered the conflict with rather hazy theories of victory built on dubious assumptions that, in the event, were proved to be unfounded.[12]

In the Vietnam War, victory relied essentially on assisting in the creation of a reasonable degree of stability (governmental, military, economic, and otherwise) in South Vietnam and compelling Hanoi to relieve its pressure on the beleaguered Saigon government. By the time it left office, the Johnson administration basically had succeeded in achieving the first goal—although it proved to be far more difficult and costly than Washington initially imagined—but had failed completely in obtaining the second. The administration's theory of victory, such as it was, required Hanoi to accept defeat, agreeing to give up on Vietnamese unification in exchange for Washington ceasing to inflict "pain" on North Vietnam through bombing and other means. There was, as noted above, no "Plan B" if Hanoi failed to be (from Washington's perspective) reasonable.

The G.W. Bush administration, by contrast, made a very different—in some respects opposite—error. There was little interest in coercing Iraq; quite correctly, the administration had come to the conclusion that Hussein was highly resistant to coercive pressure. The administration was aware of the unhappy US history in Vietnam, and wanted to avoid becoming trapped in an endless, fruitless negotiation with its Iraqi enemies. Thus, it was concluded that regime change was a prerequisite to any meaningful strategic victory in Iraq. However, the American strategy in Iraq might reasonably (if a tad ungenerously) be described as "the Incredible Hulk theory of victory": the United States would utterly smash the Hussein regime and, once the dust settled, Iraqis quickly would create a functional democratic government. In short, the American government would not *need* to create any real medium- or long-term strategy for Iraq. The United States did not wish to fight a long counterinsurgent campaign in Iraq, so it would not; hopefully, there would be no significant insurgent activity after a short time, but, if there was, the Iraqi government would be able to cope with it.

The Bush administration's desire to avoid fighting an extended counterinsurgency is quite understandable, but its refusal to acknowledge the very great likelihood that destroying the Hussein regime would create the conditions for a major *multi-sided* insurgency that would overwhelm the capabilities of Iraq's new democratic government was a clear example of calamitous wishful thinking. All the basic points laid out in the previous discussion of Iraqi government and society were known publicly before the invasion. Iraq, far from being some sort of mysterious entity unknowable to outsiders, was studied intently by many individuals both within and outside government; moreover, the general characteristics of tribal societies have been a matter of enormous interest to anthropologists for many decades. Just as senior Johnson administration policy makers could not justifiably plead ignorance of Vietnam and its society, their successors in the G.W. Bush administration cannot be excused by any shortcomings in their command of anthropology. This is because any strategic analysis of how to win in Iraq should have accurately accounted for such factors from the beginning—the fact that they are not "military" in the strict sense of the term is irrelevant. In short, the information required in order to construct a realistic Iraq strategy was available—yet American leaders failed to realistically account for these factors in constructing their initial strategy, and this, in turn, has shaped the course of the conflict in ways highly unfavorable to the United States.

Any strategy, unless it is based on straightforward genocide, ultimately requires the manipulation of human conduct—coercion, deterrence, and similar concepts are, ultimately, about *convincing* individuals to engage in a particular form of behavior.[13] Although weapons technology and similar matters are extremely important, a good strategy is founded on a sound analysis of likely human behavior. At least for its first few years, the Bush administration's strategy in Iraq failed that test spectacularly, and it did so, in essence, because US leaders engaged in the very American vices of ignoring the past—as with any country, Iraq's history tells much about the character of its society, and informs one about the tensions within that society—and dismissing ideologically inconvenient truths.

An excellent example of both of these failings was provided by President Bush in a February 2003 speech to the American Enterprise Institute. The then-president appears genuinely to have adopted the ahistorical view that democracy can flower anywhere in the world with only the most minimal encouragement:

> It is presumptuous and insulting to suggest that a whole region of the world or the one-fifth of humanity that is Muslim is somehow untouched by the most basic aspirations of life. Human cultures can be vastly different, yet the human heart desires the same good things everywhere on earth. In our desire to be safe from brutal and bullying oppression, human beings are the same. In our desire to care for our children and give them a better life, we're the same. For these fundamental reasons, freedom and democracy will always and everywhere have greater appeal than the slogans of hatred and the tactics of terror.[14]

The first sentence quoted merely attacks a straw man—no serious person opposed to the 2003 invasion of Iraq argued that every Muslim in the world was "untouched by the most basic aspirations of life." What follows, however, is, from a historical and sociological perspective, astonishing: an assertion that human beings everywhere more-or-less share the same values and, given the opportunity, any group of people will choose "freedom and democracy" over other available alternatives. This is obvious nonsense, as even the most superficial scan of the human experience over the last several thousand years of recorded history demonstrates.

Certainly, most people do enjoy *personally* being free from oppression that is "brutal and bullying," though a disturbingly great number of people seem to enjoy bullying others, if given the opportunity. Yet many humans find political oppression in general quite tolerable, even amenable. The Hitler regime clearly was popular with Germans in, say, 1940—certainly more popular than the Weimar Republic had been during its brief, unhappy life. (Many Germans also appear to have found "slogans of hatred" rather compelling.) More recently, Russians had a plausible opportunity to create an enduring democracy; they did not do so, and the moderately oppressive (but reasonably well-organized and stable) pseudo-democracy that solidified during Vladimir Putin's time as president has consistently enjoyed a good deal of public approval. This is not because Russians are so dim as to believe that they are freer now than they were, say, during President Yeltsin's first term; instead, they appear to have become convinced that a mildly authoritarian government is more likely to ensure themselves and their children a good life than a democratic one would. One also might note events in Venezuela, which, until recently, was a fairly stable democracy with a free press. Today, President Hugo Chávez is progressively eliminating the latter nuisance and busily replacing Venezuelan democracy with a dictatorship built on his cult of personality—and while doing so enjoys support not only from many Venezuelans but also from a surprising number of cheerleaders who live in actual democracies but endorse his "Bolivarian Revolution."[15] Of course, the German, Russian, and Venezuelan examples are only three of the thousands which one could cite that contradict President Bush's hopeful assertions.[16]

The American war in Afghanistan provides yet another example of strategic failure, and although it (unsurprisingly) bears some resemblance to that in Iraq, it nonetheless is distinct. Like Iraqi society, Afghan society has tribal characteristics (indeed, given its essentially premodern economy and other factors, Afghanistan is far more traditional and tribal). However, there has never been a reasonably modern and stable central government that efficiently controlled the entire country. In this regard, Afghanistan is quite unlike Iraq, which was ruled, brutally but effectively, from Baghdad until the Persian Gulf War and the no-fly-zones that denied Hussein military access to parts of the country. Even the Soviet Army found Afghanistan to be ungovernable; demographic maps of the country are reminiscent of a Jackson Pollack painting, with a chaotic distribution of myriad ethnicities.

There is no Afghan nation, in any reasonable sense of the term; "Afghanistan" essentially is just a geographical expression that history turned into a parody of a nation-state. Moreover, the landlocked country is desperately poor, overpopulated (given its largely agricultural economy and shortage of arable land), and has a staggering rate of illiteracy. In gross domestic product terms, it still is rated as a least-developed country. Afghanistan's main export product is opium, the growing of which is illegal. Afghanistan is, in short, one of the least promising states in Eurasia for would-be nation-builders; a basic examination of the country's circumstances makes it clear that its prospects for becoming stable would, under the best of circumstances, appear to be extremely dim. Nevertheless, after the September 11 terrorist attacks and the subsequent refusal of that country's Taliban government to surrender Osama Bin Laden to the custody of the United States, the Bush administration promised to engage in "fixing" Afghanistan,[17] providing the country a better future. Vague promises soon expanded to a full-fledged commitment to democratization, modernization, and stabilization that became the metric by which American success would be judged.

The decision to yoke American victory in Afghanistan to the success of nation-building in Afghanistan was a very imprudent one, and represented a failure of strategic imagination of the first order. In the days following the 9/11 attacks, the American citizenry clearly demanded that *Al Qaeda* be dealt with harshly. Although a simple desire for rough justice drove the public, retaliating for the attacks also was the only strategically sound response that the administration could make; it was incumbent on the Executive branch to demonstrate that terrorist attacks on US soil, or the sponsorship and protection of those who would commit such crimes, would not be tolerated.[18] After the Taliban did not promptly and meekly surrender Bin Laden, therefore, invading Afghanistan was the correct decision in both domestic political and strategic terms: the US public would enjoy the satisfaction of seeing a particularly nasty Islamist government crushed by its armed forces, while the act of doing so would serve as a useful warning to other governments that might be inclined to harbor groups such as *Al Qaeda.*

It was not, however, necessary to offer to reconstruct (or, more accurately, construct) Afghanistan after removing the Taliban from power. There was very little demand on the part of the American citizenry that their government take responsibility for Afghanistan's fate—frankly, most Americans did not care much whether or not Afghanistan became a thriving country. The notion that the United States would take responsibility for Afghanistan helped somewhat to blunt criticism of the US invasion, but, strategically speaking, this was a poor trade, as the actual benefits for Washington were quite minimal. Given the international "state of play" in late 2001, it was obvious that, regardless of whether the United States took responsibility for Kabul's long-term fate, many states and organizations would oppose an American invasion of Afghanistan and the United Nations would not sanction such an endeavor.

In fact, the commonly accepted belief that the United States enjoyed overwhelming international sympathy and support for its actions in the months immediately following Afghanistan and that this support only waned because Washington acted in an increasingly unilateral manner is gravely flawed. Two months after the 9/11 attacks President Bush addressed the UN General Assembly; notably, the UN was an institution that had been specifically threatened by Osama Bin Laden and, of course, the headquarters where Bush spoke is located in New York City itself. As the *New York Times* tartly noted, "Mr. Bush's address seemed to affirm a new faith in multilateralism. Nonetheless, the speech was not interrupted by applause. Neither was the speech of Mayor Rudolph W. Giuliani at the United Nations in October."[19] This silence was significant, as it demonstrated graphically how much support the United States truly enjoyed from the broad international community after the 9/11 attacks.

Even if the international community's support could have been purchased in exchange for American guarantees in regard to Afghanistan's future, it likely would have been of relatively little practical value. Militarily—contrary to many agitated media predications about supposedly battle-hardened *jihadis* and the clichéd "brutal Afghan winter"—the Taliban was very weak. The Afghan government lacked a modern air force, or much in the way of advanced weaponry in general, and Taliban forces essentially were an undertrained and ill-disciplined rabble. The *Al Qaeda* fighters in Afghanistan were, man-for-man, somewhat more formidable, but small in number; lacking air support and high-technology weapons, there was little they could do to resist the American onslaught.

The only truly important military help that the United States required for its Afghan expedition was the cooperation of the local Northern Alliance—which of course was fighting the Taliban and therefore was delighted to collaborate with the Americans—and the granting by Pakistan of overflight rights to the United States. The United States accomplished the latter through old-fashioned bribery and threat: very substantial US military and other aid to Pakistan was announced shortly after the 9/11 attacks and Washington made it quite clear to Islamabad that its assistance in the Afghan campaign was not optional.[20]

Given these realities, the most strategically sensible course for the United States to pursue was a straightforward one: a grand raid whose purpose would be to displace the Taliban government and capture or kill as many Taliban and *Al Qaeda* fighters as possible, with Osama Bin Laden being (for obvious reasons) by far the most important individual target. Thus, while the wisdom of specific military choices (such as the decision to pause combat operations during the Battle of Tora Bora) during the winter of 2001–02 may be debated, the general character of American operations during the early period of the Afghan conflict was appropriate. The fundamental error was not an operational one, but the political-strategic one of accepting a task—the reformation of Afghanistan—that would be extraordinarily difficult (if not impossible), expensive, and would guarantee that Washington could not show its friends and enemies alike that it was capable of winning a speedy and decisive victory *on its own terms* over terrorists and their allies. There are two broad objections to framing the Afghan conflict in this way, but neither of them can withstand cold-eyed scrutiny.

The first objection, and the more narrowly "strategic" one, is the contention that only a long-term presence in the country would ensure that the Taliban would not return to power and that Afghanistan would not again become a terrorist haven. This is true, insofar as it goes—only a comprehensive nation-building exercise would turn Afghanistan from a potential enemy to an American ally, and, indeed, Kabul officially now is a US partner in the struggle against *jihadist* terrorism. It would be more accurate, however, to describe it as a weak client state whose government is entirely dependent on Washington for its survival.

This relationship is not, substantively speaking, any more beneficial to Washington than a less formal relationship would be. It makes perfect sense to prop up an anti-Taliban regime with military and financial aid, but this does not require that the United States take responsibility for its survival. Indeed, that is the usual case with US relationships with dubious or unstable regimes, including those in the Muslim world—for decades, the United States enjoyed fruitful relationships with many Arab countries, and had never publicly guaranteed that their citizens would enjoy domestic political stability, much less democracy. (In recent months, unfortunately, the United States has begun to deviate from this sensible policy, as its Libyan adventure demonstrates dramatically.) Certainly, the government of Hamid Karzai should have been supported generously, but it was unnecessary and counterproductive for US/NATO troops to stay in the country and take responsibility for the survival of the new regime. A well-supplied Afghan government should have been able to keep control of Kabul and other major cities, though it probably would not have de facto authority over much of the countryside—a situation not very dissimilar from the one today. If the Taliban seriously threatened the Afghan government's position in any of the major cities, the temporary provision of US air support—and, if absolutely necessary, small numbers of ground troops—should have sufficed to ensure that the Taliban was beaten back.

The notion that it was necessary to remake Afghanistan in order to prevent it from again becoming a terrorist haven was doubly flawed. There is the obvious point that much of rural Afghanistan still is controlled by the Taliban—a situation that was entirely predictable, given the geographical character (physical and human) of the country. The United States could permanently have maintained a far larger force in Afghanistan, and this still would not have prevented the reconstitution of the Taliban. Afghanistan, after all, is a country noticeably larger than Iraq in both physical and population terms, and the portion of the state bordering Pakistan is wild country that clearly is beyond the control of any occupier unwilling or unable also to operate on the ground in Pakistan. Moreover, an international terrorist group is, by its nature, mobile. While it was certainly useful to Bin Laden to have the full resources even of a weak country at his disposal, once the control of the machinery of the Afghan state no longer was in the hands of his allies there was no special advantage to operating in Afghanistan, as opposed to any of numerous other feeble or failed states (or even the relatively ungoverned portions of otherwise fairly stable states) where there is some popular sympathy for Islamic radicalism.

Given that the entire world cannot be "fixed" there was no reason to focus particularly on fixing a piece of it located in the center of Eurasia. For obvious reasons, "draining the swamp" in principle indeed is preferable to periodically spraying DDT, but in actual practice the costs of doing the former often are so great that the latter clearly is the more sensible course. This point also all-too-clearly applies to Iraq. The Bush administration quite justifiably was exasperated by Iraq's constant troublemaking, but after its invasion quickly discovered that the price of containing Iraq and coping with Hussein's misbehavior was infinitesimal in comparison to that of implementing a comprehensive solution to "the Hussein problem."

The second objection to implementing a raiding strategy in Afghanistan is based primarily on humanitarian concerns: in short, that a mere raid would do nothing to provide the people of that country with the opportunity to grasp a better future. There perhaps was a strong moral case to be made that the United States should take on the burden of creating a more humane Afghanistan. The plight of Afghan women, in particular, shocked the conscience. Leaving aside the complex ethical question of whether Western countries should engage in Kiplingesque imperial endeavors, however, the strategic answer as to whether the United States should have attempted this project is a resounding "no." Afghanistan's human rights record—and, again, especially the mistreatment of woman in Afghan society—was appalling, and one certainly can argue that Afghanistan's human rights violators should be dealt with using military force. *However, that is a moral, not a strategic, argument and it is vital that the two not be confused.* If Americans and others wish to use their armies to slay monsters, they are free to do so—and perhaps should be congratulated on their vigorous enforcement of decency—but such endeavors should not be expected to render any profit strategically.

Indeed, it is somewhat perverse that the United States decided that it must help the people of Afghanistan because their country contained a great many people who dedicated themselves to inflicting harm on innocent Americans. By contrast, few individuals in the Democratic Republic of Congo, for instance, have dedicated themselves to anti-American terrorism or similar activities and, thus, the United States has done virtually nothing to bring order and prosperity to a country whose horrific and long-running civil disorder claims lives every day—the endless strife in that country has killed millions and left millions more impoverished, emotionally or physically damaged, forced to flee their communities, or otherwise suffering.[21] Compared to Afghans, however, the Congolese have received little help from the United States—or the international community in general—and certainly no multi-hundred billion dollar guarantees to rebuild their country into a prosperous and stable democracy. Indeed, their plight has not even received significant notice in the US media—most Americans have little, if any, knowledge regarding the situation in Congo.

The tragedy of the Congo is, of course, only one of many that could be cited to make the point that the nation-building project in Afghanistan is fundamentally different from the American reconstruction of Japan and (West) Germany after World War II. The latter enterprises *were* fundamentally strategic, not humanitarian, in character: American leaders believed, correctly, that if those countries did not become stable and prosperous democracies, they might eventually present a significant threat to the United States, either as Soviet allies or rogue powers. Relieving the personal plight of German and Japanese citizens was an incidental benefit—a very great one, in humanitarian terms, but not the driver of US policy. While many US leaders no doubt believe sincerely that the reconstruction of Afghanistan is important to US security, it frankly is not—it is a humanitarian endeavor masquerading as a strategic one. Even if nearly every Afghan were to reject Islamism and come to respect the United States—a highly improbable development—this would merely eliminate some potential recruits for organizations like *Al Qaeda*; the overall strategic threat presented by Islamist terrorism would not decrease dramatically.

While there are threads linking the US strategic errors in Vietnam, Iraq, and Afghanistan, in certain respects Vietnam and Iraq are more similar to each other than either is to Afghanistan. Most fundamentally, the taking of some form of military action against the Taliban clearly was necessary for the reasons discussed above, while the latter two conflicts ultimately were "wars of choice." Both the Vietnam and Iraq Wars were entered into on understandable strategic grounds: from the perspective of the United States, a communist takeover of South Vietnam and the continuation of Hussein's rule over Baghdad both were undesirable (albeit for quite different reasons). In both cases, US leaders erred fundamentally in failing to comprehend the sort of conflict into which they were entering.

Because the Johnson administration did not wish to face the actual cost of preserving the Republic of Vietnam, it was unwilling to commit the human and financial resources necessary to win the war quickly. Thus, the United States paid an enormously higher price over a long period of time—and nonetheless eventually lost the war. The Vietnam War was winnable insofar as a non-communist Republic of Vietnam could have been preserved, though almost certainly not winnable at a price that Washington would have considered acceptable when debating the "Vietnam Question" in 1964. That the United States ultimately will win the Iraq War—in the sense of creating a stable, pro-American bulwark against Iran—remains doubtful, but even if it does, it will be a model Pyrrhic victory.

Colin Powell's "Pottery Barn rule" essentially was correct—if the United States broke Iraq, it owned it. The failure of many American leaders (though not Powell himself) was to grossly underestimate what those costs would be.

Indeed, in at least one area the United States simply lacked the resources necessary to win quickly in Iraq: in 2003, the US armed services, the Army and Marine Corps in particular, simply were far too small to occupy Iraq in the numbers necessary to make rapid, comprehensive victory possible—overawing potential resistors, guarding weapons depots, imposing order, and rapidly rebuilding Iraq's infrastructure. For instance, the occupation ideally might have deployed, say, one uniformed individual and one civilian (administrator, private security contractor, engineer, aid provider, or similar worker) for every twenty Iraqis, giving a total foreign presence of roughly 2.5 million.[22] Of course, killing the insurgency in its cradle and undertaking rapid reconstruction still might have been possible with half that number, or perhaps even a mere one-quarter of it, which would translate to a military force equaling only about 1.25 percent of the Iraqi population, as well as a similar number of civilian occupiers. Yet, even considering that not all foreigners in Iraq would be American, the United States did not possess anything near the number of military or competent civilian personnel necessary to place a force of the latter size in Iraq.

The combination of Iraqi socio-political conditions and the dearth of American occupiers meant that the Iraq project was almost certain to be long and difficult. Bush administration leaders perhaps can take some cold comfort in the fact that they at least did not throw an easy victory away. Rather, given the resources they had at hand, the Iraq War always was likely to be lost or, at best, be won at a cost grossly disproportionate to the plausible benefits that Washington might enjoy from the creation of a reformed Iraq. As of this writing, the latter, better, outcome remains at least somewhat plausible, largely thanks to the Surge of 2007, a bold (if belated) move for which the administration does deserve credit. This surprisingly successful desperation play does not, however, outweigh the many operational and political mistakes that the United States made in Iraq in the pre-Surge years, such as disbanding the Iraqi Army, the only local institution capable of imposing order in an Iraq in which there was only a minute occupation force.[23]

The Afghanistan conflict, unlike Iraq and Vietnam, was not a "war of choice." As noted above, if, following the 9/11 attacks, Afghanistan would not hand Bin Laden over promptly, American leaders had no responsible option other than to invade that country, overthrow the Taliban, and hunt Bin Laden. Moreover, the overthrow of the Taliban was not a dishearteningly difficult mission for the US military—although operating in a landlocked country deep in Eurasia presented some very considerable logistical challenges, they could be, and were, overcome. Thus, if properly defined, the war in Afghanistan was both necessary and winnable quickly at a modest cost. However, the Bush administration failed to define the conflict properly—as a mighty raid, not a nation-building exercise.

The international politics surrounding the Afghan and Iraqi situations were radically different, and thus the Pottery Barn rule had much less salience in regard to Afghanistan. Of course, many individuals and organizations would be appalled by and critical of the supposed callousness of American policy, but, bluntly speaking, there is little reason to believe that this would have had significant real impact on US interests. (Although one hastens to add that it would have been desirable, both for ethical and international public relations reasons, for the United States to airdrop food for refugees and otherwise assist vulnerable civilians in immediate physical peril—in short, to do precisely what it actually did do during the early months of the Afghan invasion.)

A demonstration of US military power unleavened by humanitarian illusions also would have been useful in planting a worry in "bad actors" that, if sufficiently provoked, the United States would be willing to swoop in, smash their own governments, and then withdraw promptly. Regardless of whether actually doing so would have been prudent—and in the Iraqi case, for instance, it certainly would not have been, for the reasons noted above—the precedent set by actually conducting a "regime change raid" would have been useful politically. This is because encouraging the leaders of rogue states to fear the *possibility* of a quick and ruthless regime change might persuade some of them to think very hard about committing acts (such as supporting international Islamist terrorists) that might gravely anger the United States, and at least a few of them therefore might refrain from such activities. Although hardly a cure-all for roguish troublemaking, forcefully demonstrating to troublesome states that they are not the only ones capable of acting ruthlessly and unpredictably would have been desirable. (The United States of course attempted to teach a similar lesson by overthrowing Hussein's government, but in that case succeeded mainly in underscoring the difficulty of occupying an unfriendly country—and thus the unlikelihood that Washington would soon undertake another such effort.)

The Vietnam, Iraq, and Afghanistan conflicts were all quite distinct, but all were similar insofar as they were marked by fundamental strategic errors. This resulted in one war being lost outright by the United States, and two as yet undetermined, with Iraq at best offering the prospect of a success obtained at ruinous cost, while nothing better than a grotesque caricature of victory is on offer in Afghanistan. These difficulties are notable most especially because they are bedeviling the state with by far the greatest military resources globally (as well as the world's largest economy and enormous diplomatic and other capabilities). That the United States—which spends over half a trillion dollars every year on its military, not to mentions hundred of billions more on intelligence gathering and analysis, veteran's pensions, and other militarily relevant activities—has had such enormous difficulty in three of four major conflicts since the mid-1960s, *even though none of the three was against a militarily first-rate foe,* indicates that the current "American way of strategy" is now dangerously flawed.[24]

Leveraging Mars: the uses and limits of military power

All strategic tools, including military ones, have limitations. Obviously, coercive force is the final arbiter of what polities may or may not do, a fact immortally summarized by Thucydides in the most famous words in the Melian dialogue: "the strong do what they can, and the weak suffer what they must."[25] However, especially in modern times, it is rare for the relationship between two particular polities to be defined simply by the threat, much less actual use, of violence. Most states are not at war with each other most of the time, nor are all of "the strong" constantly confronting all of "the weak" with the sort of stark, non-negotiable demands that the Athenians presented to the Melians. The actual global security environment is an intricate and ever-shifting tapestry of bilateral and multilateral relationships. Every one of these interactions is unique, and in a given one the possibility of violence may play a critical role or, conversely, virtually none at all.

The historical record of polities that attempted to rely almost exclusively on military power to achieve national goals is mixed. Certainly, there have been very successful political entities that relied far more on the mailed fist than on other instruments. For instance, two of the most spectacularly successful examples of heavily militarized strategies were the empire-building projects of Alexander the Great and Genghis Khan. These impatient warlords relied chiefly on military power to rapidly construct huge empires, and their success in doing so is unarguable. It should be noted that the Macedonian Greeks and Mongols did not rely exclusively on the *direct* use of military violence—Mongol diplomacy, for instance, was sophisticated, albeit quite different in style from diplomacy as practiced at Turtle Bay. Nevertheless, military force clearly was the cornerstone of the grand strategies of Alexander and Genghis.[26]

Perhaps more significantly for this discussion, both the Macedonian and Mongol Empires did not endure very long as unitary entities. Alexander's empire splintered almost immediately upon its founder's death, an unsurprising result as Alexander died at the age of thirty-three and left no adult male son—such an heir might (if he were clever and talented) have been able to hold the empire together, but we cannot know. Genghis Khan lived to a far riper age, but his initial rise to power was far more difficult and time-consuming than was the case for Alexander (at the age of eighteen, the latter took control of the Macedonian Army, already an extraordinary military instrument thanks to efforts of Alexander's father,

Philip II). Thus, he too had relatively little time to consolidate his imperial gains during his lifetime. Unlike Alexander, however, the new Mongol Empire survived for some time after its founder's death as a more-or-less unified entity; Genghis arranged for his respected adult son Ögadei to be his successor as great khan, and named other descendants as subordinate khans in control of specific geographical portions of the empire. Indeed, the territory under Mongol control continued to expand after the death of the imperial founder, although within a matter of decades centrifugal forces caused it to splinter into several distinct polities.

Even if a highly militaristic grand strategy is unlikely to succeed in creating a huge and long-lived empire—and the endurance of an imperial project surely is one of the main criteria for judging its overall success—one would not be justified in calling Macedonian or Mongolian grand strategy a failure. After all, it is difficult to call the successful conquest of a very extensive portion of the Eurasian landmass anything less than a spectacular, even if fleeting, accomplishment. Recent practitioners of highly militarized grand strategies have not, however, tended to be as fortunate as their Macedonian and Mongol predecessors. Napoleon, Wilhelm II, and Hitler all implemented grand strategies based on military victory, and all three enjoyed considerable success, for a time. However, the first two died without crowns and in exile, while the third chose to shoot himself while still nominally in command of a dying Nazi polity.

While the United States certainly does not have a grand strategy based on ever-greater military conquest, Washington's enormous current military strength has a hugely distorting effect both on the perceptions of American leaders and those of foreign nations. Because America's leaders—and its citizenry—assume that their country's military strength greatly surpasses that of its potential foes, they greatly underestimate the seriousness of the challenge that it may face in coming decades from one or more other great powers. *Most American leaders, and voters, are profoundly unserious about great power strategy because they do not truly believe that their country's preeminent status ever will be challenged successfully.* Thus, discussions of national security issues tend to focus on second-rate short-to-medium-term menaces such as North Korea, Iran, and, most of all, *Al Qaeda* and other Islamist terrorist groups.

This casual attitude toward other great states is, in essence, a case of "grand strategic victory disease": most Americans, including very knowledgeable ones, find the notion of a truly fundamental challenge to Washington's international status so incredible that they prefer to focus on lesser threats whose reality they can accept. Horrible though it would be, American leaders *can* envision a terrorist group's nuclear weapon being detonated in Los Angeles—and, unquestionably, they are correct to loathe this possibility and work energetically to prevent it from occurring. By contrast, however, they cannot believe that the United States could be displaced from its present position as the greatest of the world's powers. This mainly is because severe American decline would involve changes in the international system that seem implausible to them.

This failure of strategic imagination occurs mainly because most American leaders (most definitely including US presidents), fail to comprehend that the fortunes of a great power may decline quickly and radically even in a generally peaceful international environment. They of course can understand how the Third Reich went so quickly from controlling most of Europe to expiring because that was a blunt military process—failure on the battlefield directly translated into political defeat. A more subtle evolution, however, also can be devastating to a great polity's global position, even if the much-weakened power survives and carries on with "business as usual." The price that Americans may pay in coming decades for presidential imprudence probably would not be direct and overwhelming—their economy likely would remain generally prosperous, they would continue to live under the protections of their Constitution, and so forth. The ability of Washington to shape the global political environment so as to make it amenable to the long-term security interests of the United States and the survival and propagation of American values could, however, diminish immensely.

The sheer quantity of military power at America's disposal itself tends to distort decision making—strategic problems often are perceived from a standpoint that encourages short-term, or at best medium-term, thinking to the exclusion of deeper issues. This is *not* to say that the US military is too mighty and should be pared back, much less to argue—as do many observers, particularly those of an anti-American bent—that the United States is a "rogue superpower," cruel, imperialistic, and destructive.[27] In fact, the truth is more nearly the precise opposite. Today Washington is the bulwark of world order; as Colin S. Gray has argued, the United States is "the Sheriff"—the organizer of global "posses" that protect and maintain world order and help to keep global villains within bounds.[28] If today the United States took off its sheriff's badge, tossed it back at the surly residents of the global village, and rode home to live in peaceful isolation, the world almost certainly soon would be a much more disordered and violent place.

Indeed, far from being too large and powerful, the US military in fact is too small, given the global ordering role that Washington has accepted. The United States certainly spends a great deal of money on defense, but much of this goes toward developing and purchasing highly capable weapons systems that are exorbitantly expensive on a per-unit basis, in part because the United States actually fields so few of them (the B-2 "Spirit" bomber and F-22 "Raptor" fighter being prominent examples of this phenomenon). More significant, however, is the fact that the two decades immediately following the end of the Cold War were abnormal insofar as only one of the world's states had both a huge economy *and* a willingness to spend a non-negligible percentage of its total GDP on defense. (It is notable that the People's Republic of China apparently is in process of correcting this anomaly[29]—and that, in turn, is encouraging others, such as Japan and India, to rethink their own spending habits.)

The relative military might of the United States, and the illusion of strategic invincibility that it feeds, obscures the fact that the brief "unipolar moment" (to use Charles Krauthammer's apt phrase) is over and can never be regained. Although there presently is no state that might reasonably be described as a true peer competitor to the United States, the global security environment increasingly is one of vigorous competition, a reality discussed in greater detail below. The temporary disproportion in US strength relative to other powerful polities such as China, India, Japan, and Russia still could be leveraged to enormous advantage, helping to ensure that Washington will remain the greatest of the world's powers, though not a global hegemon, for many decades. However, that would require very serious long-term grand strategic thinking of precisely the sort that has been in short supply in recent years.

The previous discussion of the wars in Vietnam, Afghanistan, and Iraq demonstrates how pitiable US efforts to translate military power into strategic advantage have been in recent decades. The 1991 Persian Gulf War is a notable exception in this regard. Even though, contrary to its (unrealistic) hopes, the G.H.W. Bush administration could not translate its victory into a "New World Order" in which the United Nations, particularly the Security Council, actually would be a useful instrument in maintaining global peace and stability, the fact that Washington handily achieved its goal of rolling back Iraq's conquest of Kuwait, and thus ensuring that Hussein would not have an excessive permanent influence over the world price of oil, should be recognized as a significant accomplishment. The other three major US conflicts of the last four decades,[30] however, point to a fatal inability to translate US military power even into operational victory, much less to leverage that power into long-term strategic gain.

The Vietnam case of course is the least directly applicable of the three to the discussion of current and future US strategic considerations. This is partly because the war is increasingly remote, with more than thirty years having passed since the demise of the Republic of Vietnam, but it also is significant that it took place within the context of a bipolar global struggle—a very different global security environment than the one prevailing today or, most likely, tomorrow. Several of the aforementioned similarities between the Iraq and Vietnam Wars are intriguing, but for this work it is most useful to note that US decision making in regard to Vietnam showed many of the failures that would reappear decades later. The failure in Vietnam provides powerful evidence that there in fact is a long-term pattern of flawed grand strategic thinking in the Executive branch that well precedes the G.W. Bush administration.

The inability to translate military power into tangible strategic gains is particularly problematic because US strategic culture is, for quite understandable reasons, increasingly focused on the application of military power to ameliorate or solve strategic problems. Generally speaking, *the American tendency to focus on military solutions to strategic challenges is not, in itself, mistaken, and actually is quite sensible, given the strength of the US armed forces.* Wise leaders focus on the most effective ways in which to use the tools in their national "strategic toolbox" and, when possible, avoid areas of national weakness. Thus, US presidents are inclined to turn to the uniformed military to address strategic matters. The problem, however, is that they often do not wield their military instrument wisely, and thus tend to be ineffective at resolving the problem which they face, or even create a new and larger one.[31]

In addition, there of course are situations in which the use of US military power is inappropriate for any number of reasons, and in recent years American leaders have appeared to find it difficult to devise plausible ways to address long-term strategic problems that defy either military or realistic diplomatic solutions. The proliferation of nuclear weapons by North Korea and Iran are exemplars of this problem.

The flight from reality: threats, diplomacy, and strategic circularity

In the 1990s, the Clinton administration decided that the risks of costs of attacking Pyongyang's nuclear weapons program outweighed the likely benefits that would flow from an attack on North Korean nuclear facilities. This was an entirely reasonable and responsible decision—given North Korea's unpredictability and paranoia, even a very limited strike might have resulted in full-scale invasion of South Korea, the devastation of Seoul (the North has thousands of artillery tubes within range of that metropolis) and tens—or even hundreds—of thousands of resulting civilian deaths, among other dreadful effects. However, the Clinton administration's solution to its strategic dilemma was, strategically speaking, farcical: the negotiation of the Agreed Framework, an arrangement in which North Korea would be provided with various forms of aid (including construction of light-water nuclear reactors) in exchange for an unverifiable promise by Pyongyang that it would suspend its nuclear program. The Kim regime proceeded to act in line with its usual modus operandi, pocketing its profits, secretly continuing its nuclear program, and, apparently, obtaining a nuclear arsenal and conducting nuclear tests in October 2006 and May 2009.

Given North Korea's longstanding record as an utterly untrustworthy negotiating partner, there was no reason for American (or South Korean or Japanese) officials to expect any outcome better than the one which actually occurred. Some former Clinton administration officials have attempted to foist blame onto the Bush administration, implying that the Agreed Framework was achieving its purpose before Washington confronted Pyongyang, as it was limiting the number of nuclear weapons which North Korea could build.[32] However, while it probably is true that the Agreed Framework helped to the limit the amount of fissile material that the North produced during the 1990s, the supposed purpose of the Framework was to prevent North Korean acquisition of *any* nuclear weapons; thus, the Clinton administration's strategy clearly failed.[33]

The Bush administration deserves credit at least for being realistic enough to confront Pyongyang with evidence of its nuclear cheating, an act that indirectly led to the final demise of the fatally flawed Agreed Framework structure. Beyond this, however, there is little sign of real progress in addressing the renuclearization of the Korean Peninsula. The Bush team supported the creation of a multilateral mechanism for resolving the nuclear issue, with six-party talks, involving China, Japan, the two Koreas, Russia, and the United States, occurring from August 2003 onward. Diplomatic efforts were redoubled after the North Korean nuclear test, and a new agreement was reached in February 2007 to close the Yongbyon nuclear reactor (the same reactor previously closed under the Agreed Framework), invite International Atomic Energy Agency (IAEA) personnel to inspect the reactor, and so forth. The six-party talks became moribund shortly thereafter; new diplomatic initiatives surface occasionally, though always with ultimately unsatisfactory results.

When one cuts through the details of the negotiations, it is obvious that nothing fundamental has changed in regard to North Korean nuclear ambitions. It is self-deluding to believe that the actual denuclearization of North Korea will result from negotiations, as there is no meaningful evidence that the character and goals of the Pyongyang regime—which, incredibly, continued its nuclear weapons program despite the emergence of famine conditions that became a permanent feature of North Korean national life—has changed fundamentally. Thus, its strategic goals should not be presumed to have altered drastically. Believing that carving a slightly more elegant diplomatic agreement, with a few thousand extra barrels of fuel oil provided to Pyongyang or a slightly tighter IAEA inspection regimen imposed on it or whatnot, will solve the problem is to engage in almost magical thinking. Only a deep-seated change in North Korean goals would make meaningful progress possible.

A similarly futile negotiating process is ongoing with regard to Iran. Like Pyongyang, Tehran has provided ample circumstantial evidence that it desires nuclear weapons. Although Iran's precise reasons for desiring a nuclear arsenal no doubt differ substantially in their details from those motivating North Korea, the former appears similarly dedicated to obtaining nuclear weapons.[34] (Indeed, Tehran's nuclear ambitions apparently predate the Iranian Revolution—and if the Persian monarchy never had been overthrown it is possible, even probable, that Iran would have obtained nuclear arms years ago.) Moreover, unlike North Korea, Iran is not a hopelessly impoverished and marginal country—it is one of the strongest and most populous Middle Eastern states and, in global terms, a respectable medium power, as well as being one of the world's major petroleum exporters. In short, while one could conceive at least somewhat plausible scenarios in which Pyongyang might be compelled to abandon its nuclear arsenal *if* Beijing decided that North Korean disarmament was critical to Chinese national interests, it would be very hard indeed to bully Tehran into surrendering its nuclear ambitions. (The most effective non-violent measure to coerce Tehran surely would be a global embargo on Iranian oil exports—and, given prevailing economic and political realities, such a sanctions program is utterly fantastical.) Iran apparently desires nuclear weapons, and if so, eventually it shall have them.[35] The Obama administration chooses to ignore this inconvenient reality, as do other governments, which continue to negotiate furiously for an end to Iran's nuclear program.

During the Bush years, there was much discussion, often hysterical, of the possibility that the United States might bomb Iran's nuclear facilities,[36] or even undertake regime change in Iran. The latter measure always was so far-fetched as to defy belief, but even the former was far-fetched, given the obvious, and large, risks and disadvantages: almost certainly, large numbers of Iranian civilians would be killed and the Iranian population—which presently appears to be one of the least anti-American in the Middle East—would be enraged. Moreover, damage to the Iranian nuclear program probably would be ephemeral, while the present Iranian regime would enjoy enormous long-term dividends in the form of domestic popular support in its war against the Great Satan.[37] Talk of imminent US action against Iran has dampened considerably in the Obama years, mercifully, though it has not disappeared altogether.

US military power should not be applied kinetically to the Iranian proliferation problem, as a limited strike probably would do no more than delay the program by a few years, while the occupation of Iran is simply unimaginable. The costs of serious military action against Iran are high enough as to discourage all but the most adventurous policy professionals. Thus, while there will continue to be much rumbling from certain quarters about how the United States could and should strike Iran, in the end, it will not do so because such a move would be self-evidently counterproductive. (Unlike, one hastens to add, in the Iraqi case, where the likely costs of an invasion were not *glaringly* obvious beforehand—partly because the United States had no experience occupying a largish Middle Eastern state.)

If the application of military power is not appropriate, and diplomacy is ineffectual—indeed, perhaps even harmful, as, like the art of distraction which magicians apply to make tricks appear real, the details of complex ongoing negotiations sometimes divert observers from more fundamental truths—then Washington simply must attempt to cope with an unpleasant reality. There is no Iranian or North Korean nuclear "crisis"—a word best used (unless one is E.H. Carr) only to describe brief historical moments of acute danger. Rather, the nuclear scheming of Pyongyang and Tehran has created a problematic international *condition*; while not necessarily permanent, that condition could endure for decades, and the United States and other interested powers should respond accordingly. Certainly, Iranian and North Korean proliferation presents real dangers; preferably, neither state would possess nuclear devices. (Nor, for that matter, would Pakistan, which—given its political instability and the substantial number of Islamists within its political and military elites—likely presents a graver long-term problem than either Iran or North Korea.) Yet the security environment never is ideal—and, in relative terms, Iranian and North Korean nuclear possession does not appear to be an especially overwhelming threat. Obviously, certain *uses* of Iranian or North Korean nuclear weapons would be horrible, and such actions might demand a similarly horrible US response, but prudent policy and strategy can minimize the odds that a "worst-case" event will occur. It is for this reason that the absence of American strategic creativity is so important—grand strategy cannot be well-designed if the universe of choices is narrowed by a poverty of imagination. Fruitless negotiations and idle discussion of military options that will not be pursued do nothing to actually improve the security environment.

The purpose herein is not to suggest ways to mitigate the North Korean and Iranian proliferation problems, but to highlight the American policy elite's worrying inability to confront high-profile strategic problems promptly and in a clear-eyed fashion. Incredibly, the North Korean nuclear "crisis" has been ongoing, in one form or another, for more than twenty years; in that time, despite endless policy debates and the composition of a library of studies, books, and journal articles about the North Korean situation, Washington still has not settled on a pragmatic strategy for coping with the reality of Pyongyang's nuclear possession.

If Washington cannot implement a strategy worthy of the name regarding North Korea, what confidence should one have that it will be able to cope with international matters that are far more complex and nuanced—such as navigating an international security environment in which there are numerous great powers, each with a very distinct strategic culture and unique national goals? The inability of the US government to tackle rather obvious realities in regard either to North Korean or Iranian proliferation is interesting for our purpose because it is indicative of a political elite (both Democrat and Republican) given to self-deception and therefore unsuited to the task of implementing a grand strategy that will be robust under real-world conditions. The US military is such an excellent instrument that it may, on occasion, rescue presidents and lesser policy makers from themselves, making military victory possible despite egregious strategic errors. It cannot, however, be relied upon to do this consistently.

No longer alone: America in a world great power competition

In a world with only one superpower, Washington's tendency toward strategic fantasy only presented a minimal impediment,[38] for the simple reason that no other state possessed the ability to capitalize on American mistakes in a manner that would result in truly significant harm. An international system with numerous great powers, however, is not so forgiving, and such a system rapidly is coming into being.

In general, the period from mid-1989 to 11 September 2001 was a time of immense satisfaction for those who made US foreign policy. The exhilarating victory over its Soviet nemesis seemed to confirm wisdom of the American policy making establishment: the Soviet empire in East-Central Europe, and then the USSR itself, collapsed without massive violence, a shocking (and, historically speaking, somewhat puzzling) occurrence. Moreover, surveying the world about them, most US policy makers saw every reason to believe that Washington would lead the world into a new and more peaceful era in which great power conflict—and thus great power war—was a thing of the past. Not only was America militarily dominant, but its economy was easily the largest (unless the EU was considered as a whole) and those countries that were rapidly developing had almost all embraced free markets—and a fair number of policy makers of both right and left accepted uncritically the hypothesis that political liberty invariably followed in the wake of economic liberty. The prevailing wisdom inside the Beltway was that, even if the world was not quite reshaping itself on an American model, the security environment nonetheless was a salubrious one and would remain so for a long while.

One of course should not overstate the degree to which the "long decade" from 1989 to 2001 was one of casualness toward potential threats. The national security establishment continued to function normally, and the United States was involved in a fair number of conflicts, including one medium-sized war and numerous smaller operations, such as the 1989 US invasion of Panama, the 1993 fiasco in Somalia, and the 1999 bombing of Serbia by NATO. All of these matters, except the successful Persian Gulf War, were, however, small in scale and their direct impact on the global security environment was modest.

There was an understandable lack of focus in regard to US national security during these years (a fact noted by many at the time). Without the existence of a great power peer or near-peer, and with the degree to which *Al Qaeda* and other Islamist groups presented a threat still very much open to debate, the answer to what the United States needed to do to provide for its national security was open to personal interpretation of what threats actually were likely to appear and in what timeframe. Most members of the policy elite mixed optimism with a degree of caution, but some were so enthused as to recommend truly radical measures; former CIA Director

William Colby, for example, taped a television commercial in which he recommended that military spending be cut by fifty percent.[39]

Interestingly, however, a substantial number of observers were not of the view that great power war was merely a problem of the past, and, particularly during the latter years of this period, many of these observers focused on China as an emerging superpower threat to the United States. Their reasons for doing so—China's population, impressive economic growth, and belligerence toward Taiwan chief among them—essentially were sound. Moreover, from today's perspective, most of the warnings of Beijing's growing power certainly do not appear wildly alarmist: China has become far more muscular economically and militarily than most analysts writing in, say, 1995, would have imagined possible. Moreover, even though it thus far has attacked Taiwan or undertaken some similar adventure, its behavior, such as the careful cultivation of relationships in Africa, Latin America, and elsewhere, indicate that it is a power with very considerable ambitions. Many analyses written during the 1990s, however, viewed the US–China relationship through a bipolar lens,[40] with many authors displaying a tendency to treat China as a sort of substitute Soviet Union, thus placing the US–China relationship in the context of a budding Second Cold War.[41] This perspective continues to influence some of the thinking about the PRC and the US relationship to it, though it appears to be waning as states such as India have enjoyed an increasingly prominent international profile.

The "China as new USSR" perspective was and is problematic because the global security environment, that of the eastern portion of Eurasia in particular, bears little resemblance to the one prevailing in the late 1940s. In the latter case, the Soviet Union was able to take advantage of the very specific circumstances created by World War II. The destruction of the Third Reich and the consequent creation of a strategic vacuum in East-Central Europe, the exhaustion of France and Britain, and an inability on the part of the United States immediately to come to grips with the fact that the USSR was a ruthless foe and adapt its strategy accordingly created perfect conditions for sealing Moscow's status as a superpower. Moreover, the destruction of Japanese power created circumstances in East Asia that made Mao's victory in the Chinese Civil War and the creation of the Kim Il-Sung regime in North Korea possible, thus providing Moscow with two key client states in East Asia (although Beijing soon would slip from Soviet influence).

There is no great local security vacuum waiting to be filled by China. Although some of China's neighbors may fall ever more under China's influence, the most obvious candidates for satellite status are states such as Burma/Myanmar—a weak, impoverished country whose corrupt and repressive government has ensured that it is left behind economically in an increasingly prosperous part of the world.[42] China has grown enormously wealthier over the last two decades, but thus far there is little sign that the Asia-Pacific is falling under Chinese hegemony. This absence of triumphal empire-building does not necessarily indicate that Beijing has no substantial ambitions; indeed, China certainly sees itself as a great state that should play a major global role. Whether this means that key Chinese leaders are consciously seeking worldwide hegemony is debatable,[43] but, in any case, such a goal likely would be unattainable unless the PRC were to fight, and win, World War III.

Instead of a simple bipolar structure, it appears more likely that unipolarity—which already is in an advanced state of decay, a fact powerfully evidenced by the US inability to convince many of its formal allies to support its occupation of Iraq—will be replaced by a multipolar structure in which the United States interacts in complex ways with several great powers (China, the EU, India, Japan, and Russia being the most obvious candidates) and a large number of medium and minor powers. Moreover, recent years have highlighted the likely importance of religion and culture as complicating factors in twenty-first century international affairs; one does not have to accept Huntington's "Clash of Civilizations"[44] in its entirety to acknowledge that the politics of this century will not be shaped only by icy realpolitikers in the Kissinger mold.

Imprudent presidents and grand strategy

If the United States is to achieve its policy goals in a complicated international environment, it is vital that it be able to apply its "comparative advantages," particularly its military power, in an appropriate and effective fashion. However, the recent historical record gives one little reason to be confident in its ability to do so. Washington certainly has outlined broad strategic goals in the *National Security Strategy* and elsewhere, but truisms and vagaries do not add up to a meaningful grand strategy.

It of course is not necessary—indeed, it typically would be counterproductive—for a grand strategy to be written down in detail and made publicly available. The absence of a definitive document does not mean that a state lacks a grand strategy, nor does the existence of such a document indicate that meaningful grand strategy exists. Colin S. Gray's elegantly brief definition of grand strategy as "[t]he purposeful employment of all the instruments of power available to a security community" illuminates the essence of the issue.[45] It is not sufficient that a state flail about like a boxer whose eyes have been shut by swelling; power—be it military, economic, diplomatic, or any other type, must be employed in a *purposeful* fashion. It is in this area that the United States is noticeably lacking, and much of the reason for this may be found in the weakness of recent presidential leadership—and this condition is unlikely to improve in the near future.

American presidents have varied enormously in their strategic acumen, as one would expect. The United States survived and thrived despite its weaker chief executives, though perhaps only barely—one can imagine, for instance, what might have occurred if, rather than Lincoln, James Buchanan had been succeeded by another strategic incompetent. Yet the last several decades have indicated a worrying trend that could be dangerous to the United States and its place in the hierarchy of states: despite its huge population of intelligent, highly educated citizens—a vast store of human capital—several of its recent presidents have been troublingly mediocre grand strategists.

Analysts of course differ over the relative merits of the past several presidents, and judging presidential "strategic performance" inherently is rather subjective. Since 1948 various institutions have undertaken polls of historians, political scientists, and similar experts, but these are of little use for the purpose at hand. First, such polls have obvious potential problems with ideological and other biases; some polls have endeavored to address the question of ideological bias,[46] but even if this is addressed adequately, a plethora of other potential issues remain, such as the particular expertise of the individuals surveyed.[47] More importantly, strategic performance is not separated out from success in passing domestic legislation and similar achievements, and only the former is relevant to this work.

Nonetheless, there is a compelling case to be made that several recent presidents have been weak strategists. For instance, the Carter presidency provides a particularly stark example of the gap between the duties of the presidency and the strategic acumen of its occupant.[48] Indeed, the mere fact that Carter was elected president of the United States, particularly during a time in which America's international position was shaky and the power of its Soviet foe appeared to be waxing, is somewhat troubling. As a one-term governor of the state of Georgia, he had no significant experience in foreign policy or related matters, nor was there any particular reason to believe that he had any substantial knowledge of such subjects or had thought deeply about them. He had served as a junior naval officer, but this, in itself, hardly qualified him to be commander-in-chief of the armed forces, much less prepared him to devise and execute the grand strategy of the United States.

Given his background (or lack thereof), it is not in the least surprising that the Carter administration's foreign policy record proved to be unimpressive, including a ham-handed attempt to grant human rights a central role in foreign policy making and, most strikingly, a gross mishandling of the Iranian hostage situation, which resulted in the long-running humiliation of the United States and a major domestic and international victory for an Islamist regime that continues to bedevil Washington today. Even many of the Carter administration's apparent triumphs today appear tarnished. The signing of the Camp David Accords perhaps was its greatest success, though even that agreement's real long-term value may be questioned. Also, the administration's intervention (alongside Britain) in Rhodesian/Zimbabwean politics was intended to create an independent

Zimbabwe that would be a stable, prosperous democracy; time has demonstrated that London and Washington failed to do so, with catastrophic results for the Zimbabwean populace.[49]

Carter's subsequent career as a freelancing would-be peacemaker (including a mission that paved the way for the aforementioned Agreed Framework) and author of simplistic analyses on global affairs[50] has confirmed his paucity of strategic judgment; to this day, the former president continues to make stunningly naïve assertions. (Ironically, Carter's campaign autobiography was entitled *Why Not the Best?*[51]) For instance, in the course of arguing in an editorial that India should not receive fissile material from the United States, he states: "If India's demand [for access to fissile material production technology] is acceptable, why should other technologically advanced NPT signatories, such as Brazil, Egypt, Saudi Arabia, and Japan—to say nothing of less responsible nations—continue to restrain themselves?"[52] One marvels at the contention that Saudi Arabia, the state which, via its extremely well-funded efforts to propagate Salafist Islam worldwide and eclipse more tolerant visions of Islam, has done more than any other (including Iran) to spread Islamism and loathing of Enlightenment values, is relatively responsible.

The Carter administration is only a particularly stark example of the malady under discussion. The Johnson and Ford records also were weak. The Johnson administration's disastrous decisions regarding Vietnam were touched on above, while the Ford administration looked on as South Vietnam died and otherwise presided over a floundering foreign policy. However, in fairness to Ford, one might note that, given the crippling of the presidency by the Watergate scandal and the domestic political circumstances of the time, effectively wielding American power was very difficult at that point in history. Moreover, Congress bears the bulk of the blame for the catastrophe of 1975—it almost surely could have saved South Vietnam, but chose not to do so, while the president's strategic options were greatly limited by the 1973 Case-Church Amendment and the general political climate in the United States.[53]

The remaining recent presidents, however, might be able to claim more successful records. Richard Nixon had some notable accomplishments, such as arranging a quasi-alliance with Mao's China. He also deserves some credit for his handling of Vietnam; while far from perfect, the Nixon policy ultimately resulted in the Paris Peace Accords, an agreement which, *if enforced*, would have provided a satisfactory result to the American enterprise in Indochina, a "Korean War solution" in which South Vietnam would have survived as an independent, non-communist US ally. The fact that it was not enforced at the decisive time, spring 1975, was not the result of a strategic failure in any usual sense, but of Nixon's self-immolation: the Watergate cover-up provided the opportunity that Nixon's enemies needed to hobble him and, ultimately, remove him from office. If Watergate had not occurred, the Case-Church Amendment or similar legislation surely would have never passed Congress, much less with a "veto-proof" margin. If the North had dared to launch an invasion in 1975, Nixon—a president possessed of foreign policy *gravitas* who had won a landslide re-election victory in 1972 against an opponent of his Vietnam policy—would have been able to protect his ally and thus assure its continued existence.[54]

Of course, the Watergate scandal *did* occur, and therefore the events that followed that hotel burglary must be taken into account when assessing Nixon's record. While it is best to avoid excessive psychological speculation—there probably already has been more than enough amateur psychoanalysis of the enigmatic thirty-seventh president[55]—Nixon's behavior was oddly self-destructive, given that the Watergate burglary and cover-up were gratuitous in a campaign where the incumbent's victory was near-certain. Moreover, Nixon had periodically sabotaged himself repeatedly throughout his career, as in the infamous "you won't have Nixon to kick around anymore" concession speech that he gave on the night that he lost the 1962 campaign for governor of California. In strategic affairs, personality matters, sometimes critically so, and whatever traits led Nixon to undertake the Watergate cover-up had an impact on his record as a strategist.

In terms of judging strategic acumen, Ronald Reagan is an unusually difficult man to assess. He clearly possessed something in the way of what Clausewitz would call *coup d'oeil*, seeing—long before he even entered politics, or even had turned to the Right—that the USSR and its ideology presented a grave threat to the United States. At a time when Hollywood had more than its share of the sort of political naïfs whom Lenin called useful idiots, the New Dealer Reagan understood intuitively that communists were not merely "liberals in a hurry."[56] During his presidency, Reagan's strategic instincts generally were sound, but his lack of formal academic or practical background in strategy also occasionally showed, as in the bungled intervention in Lebanon.[57] Overall, however, his strategic record is a respectable one—and, though it would be a gross exaggeration to grant the Reagan administration sole credit for the demise of the USSR, the administration's military buildup and vigorous containment policy helped to create the conditions for the events of 1989–91.

Finally, it is important to give proper credit to the underrated G.H.W. Bush. While he certainly could not be placed in the same class as Lincoln, having never faced a crisis as acute as the sixteenth president did, he did confront a rather substantial number of foreign policy difficulties during his one presidential term, and generally managed them well. The 1991 Persian Gulf War is his most obvious success,[58] but the administration's handling of the collapse of the USSR and then the Soviet Union itself also is deserving of considerable praise. While his administration perhaps was excessively cautious, at one point even trying to keep the USSR alive by containing the centrifugal forces that were killing it,[59] in the circumstances of that time the vice of timidity was far preferable to that of excessive adventurousness, and an extraordinarily dangerous strategic problem—the demise of a vast, (heavily) nuclear-armed, and unashamedly thuggish empire—was resolved with minimal violence.

When the presidents of the last several decades are considered together, the recent record of American voters in choosing strategically talented presidents appears quite mixed. While it must be granted that voters did avoid some probable disasters—a George McGovern or second Carter administration, for instance—it also is of note that G.H.W. Bush failed to win reelection despite his obvious strategic successes.[60]

It is too early to provide a truly long-term judgment of Bill Clinton, much less his immediate successor. However, for reasons discussed above, the auguries are rather dubious for both men. The current administration of course is a "work in progress," so many of its successes and failures have not yet occurred. However, though it is too early to speak conclusively on President Obama's capabilities as a grand strategist, there is reason for concern, given both the administration's apparent lack of a coherent grand strategy that is not based on counterterrorism and the unfortunate decision to involve the United States in Libya.

Tyranny's rewards: America's great power competitors

For a very long time, and particularly since the collapse of the Soviet Bloc, it has been widely believed that democracies enjoy massive inherent advantages over other forms of government. The reasoning for exactly why this is the case varies from one author to the next, but it commonly is assumed that the free flow of ideas and the freedom of citizens to criticize government failings, as well as the advantages that come from the rule of law and the consequent respect for property ownership, rewards democracies over the long term and allow them over decades to gain ground relative to authoritarian competitors.

Without doubt, there is more than a little truth in this perspective, and the Cold War provided an unusually stark example of how a democratic superpower could outlast an undemocratic competitor. However, it should always be kept in mind that the Cold War *was only one case.* Its ultimate outcome most certainly does not prove that democracies always will emerge triumphant from peaceful competition, and World War II does not demonstrate that they invariably will win wars against non-democrats. As a form of government, democracy had a very strong run during the twentieth century, but past victories do not necessarily guarantee future ones.

Speaking globally, at this point in history the future of democratic governance at best is uncertain. The most populous state on the planet has enjoyed several decades of stunning success under a nominally communist government. The rise—from the long view, actually the recovery—of

China surely will prove to be an historical process of first-rank importance. Indeed, it is not difficult to imagine that historians of the future will regard China's new affluence as the closing of a period that began when the Industrial Revolution made Northwestern Europe the center of human economic activity. Defying many optimistic predictions, however, China has not yet transformed itself into a democracy and at the moment most of its leaders appear more than slightly uninclined to do so.

Russian policy makers perhaps should not be as sanguine as their Chinese counterparts about the future: Russia appears to be in long-term decline, a former superpower with an economy based on the extraction of natural resources. At least when energy prices are high, oil and gas revenues provide enough money to enrich Russia's small, avaricious elite while still leaving a decent revenue stream for the state.[61] Moscow, however, lacks a plausible plan for moving beyond its current status as a middle income state with a declining population and a military establishment of increasingly dubious overall quality. Russian democracy has degenerated into bleak farce[62]—particularly troublesome opponents of the current regime tend either to be shot by mysterious assailants or railroaded into prison by a lawless "justice" system—and Moscow seems unable to modernize its economy and effectively address its deep social problems.

In their relationship with the United States, however, Russian leaders do share some major advantages with their Chinese peers, including enormous freedom in foreign policy making and the construction of grand strategy, opacity in decision making (which makes it very difficult for outsiders to anticipate future actions), and an ability to take ruthless advantage of opportunities in a timely manner. China and Russia, like many undemocratic states, can, when they are determined to do so, navigate the geopolitical environment with an athletic combination of speed and muscle, creating and capitalizing upon opportunities.

Washington, by contrast, is both sluggish and relatively transparent in its actions, sacrificing swiftness and surprise for formal interagency processes, as well as freedom of the press and of public criticism. As noted previously, public input in foreign policy and defense decision making has both good and ill effects, and the former should not be underestimated. It is not argued herein that openness in the policy process is, on balance, negative, much less that the United States government should attempt to model itself on authoritarian ones. (American airports provide a vision of what a more authoritarian United States would look like and it is a very disagreeable mixture of humorless bossiness on the part of officialdom and gratuitous inconvenience and indignity for travelers.) Affection for democratic ideals, however, should not blind one to certain specific advantages that Washington's authoritarian competitors might enjoy in the strategic environment of the twenty-first century.

Technological, social, and political changes are intertwined deeply. Clearly, technological developments can drive political and social change:

the Protestant Reformation cannot be discussed properly without reference to the spread of the printing press in Europe, nor can the social history of the United States in the twentieth century be understood if one does not account for the importance of the American population's access to affordable automobiles. However, political choices can determine whether technological change is speedy or sluggish. It surely was not a matter of simple chance that the Shanghai of 1960 was an intellectual backwater but today that city is one of the world's major centers for research in science, technology, and medicine. If the CCP's priorities had not changed enormously after the Great Helmsman's death, Shanghai would have remained what it was half a century ago—a world leader in the production of stultifying Maoist doctrine, and little else.[63]

At present, the speed of both technological and social change is extraordinarily rapid, and this will impact global politics in ways that cannot be predicted reliably.[64] In coming years, advances in genetics and bioengineering, computer science,[65] robotics,[66] nanotechnology,[67] and other areas may have very significant military and political implications. Many of those advances will be made by scientists employed by non-democratic competitors to the United States. However, even breakthroughs occurring in Western laboratories may ultimately be used to Washington's disadvantage. Whether a technology can be developed and whether it can be leveraged effectively for military and strategic advantage are two quite distinct issues.

In past decades, the United States has been proven quite adept both at developing technologies and applying them so as to enhance its military power, with the result being that it was at the leading edge of two distinct revolutions in military affairs (RMAs):[68] the nuclear revolution of mid-century and a still-ongoing guidance/computerization/space power revolution that began in the latter twentieth century. The more recent of these often is referred to in defense and policy circles as "the" RMA—an unfortunate phrasing, as it implies that there has only been, and presumably only can be, one RMA in human history; it is more precisely referred to as the Second American RMA. This latter RMA, it should be noted, largely was a reaction to its nuclear forerunner: Washington hoped that the development of highly potent conventional weapons would make nuclear war less likely, as NATO thus might have the capability to fend off a Soviet invasion without resorting to the use of tactical nuclear weapons. (The belief that the Soviet Union would prove so obliging as to refrain from nuclear use even as its own forces were being defeated probably was an extravagant exercise in wishful thinking, but that point is tangential to the question at hand.) The first American-led RMA had been *too* revolutionary, resulting in the creation of nuclear arsenals so destructive that war easily could degenerate into the mass butchery of non-combatants. Its successor was intended to correct this deficiency, making it possible for the United States to conduct military operations that not only were infinitely more discriminate than a large-scale nuclear exchange, but also considerably more nuanced than the conventional warfare of previous decades. Precision air strikes against Taliban and *Al Qaeda* targets in Pakistan, for instance, undoubtedly have resulted in a number of civilian casualties (the exact size of that number, however, is quite controversial). Yet, the damage inflicted is tiny compared to that which US airpower inflicted on the Low Countries and northern France during World War II.

It should not nonchalantly be assumed that democracies in general, much less the United States in particular, in the future will prove more adept at leveraging technological change for strategic advantage. The fact that the United States was responsible for the two most recent RMAs does provide some historical support for "democratic confidence," but it also should be kept in mind that the political and technological conditions of tomorrow will differ greatly from those prevailing in the past. There are many reasons for this, but for the moment three general points should suffice.

First, applying certain promising technologies for military purposes can be highly controversial publicly—or even, as in the case of new and potentially terrible next-generation biological weapons, already outright banned by international treaty. Governments such as that of the United States may be inclined simply to avoid research whose implications may be ethically or politically troubling. Even pursuing classified research in certain areas potentially has political consequences,[69] and openly pursued research, much less actual application of the knowledge gained thereby, certainly would have political costs. Even a phrase such as "genetic modification of soldiers" is likely to make policy makers in a democracy woozy—at least partly, for good reason: some areas of research inherently are highly vulnerable to unethical abuse. This, however, actually creates a potential advantage for unscrupulous and secretive powers, which might seek to gain a critical advantage in areas where their more virtuous peers fear to tread.

Second, the United States was financially and scientifically/industrially very well-positioned to "launch" the two aforementioned RMAs. The United States of World War II era was not only easily the wealthiest state on the planet, but in recent years it also had enjoyed a major influx of talented scientists who were fleeing Nazi repression. After the war's end it became clear that Berlin had devoted so much of its intellectual and material resources to other programs that it never came close to creating an actual device. The Soviet Union did not explode a nuclear device until 1949, and its own bomb program relied partly on data obtained from its "atomic spies" in the United States.

The Second American RMA was much less abrupt, unfolding over the latter decades of the Cold War. For most of that time, the overall advantage in US military technology over the USSR was far from obvious. Indeed, it was only in the closing years of the Cold War that the United

States arguably might have come to possess a critical advantage in conventional technology: the US military was far more technologically impressive in 1989 than it was in 1979, much less 1969. As with the Nuclear RMA, the United States enjoyed critical structural advantages: not only was Washington confronted with only one real military competitor, and not only did that foe have a far lower GDP per capita, but it had—out of a mixture of necessity and ideologically driven naïveté—created a monolithic technological-military-industrial complex. Almost all Soviet scientific effort—and there were many fine scientists in the USSR—was geared toward military progress; supposedly wasteful consumer-driven research was minimal. The Second American RMA, however, was largely the result of the interbreeding of military- and consumer-driven research. The Soviet Union was exceedingly good in some areas of military technology, but it could not assemble its own Silicon Valley. Indeed, its leaders could not even envision how such a hothouse of innovation could be built: the notion that consumer-driven creativity was important was problematic enough, but the idea that "parasitic" unemployed university drop-outs building toys in their parents' garages might contribute to a country's military power was beyond their imagination.

Third, as Edward Luttwak informed readers of his classic *Strategy: The Logic of War and Peace*, victory in strategic endeavors often is the parent of future failure (and failures, if a polity draws the correct lessons from them, make future successes possible).[70] Throughout this work, there has been discussion of how excellence in grand strategy can allow for a virtuous cycle, with success feeding success; this theme has been a powerful one throughout American history. Yet, winning can, and often does, breed overconfidence. It has been a very long time since Washington has tasted a stinging strategic defeat at the hand of a great power; indeed, one of the remarkable facts of US history is how very few times America actually has suffered gravely at the hands of peers or near-peers. The raiding and burning of Washington, DC, the bombing of Pearl Harbor and the retreat of the Eighth Infantry Division in Korea all were humiliating at the time, but in the grand scheme of history they were small setbacks for a usually very lucky polity.

Given recent US experiences in Afghanistan and Iraq, the current generation of American leaders is quite aware that conventional military excellence does not automatically translate into counterinsurgency competence. It is much less likely, however, that many of them appreciate how tenuous US conventional (itself a problematic word, but the common stand-in for "non-nuclear/chemical/biological") military supremacy could be in a time of extraordinary technological, economic, and social change.

Conclusion

Washington's current and future competitors have access to the lessons of the past. How they attempt to apply those lessons one cannot say, but it is entirely possible that Beijing, Moscow, or another power will prove adept at sidestepping seemingly overwhelming US strengths, much as *Al Qaeda* did in the 9/11 attacks. Strategic success breeds complacency; assumptions about how the world system is organized and what threats are plausible go unquestioned. The formula for addressing this is simple in conception, but difficult to apply in practice, as it requires the *constant* questioning of the premises upon which policy is built and a dedication to rigorously challenging culturally comfortable assumptions.

This of course is entirely alien to the natural inclinations of bureaucracies,[71] which tend to reward consensus and reject challenges to the worldview prevailing within the organization. This is understandable. If policy makers are confronted with a staggeringly complex reality that defies easy comprehension they may become confused and unsure of how to respond; institutional paralysis can result. A government whose worldview is profoundly flawed might enjoy strategic success despite wrongheadedness—serious mistakes may be survivable, if enemies make even worse mistakes. However, a "bureaucracy of anomie" in which decision makers have given up any hope that they can shape the future cannot function at all.

A great potential advantage of the US system is that Washington need not be trapped by either unexamined wrong assumptions or intellectual bewilderment. The president can question verities and impose course corrections in foreign policy, crafting a grand strategy that is prudent and elegant. However, in order to do so, he or she must know both the right questions and the right (or, in any case, right enough) answers. That is a lot to ask of a human being, and it returns us, once again, to the slippery, frustrating concept of strategic genius.

Conclusion

The strategic history of the United States has been an enviable one. This has been the result of both a distinctive combination of favorable geopolitical factors and a large portion of good fortune. At several points in its history, the United States has been extraordinarily lucky—more than once the White House has been occupied by the right man at the right moment, and the result was a strategic windfall for the United States.

Nevertheless, luck is not a plan. Washingtons, Polks, and suchlike are in perennially short supply and they do not always appear when needed. At the moment of decision, the commander-in-chief might be either an Abraham Lincoln or a Jefferson Davis. Strategic history is punctuated by critical events that occur irregularly. Sometimes the spark that might light a conflagration does not land on dry enough tinder (World War I conceivably could have started in 1905 as a result of the First Moroccan Crisis, but did not), yet at other times it does. A state cannot predict when it will need its great men or women. The disheartening reality is that no matter how carefully a polity tends to its long-term grand strategy, a supreme commander who has the wrong stuff but is in charge at a critical point in history can bring ruin. This certainly is true for the United States, which grants its commanders-in-chief a fixed term in office and wide powers.

There is no feasible solution for this potential weakness in the American constitutional regime. While clever political theorists might invent all manner of alternatives to the current system, there is near-zero probability that such notions might be implemented *before* a strategic disaster occurs. The US Constitution began as an exercise in applied political theory, but it now has been developing organically for well over 200 years, and both the citizenry and policy making establishment basically are uninterested in alternatives to the current, "imperial" presidency.

This is made all the more problematic by the fact that in recent decades most of the individuals raised to the highest American office have taken it despite having little practical experience of foreign and defense policy. In the last several decades, the résumé of most Republican and Democratic presidential nominees has been thin. There of course have been exceptions to this rule, but figures such as Dwight Eisenhower and George H.W. Bush stand out as being unusual in an assemblage dominated by governors and senators with little experience in the day-to-day management of foreign and defense policy. Whereas it once was not unusual for presidents to have previously served as ambassadors or general officers, or even to have sat in the Cabinet, that is now rare. Most presidents take office having never personally handled the policy machinery of the American state.

The lack of relevant experience, however, perhaps is less troubling than the absence of intellectual preparation that most presidents have for their office. Presidential candidates and presidents-elect are briefed intensely on issues, and they thus take office with a good working knowledge of current affairs, but this decidedly is not the same thing as an understanding of strategy, grand or otherwise. Current affairs are just that—ongoing policy problems that require attention. How successfully those problems are addressed, however, often is dependent on how well an individual has honed his or her mind before holding power.

Before the latter twentieth century, most presidents had, since their youth, been exposed deeply to classical history and other subjects which hone the mind, allowing for the development of an intuitive, if not necessarily an explicit, understanding of grand strategy as an art form, the coming together of military, economic, and other forms of power so as to advance the interests of the state. They had learned how to think in long, even very long, timeframes; Manifest Destiny merely is the popular expression of an extraordinarily ambitious grand strategic conception. If great swathes of the American populace thought in such terms, it would be very surprising indeed if their presidents were unable to muster the intellectual energy to craft a rather more nuanced vision.

In principle, the presidents of tomorrow should be just as capable as their predecessors of thinking about grand strategy in a sophisticated manner. Indeed, in the post-World War II period strategic studies developed as a distinct field of study,[1] creating a class of academics who explicitly strive to separate strategic gold from the ore of history. The resulting products fill bookshelves and are available to all comers. The problem, however, is that even to possess an awareness of one's own ignorance requires some conception of what one does not know. We can expect that most future would-be presidents will think they understand strategy because they understand current affairs and are unaware that there is a meaningful distinction between the two categories. Indeed, the difference between the two is not immediately obvious even to most highly intelligent observers—to perceive it requires either an appropriate intellectual background and/or natural gifts. The latter is rare, while too few of those who would be president receive the former. This, however, does not mean that it is impossible to mitigate the dangers that accompany vesting great authority in a single individual.

In principle, the United States can increase the likelihood that it will have future presidents possessed of real ability as strategists *if* an awareness of the "strategy deficit" and the reasons for it is cultivated. Unfortunately, this is difficult to do, given the current deficiencies in public strategic discussion in the United States. Moreover, the presidential "strategy deficit" is an uncomfortably bipartisan issue—neither the Republicans or Democrats can claim to be innocent of placing strategists of dubious talent in the White House. Even-handed public discussion is difficult when activists in both parties are not inclined to make frank, public statements that the other side conceivably might exploit. Yet, intellectual seriousness on the part of policy makers and journalists would encourage positive change in the US political culture and likely have a ripple effect, ultimately generating, one would hope, a demand on the part of voters for deeper discussion of security and foreign policy issues from presidential candidates, with the electorate showing favor toward those who can demonstrate depth and competence in these areas.

Although this should happen, however, it most likely will not, at least in the near term. Good strategic analysis requires confronting uncomfortable truths, and the fact is that at this point in history there is little sign that a revolutionary improvement in public and elite understanding of strategy, and the critical role that presidents play in it, is imminent. Most likely, US grand strategy will continue to be unfocused and inadequate for some years, perhaps even for decades. In the meantime, there will be strategic incoherence, with wild vacillations between administrations in their general worldview, and thus in their behavior toward allies, neutrals, and foes. The United States will react to great events, rather than anticipating, channeling, and using them to achieve its national goals. This will have regrettable results, as continuity and consistency are critical to grand strategic success. US unipolarity was never destined to be permanent, but continued strategic confusion will encourage the decline in American power and speed the rise of other powers, including potential future peer and near-peer competitors.

We can expect that in virtually every one of the next fifty years, the percentage of the global GDP which is accounted for by the United States will continue to drop, continuing a decades-long trend. This is anything but unforeseeable, and merely reflects basic economics. The outsized American economic power in the mid-1940s reflected a unique historical contingency, and it was not permanently sustainable.[2] Today, many poorer states are gaining ground on the United States in relative terms, and this group includes potential future enemies. The progress made by the latter is not entirely unwelcome—it would be both pointless and repugnant to wish continued desperation on presently impoverished people—but it ensures futures challenges for the United States. While there is no simple equation by which economic prosperity is translated into international political power[3] (as noted above, the USSR was economically pitiable, but for decades maintained an awesome military establishment), there nevertheless most definitely is a correlation between economic and military power. The global distribution of wealth also clearly is relative in diplomacy and other areas. Gold fuels the machinery of statecraft. Thus, it can be taken as a given that the global distribution of power will change, and American power in the international system will decline.

An overall lessening of US global power would not necessarily have tragic results. Unfortunately, however, the reemergence of multipolarity does mean that it is possible that such a global war or similar event will occur at some point in the future. The task of American policy and strategy is to prevent such a disaster from occurring, and most certainly that such a cataclysm does not result in the birth of world order in which the United States is weak and permanently on the defensive, its prosperity and Constitutional order threatened by powerful antagonists. In order to guard against this, Washington must strive to remain the greatest single power—not the unipolar "capital of the world," but a diplomatically clever and militarily potent balancer capable of deterring would-be enemies of great power peace.

There is an immense qualitative difference between managed relative decline and an unregulated, chaotic freefall. The former implies the adaption of strategy to reflect disagreeable realities, and it is the prudent approach to intractable geostrategic problems. It is the exercise of wisdom, not the surrender to despair. It also is very difficult to achieve, perhaps even more so in a great republic than in most other sorts of state: proud citizens do not want to confront the corrosion of their polity's influence and are apt to find alluring flattering humbug that emphasizes national "specialness" and offhandedly dismisses decline. Thus, not only is strategic acumen required on the part of a leader, but also tact and wisdom.

This is very much to ask of any president. It is, however, not to ask for the impossible—and the United States produces many individuals who could do very well indeed at the task of managing national security affairs and crafting grand strategy. For a country with as much in the way of human and material assets as the United States, strategic success does not require perfection. Strategists compete with other strategists, and they all have emotional and intellectual weakness and imperfections. From the Revolutionary War onward, US strategic history is littered with poor judgments, cultural biases leading to miscalculation, and all manner of other errors. That did not prevent the United States from becoming the most powerful country in the world less than two centuries after achieving its independence. A very large part of continuing US strategic success in the future is a question of whether US presidents consistently are talented enough to ensure that their country has a sound and reasonably steady grand strategy.

Notes

Introduction

1 However, Paul E. Peterson accurately points out that, structurally speaking, "[T]here is little in the US constitutional framework that encourages executive dominance of the foreign policy-making system" (Peterson 1994: 220).
2 Colin S. Gray provides a definition of grand strategy that has the virtues of clarity and completeness: "The direction and use made of any and all among the total assets of a security community in support of its policy goals as decided by politics. The theory and practice of grand strategy is the theory and practice of statecraft itself" (Gray 2010: 18).
3 One should note that, in some important respects, technological developments have diminished, or even entirely negated, defensive advantages that the United States once held—for example, while geographic isolation from the Old World provided protection from the armies of potential enemies, during the Cold War the mating of nuclear warheads to long-range bombers and missiles made it physically possible for the Soviet Union to promptly and grievously damage the American homeland. However, this vulnerability was not unique to the United States; any state that might once have leveraged its geography to make invasion problematic (a category that most certainly included Washington's Soviet foe) confronted this new vulnerability. Thus, in certain respects, the United States today is more vulnerable than it was even in the eighteenth century, but these vulnerabilities flow from technological advances rather than military weakness.
4 On the speed and severity of Moscow's collapse, see Walton (1999).
5 Indeed, from the 1960s onward, Beijing had some success in staking out a position as a power that was not subordinate to either Moscow or Washington and which enjoyed some ability to act independently on a global level. An interesting small illustration of China's attempt to do so is provided in Chau (2007).
6 On the junta's reasoning for invading the Falklands/Malvinas, see Arquilla and Rasmussen (2001).
7 See, for example, Bialer (1980, 1981) and Valenta and Potter (1981). A particularly influential early work is Fainsod (1953).
8 See Grant (1993) and Meier (1995).
9 For the views of two (decidedly anti-Nixon) contemporary observers on the successful marketing of the less-than-charismatic Republican presidential candidate in, respectively, 1968 and 1972, see Thompson (1983) and McGinnis (1988).
10 For a critique of the use of advertising in modern presidential campaigns, see Jamieson (1996). The argument that campaign advertising actually is healthy for democratic politics is made in Freedman *et al.* (2004).

11 The argument that US voters do care much about foreign and defense policy issues is made in Aldrich *et al.* (1989) and Torres-Reyna and Shapiro (2002).

12 Precisely why this is the case is somewhat beyond the scope of this work, but clearly the psychology of political campaigns plays a non-negligible role, with voters deciding that, for whatever mix of reasons, they "like" a candidate and then ascribing competence in all sorts of areas to that candidate regardless of whether he or she has demonstrated it. This tendency is unsurprising for the very simple reason that it is profoundly human—people generally ascribe positive qualities to those leaders whom they approve of, while discounting the accomplishments of those whom they dislike. When this is added to the "us versus them" mentality inherent in a presidential campaign, it is hardly surprising that voters tend to paper over their preferred candidate's likely weaknesses.

13 For example, voters could consider factors such as high-level service in the uniformed military and/or as a civilian in an agency with defense, diplomatic, or intelligence responsibilities. Also, some candidates leave a record of interest in foreign and security affairs over the course of their careers. In the 1992 election, for instance, even the most inattentive voter would have found it difficult to miss the fact that the incumbent president both had substantial experience in foreign affairs and had enjoyed some very considerable successes in this area during his first term in office, while his two opponents in the general election, Bill Clinton and Ross Perot, did not have comparable credentials.

14 See Andrew and Mitrokhin (2005).

15 This point is illustrated brilliantly in Schroeder (1994).

16 Indeed, despite Fredrick's undoubted genius, if not for bafflingly good luck Prussia would have been smashed decisively in 1762.

17 On George Kennan's role in the shaping of the containment strategy, see Kennan (1967), Stephanson (1992), and Thompson (2009).

18 "Whatever the US errors of omission and commission, its grand strategic performance self-evidently was good enough to be compatible with the comprehensive political rout of the foe in 1989–91" (Gray 1999: 242).

19 Notable recent histories of the conflict in Korea include Varhola (2000), Millett (2005, 2010), and Halberstam (2007). Intriguing perspectives on Mao's views regarding the war are offered in Zhang (1995) and Chang and Halliday (2006).

20 As Gray notes,

> The American national experience provides ample evidence for an optimistic ideology. "Americans" survived and triumphed in the seventeenth and eighteenth centuries against the might of intermittently hostile, and numerically vastly superior, Indian tribes, against the might of France and Great Britain—and, perhaps, most impressive of all—against a very challenging physical geography.
>
> (Gray 1981: 27)

21 The most notable example of this in recent decades was the impact of Kennedy (1987). A thoughtful critique of this work is offered in Black (2008: 1–26).

22 See, for example, Brzezinski (2000, 2005), Kagan (2000), Kissinger (2001), and Frum and Perle (2003).

1 Beyond all expectations: the American rise to preeminence

1 This was not a uniquely British perspective. Later, many US professional soldiers would have similar feelings about militiamen:

> Regulars viewed their counterparts in the militia with concern and contempt. To some professionals, these men seemed too preoccupied with

> their individual rights to become good soldiers. Indeed, the unwillingness of militiamen and volunteers to accept fully the self-abnegation demanded by military discipline caused some professionals to doubt their patriotism.
> (Herrera 2001: 27)

2 Regarding the latter, interesting perspectives are offered in Millett and Maslowski (1992) and Black (2002).
3 Cunningly, the American Founders devised a Constitution that divided power among branches and levels of government and created a sustainable rule of law. That Constitution and its Amendments not only protected explicitly political rights—such as the right to assembly, free speech, and so forth—but has an implicit, and sometimes explicit (as in the Third and Fourth Amendments) protection for the property rights of individuals. It also is notable that the Constitution is largely negative in its emphasis—it is a document focused as much on the federal government's limits as on the powers and duties of that entity.
4 Certainly, the physical geography of the United States was fortuitous, insofar as the central section of North America contained enormous agricultural potential and mineral resources but had the incalculable advantage of being distant from the center of great power competition, and thus from the most dangerous of potential enemies. Undistracted by serious external threats, the United States was freed to advance westward; over the long term, the American Indian tribes, divided and relatively small in population, proved incapable of effective resistance against this onslaught.
5 The intellectual and ideological currents encouraging the outbreak of the Revolution are discussed at length in Tucker and Hendrickson (1982), Wood (1991), Bailyn (1992), and Draper (1996).
6 A highly readable history of the repression of the Cathar sect is offered in O'Shea (2001).
7 See Anderson (2000: 50–65).
8

> Although he actually lost more battles than he won, and although he spent the first two years of the war making costly tactical mistakes that nearly lost the American Revolution at its very start, by 1778 he reached an elemental understanding of his military strategy; namely, that captured ground—what he termed "a war of posts"—was virtually meaningless. The strategic key was the Continental Army. If it remained intact as an effective fighting force, the American Revolution remained alive.... [A]s long as Washington held the Continental Army together, the British could not win the war, which meant that they would eventually lose it. Like all of Washington's elemental insights, this one seems patently obvious only in retrospect.
> (Ellis 2000: 130–131)

9 On the awareness of many British officers regarding the need to win American "hearts and minds," see Conway (1986).
10 Even within just the Western Hemisphere, the importance of Britain's non-North American possessions was an important consideration. T.G. Burnard argues that Jamaica was the wealthiest and most critically important individual colony in the eighteenth century British Empire (2001: 506–507).
11 On Britain's strategic perspective in regard to the conflict, see Black (1999: 155–220).
12 See Ellis (2000: 130).
13 "The First Printing of the Declaration of Independence, as inserted in the Rough Journal of Congress," from Boyd (1943: Plate X); reproduced in Jayne (1998: 175).
14 Richard Pipes notes the grim fact that:

> Revolutionary movements and regimes tend, up to a point, to grow more radical and more ruthless. This happens because, after successive failures, their leaders, rather than reexamine their fundamental premises, since these provide the rationale for their existence, prefer to implement them more ruthlessly in the conviction that failure was due to insufficient resolve. Ultimately, when nothing succeeds, fatigue sets in and the heirs of the founding fathers settle down to enjoy life, but not before resorting to the most extreme forms of inhumanity.
>
> (Pipes 2003: 132)

15 This is not to deny that events of a terroristic character, such as the burning of Loyalists' homes, and in some cases even the lynching of Loyalists, did not occur. Such atrocities did happen, but, critically, were not publicly endorsed by most of the Revolution's military or civilian leaders. These crimes therefore were clearly different from, for example, Lenin's use of "Red Terror" during the Russian Civil War—unlike goons who persecuted suspected Loyalists, Communist party cadres were explicitly authorized and encouraged to seize property and organize summary executions of "class enemies" and other unfortunates. See Pipes (1996) and Gellately (2008).

16 The sheer scale of Mao's ambitions in this regard are explored in Chang and Halliday (2006).

17 A point noted by the anonymous "Federal Farmer"—likely, but not certainly, Richard Henry Lee—in "Letter from a Federal Farmer #1" (8 October 1787): "If we remain cool and temperate, we are in no immediate danger of any commotions; we are in a state of perfect peace, and in no danger of invasions; the state governments are in the full exercise of their powers; and our governments answer all present exigencies, except the regulation of trade, securing credit, in some cases, and providing for the interest, in some instances, of the public debts; and whether we adopt a change three or nine months hence, can make but little odds with the private circumstances of individuals; their happiness and prosperity, after all, depend principally upon their own exertions" (McDonald 1999).

18 In this regard, one might reasonably describe the European project as stagnant, at best. This author argued in the 1990s that if the EU could meet the challenge of crafting a *true* Common Foreign and Security Policy, it would be well-positioned to become a legitimate superpower (Walton 1997). However, a decade-and-a-half on, Brussels still has not discovered a strategy allowing it to climb that particular wall—and it appears most unlikely that it will do so in the medium-term future. For other views on the EU's potential to act as a great power, see Kupchan (2003) and Leonard (2005).

19 Some authors contend that the intellectual foundations for both the Articles of Confederation and US Constitution largely were based on the governance of the Iroquois Confederacy (also known as the Iroquois League or the *Haudenosaunee*, among other names). However, it seems quite unlikely that this in fact was the case. See Payne (1996).

20 For an interesting example of how a thoughtful observer might have viewed the larger significance of the Louisiana Purchase *before* the United States became a continuous player in great power politics, see Sloane (1904).

21 The most straightforward way to address the constitutional question would have been to secure the passage of an amendment explicitly authorizing the purchase of foreign territory, and Jefferson actually authored such an amendment. However, fellow Republicans—fearing, quite reasonably, that Napoleon might withdraw his offer at any time—convinced the president promptly to place the Louisiana Purchase Treaty before the Senate, where it passed by a solid margin.

22 Even after its acquisition, the United States was concerned about Louisiana's security—a worry that encouraged further territorial expansion: "With Louisiana pinched between the Spanish colonies of Texas and West Florida, American officials considered Louisiana a precarious holding. It was this sense of insecurity that made the acquisition of West Florida such a high priority in the Jefferson and Madison administrations" (Kastor 2001: 823).
23 Much insight into Jefferson's leadership in regard to the Louisiana Question is offered in Tucker and Hendrickson (1990).
24 See Fatovic (2004: 434–435).
25 The question of what the limits should be on executive power of course is central to various interlocking controversies relating to the Global War on Terrorism. See Aldrich (2002), Martinez (2004), Yoo (2005), Posner (2006), and Vázquez (2007).
26 Thomas Jefferson to John B. Colvin, 20 September 1810, *The Founder's Constitution* online edn., Volume 4, Article 2, Section 3, Document 8, accessed online at: http://press-pubs.uchicago.edu/founders/documents/a2_3s8.html. Emphasis in original.
27 Jefferson believed, correctly or not, that the people would be able to "discriminate correctly between a meritorious and a pernicious exercise of prerogative," and thus "that the scrupulous and patriotic executive had nothing to fear" (Fatovic 2004: 435).
28 See, for example, Vidal (2002) and Wolf (2007).
29 John C. Calhoun certainly was the most intellectually influential advocate for the crafting of an explicitly pro-slavery philosophy of American government. See Calhoun (1992) and Read (2009).
30 For a deeply thoughtful, and very influential, exploration of the incompatibility between founding US principles and chattel slavery, see Jaffa (1999, 2000).
31 On the Russian consolidation of Siberia, see Lincoln (1994). The Mexican and Canadian military struggles with indigenous tribes are described in Vandervort (2006).
32 As Jeremy Black points out,

> In 1830, after the close of the Latin American Wars of Independence, [Native] peoples still controlled much of North and South America, but, by 1880, the situation was radically different. This was true of the USA, transforming its geography, in part at the expense of the "sub-imperial" forces, native confederations, that can be described as secondary empires. There was also a major process of expansion by Canada, and by the states of Central and South America, notably Mexico, which expanded at the expense of the Mayas; Argentina and Chile, both of which extended their power into Patagonia; and Brazil, which did the same in Amazonia.
>
> (Black 2008: 124)

33 The settlement of previously disputed borders, such as that between the United States and Canada in the Old Northeast, had the significant side effect of limiting the diplomatic maneuver room of tribes that occupied formerly disputed territory. See Adelman and Aron (1999: 816).
34 On the characteristics of tribal warfare, see Keeley (1997) and LeBlanc with Register (2003).
35 Precisely how many repeating rifles the Native American forces possessed and how great an advantage they provided is, however, a matter of dispute. See Marshall (2007: 102–104).
36 Howe (2009: 74).
37 The Treaty was not agreed to by the government of Principal Chief John Ross, but by a dissident Cherokee faction that was especially fearful of what Jackson

might do to the tribe if it did not agree to leave its Eastern lands. It ultimately led to the removal to Oklahoma, which was carried out by General Winfield Scott on the orders of Jackson's successor, Martin Van Buren. See Hoig (1998). On the arguments used by Jackson to justify forcible resettlement of the "Five Civilized Tribes," see Young (1958: 31–32).

38 Crook's career is described in detail in Robinson (2001).

39 See, for instance, Hershberger (1999).

40 However, there are a number of recent biographies and works discussing aspects of his presidency. See Leonard (2000), Seigenthaler (2003), and Borneman (2008).

41 Insights into the military aspects of the conflict are offered in Eisenhower (2000) and Wheelan (2007).

42 Scott's fascinating and unjustly ignored career is addressed in Eisenhower (1997) and Johnson (1998).

43 Howe (2009: 750).

44 Polk himself was a slaveholder; his slavery-related business activities are explored in detail in Dusinberre (2007).

45 James M. McPherson places considerable emphasis on how the war with Mexico shaped the years leading to the Civil War. See McPherson (2003: 3–116).

46 See, for instance, Ellis and Wildavsky (1990), Pierson (1995), and Grant (1998). The differing Northern and Southern visions of property rights, with the latter permitting humans to be treated as chattel while the former did not, is explored in Huston (1999).

47 These differing perspectives led to controversy within, and in some cases the outright division of, several Protestant denominations. See Staiger (1949), Purifoy (1966), and Goodheart (1985).

48 The Southern sense of national identity is explored thoughtfully in Gallagher (1997: 61–112).

49

> [D]uring the thirty years preceding the Civil War, the South produced an extraordinary torrent of pro-slavery propaganda—propaganda that was for the most part bold, unapologetic, and insistent on the virtues of slavery. Whereas previous pro-slavery advocates had stressed the "political" arguments of expedience, economy, and race, the new polemicists, who included many of the South's best minds, based their case on the higher ground of social theory: slavery was simply the best way to organize society.
>
> (Kolchin 1980: 820)

50 Marc M. Arkin argues that in 1831 the abolitionist movement decisively altered its goals:

> Before 1831, American antislavery was characterized by gradualist measures and a colonizationist program intended to transport all freed black people out of the country. After 1831, suddenly energized abolitionists insisted on immediate emancipation and committed themselves to creation of a society in which blacks would enjoy at least civil equality with whites.
>
> (Arkin 2001: 75)

51 See Etcheson (2004).

52 On the contrast between US and Confederate military resources, see Current (1996).

53 This category certainly would include General Thomas "Stonewall" Jackson. An especially admiring portrait of this exceptionally talented operational commander is offered in Alexander (1992).

54 See Woodworth (1992).

55 On this point, see Walton (2002a: 136–137).
56 On Davis' career, see Cooper (2001).
57 A more generous view of Davis' performance is offered in Jones (1992). For a short, direct comparison of the two men, see Donald (2001).
58 See Clausewitz (1984: 100–112).
59 Some of the many useful discussions of Lincoln's performance as a strategist include: McPherson (1992, 2008); Cohen (2002: 15–51); Symonds (2008); Stocker (2010); and Williams (2011).
60 The life of another Civil War figure, General Grant, illustrates this well. The young Grant was a brave and capable junior officer, but after leaving the service he failed at several professions. However, when he returned to the Army he soon proved to be a brilliant general, which in turned launched him into the White House for two terms. Finally, in his closing months of life, Grant, in great pain from throat cancer, rounded out his improbable career by writing a classic memoir that showed him to be a prose stylist of immense talent. See Grant (1999). Grant's literary skill was perhaps his most surprising asset—not an especially bookish man by the standards of his time, Grant displayed little interest in writing for publication for most of his life; his chief motivation for composing his memoirs was to ensure that his family would not live in poverty after he died.
61 Cohen (2002: 16).
62 For a discussion of how Clausewitz's ideas are applicable to today's US Army, see Duggan (2005).
63

> *Coup d'oeil* ... refers not alone to the physical but, more commonly, to the inward eye. The expression, like the quality itself, has certainly always been more applicable to tactics, but it must also have its place in strategy, since here as well quick decisions are often needed. Stripped of metaphor and of the restrictions imposed on it by the phrase, the concept merely refers to the quick recognition of truth that the mind would ordinarily miss or would perceive only after long study and reflection.
>
> (1984: 102)

64 See Zimmermann (1992) and Brands (2002).
65 Michael Dunne makes the interesting point that

> the war and its aftermath did register an American form of imperialism, for American power (in its broadest sense) was projected abroad and imposed over unwilling subjects; and in taking American power overseas so forcefully and dramatically, the war represented both the *continuity* of American territorial expansion and its *discontinuous* passage into the Caribbean and western Pacific.
>
> (Dunne 2000: 27; emphasis in original)

66 One cannot, however, dismiss the significance of domestic politics, and perhaps even "national anxiety," and how such factors shaped the public reaction to the sinking of the *Maine*. See Dallek (1982).
67 The argument that a lack of willingness to attempt to "balance" the US effort to attain North American hegemony was vital to Washington's ability eventually to do so is offered in Elman (2004). The analysis is interesting, but perhaps gives insufficient consideration to events such as Napoleon III's adventure in Mexico.
68 Even while the war was ongoing, the Lincoln administration was concerned about the possibility of the eventual annexation of Texas by Mexico (Westwood 1984: 169).

69 Even in the closing months of the war, Northern journalist Francis Preston Blair, Sr. undertook a curious diplomatic effort centered on his proposal that the United and Confederate States agree to a ceasefire and then undertake a joint military effort to oust Maximilian (Saunders 1997). The February 1865 Hampton Roads Peace Conference, at which Lincoln and Secretary of State Seward met with a delegation of Confederate commissioners, was the ultimate result of his effort, but at the Conference itself Lincoln made it clear that Southern surrender was non-negotiable. Certainly, the president had no interest in implementing a peace based on Blair's scheme.
70 A thoughtful perspective on the Emperor Napoleon III's strategic goals with regard to Mexico is offered in Hanna (1954).
71 Precisely when the North chose to move in the direction of—even if it did not altogether adopt—"total war" is the subject of debate among historians. See Sutherland (1992).
72 See Streeby (2001: 3–5).
73

> The Great rule of conduct for us, in regard to foreign Nations is in extending our commercial relations to have with them as little *political* connection as possible. So far as we have already formed engagements let them be fulfilled, with perfect good faith. Here let us stop. Europe has a set of primary interests, which to us have none, or a very remote relation. Hence she must be engaged in frequent controversies, the causes of which are essentially foreign to our concerns. Hence therefore it must be unwise in us to implicate ourselves, by artificial ties, in the ordinary vicissitudes of her politics, or the ordinary combinations & collisions of her friendships, or enmities.
>
> (Washington 1796)

74 When he was president, even the relatively ideological and theoretically minded Jefferson conducted foreign affairs in a nuanced manner—this despite the fact that many Federalists had been convinced that he more-or-less was a crazed Jacobin who would goad Britain into war, if not bring the guillotine into domestic politics. Yet, Federalist fears were not entirely unreasonable, given Jefferson's reluctance to acknowledge the ever-darker character of the French Revolution and his occasional lapses—particularly in letters—into dramatic revolutionary rhetoric.
75 On US arbitration of the conflict, see Zimmermann (1992: 465–474).
76 See Fleming (2004) and Stevenson (2004).
77 On the evolution of the British attitude regarding restrictions on the practice of blockade, see Offer (1988).
78 For a fascinating, and unfortunately now largely forgotten, assessment of Woodrow Wilson, see Hoover (1958). It is a surprisingly frank work, reflecting both Hoover's admiration of Wilson's ideals and Hoover's resentment of the ways in which, in his view, Wilson had unfairly slighted him.
79 The failure of the *Kaiserschlacht* is explored in Zabecki (2006).
80 Indeed, Wilson was not trying to shatter the Austro-Hungarian and Ottoman Empires, and in fact the Points confronted the ravenous attempt by the other Allies to apportion the latter: "Points X and XII envisaged autonomy, not independence, for the subject peoples of Austria-Hungary and the Ottoman Empire (thus challenging the Turkish partition agreements)" (Stevenson 2004: 319).
81 See Stevenson (2004: 454).
82 On wartime industrialization, see, for example, Nash (1990).
83 The staggering size and capabilities of the Soviet armed forces are detailed in Glantz (2005a, 2005b).

84 Two of the many strong general works on the Pacific War are Spector (1985) and Hopkins (2008). A classic on the US Marine experience in particular is Leckie (2010).

2 Victory disease: Cold War triumph and its aftermath

1 Kennan (1991: 213).
2 For a critique of how the United States misfought the Vietnam War, see Walton (2002a).
3 Tzu (1994: 177).
4 As Edward Luttwak warns in a work published during the early 1980s,

> [T]oday's Soviet army is as different from the brute-force army of 1950 as the latter differed in turn from the bewildered troops which the Germans defeated by the million in 1941 and 1942. Continuously supported by self-propelled artillery and accompanied by armoured infantry, Soviet tank assaults would no longer need to stop after each successful thrust to allow the infantry and the towed artillery to catch up. Instead of ponderous step-by-step offensives, separated by weeks and months of laborious preparation, the Soviet army can now mount a continuous offensive that would persist by day and by night till its goal is reached.
>
> (Luttwak 1983: 49)

5 On the latter point, see Biddle (1996: 140).
6 The intellectual and political scope of that contest is ably conveyed in Nichols (2002).
7 On the excesses of Soviet military spending, see Walton (2007a: 207).
8 Steven Rosefielde argues that this unhealthy practice did not represent a Soviet break from traditional Russian behavior, but, rather, was entirely in keeping with Russian strategic culture—and, moreover, that Moscow may be expected to continue on this course in the future. See Rosefielde (2005). The fact that Russia presently is flush with oil and gas revenue but shows little sign of developing the sort of institutions that encourage long-term prosperity—such as an independent judiciary enforcing the rule of law—would appear to provide strong support for this argument.
9 Explicitly pro-Soviet Westerners remained a minority, distinctly so in the United States, but even in the latter country they nonetheless were a notable cultural presence. See O'Neill (1982), Lewy (1988), and Ottanelli (1991). Much more important politically, however, was the considerable faction in every NATO country that was inclined to self-flagellating criticism of the West and sympathy for supposed Soviet ideals. The friendliness which European Greens showed toward the Soviet Bloc was particularly curious, given the obvious apathy in the East in regard to even the most rudimentary environmental protections.
10 Two of the more eloquently written warnings are Chambers (1952) and Ravel (1984).
11 The argument that it did is made in Pry (1999).
12 See Nitze *et al.* (1989) and Thompson (2009).
13 See Acheson (1987) and Beisner (2006).
14 The intellectual milieu in which this elite operated is evocatively described in Acheson (1961), Kennan (1967), and Isaacson and Thomas (1986).
15 It should be noted that the Eisenhower administration did call for a more assertive "rollback" of Soviet power. However, this was a rhetorical posture, not a true change in course, a fact all too clearly demonstrated when the administration stood by while Moscow crushed the 1956 Hungarian uprising. Also, the Reagan administration pursued a strategic vision that one might call

"containment plus," seeking to undermine Soviet control in Eastern Europe and elsewhere through a mixture of public diplomacy and covert actions such as providing support for Poland's solidarity movement. In any case, though, neither president rejected the basic structure of the containment paradigm.

16 On Truman's formative influence, see Gray (2011).

17 It was a happy historical accident that Truman, rather than his vice-presidential predecessor, Henry Wallace, took office in 1945. Wallace indicated his strongly left-leaning and pro-Soviet disposition in various ways, including in his famous 1942 "Century of the Common Man" speech and subsequent book. Wallace's known leftism and Roosevelt's clearly shaky health excited opposition to his inclusion on the 1944 Democratic ticket. Moreover, it was known in high Democratic circles that Wallace had dabbled in spiritualism—a potentially embarrassing matter politically, especially as Wallace had traded rather bizarre coded letters with the Russian émigré painter and Theosophist Nicholas Roerich. The Republicans actually had obtained copies of some of these letters in 1940, but were dissuaded from using them, as the Democrats threatened "massive retaliation" in the form of revelations concerning an extramarital affair in which Republican candidate Wendell Willkie had engaged. While Wallace's assorted "baggage" was sufficient to ensure that he was not on the 1944 presidential ticket, it should be noted that his political self-destruction was fundamentally rooted in his own decisions—if he had attempted to appear somewhat more moderate in his publicly stated views and refrained from sending strange letters to a religious guru, he very likely would have become president in 1945.

18 Most famously, in a January 1950 speech at the National Press Club, Secretary of State Dean Acheson left South Korea outside the US military defensive line in the Pacific. It would be excessive to attribute the outbreak of the war to this single incident, but it was indicative of the administration's failure to send a strong message that the US was dedicated to South Korean independence.

19 Eisenhower's cleverness and cunning were underestimated by many of his contemporaries, an oversight which he perhaps subtly encouraged. See Greenstein (1994).

20 Interestingly, the inability of the Soviet leadership to grasp Eisenhower's insight that, in a long-term contest such as the Cold War, consistent overemphasis on military power undermines long-term strategic competitiveness arguably was the most important factor in Soviet defeat. The USSR's effort perennially to maintain enormous and well-equipped forces required that its economy be maintained on a permanent wartime footing—a very unhealthy state of affairs, economically speaking. The overmuscled Soviet military both justified the containment strategy and made the ultimate political vindication of that strategy possible.

21 For a variety of views from individuals within the CIA on the reasons for the invasion's failure, see. Kornbluh (1997), Blight and Kornbluh (1998), and Lynch (1998).

22 The argument that Kennedy would not have done so is made vigorously in Kaiser (2000).

23 On why and how the Saigon government might have endured, see Walton (2002a).

24 See Durschmied (2001: 361–363).

25 The argument that Reagan's policies had a profound effect in this regard is made in Schweitzer (1994, 2003).

26 A thoughtful contribution to the discussion is Kotkin (2001).

27 It is, however, important not to overstate the degree of consensus regarding containment—throughout the Cold War, it had powerful critics. For instance, shortly after the publication of the "X" Article, the journalist Walter Lippmann attacked the containment strategy in print. See Wright (1976).

28 It is important to note, however, that Kennan was not a lone voice in the wilderness regarding the threat presented by Moscow. During World War II, official US propaganda encouraged a friendly view toward the USSR, but with the end of the war—and of government-encouraged suppression of anti-Soviet views—valid suspicions of Soviet intentions resurfaced publicly throughout popular and elite discourse. For instance: "The Soviet Union is aiming at consolidation of world leadership.... One idea will dominate everything—the fighting idea of the Soviet state and the doctrines of Lenin and Stalin. Communism is getting ready for action" (Guins 1947: 32).

29

> As an organicist conservative Kennan tended to think of international relations as living matter, like any organism sometimes developing in natural balance, at other times afflicted with disease or disturbed by extraneous elements. Artificial tampering with the natural—"mechanical," "legalistic," or "universalistic" solutions to the problems of foreign policy, as arrantly exemplified for him in the United Nations—he found odious, almost perverse. Moreover such schemes were unrealistic, for eventually the fundamental nature of things would reassert itself, returning to haunt and punish the conjurers of total perfection. Nature (or the real) in this particular domain was *power*, embodied in a series of states with differing interests.
>
> (Stephanson 1992: 176; emphasis in original)

30 The effort to control the CIA was all too successful. A quarter century later, in the aftermath of the 9/11 attacks, it became increasingly clear that that organization had developed a very cautious institutional culture which made it difficult for it to assertively address the threat presented by *Al Qaeda* in the 1990s. See Coll (2004).

31 Perhaps most arrogantly, American "defense intellectuals in the 1960s and early to mid-1970s had difficulty even conceiving of the possibility that there could be more than one strategic theoretical enlightenment." Thus, undesirable Soviet attitudes and behavior merely reflected a slight backwardness in strategic thinking that would be corrected by time and exposure, particularly through the arms control process, to supposedly more sophisticated American thinking regarding concepts such as strategic stability (Gray 1981: 41–42).

32 On the contrast between Soviet and American attitudes regarding arms control, see Rowny (1992).

33 The problems with arms control as a concept are laid out in Gray (1992).

34 See Nichols (2002).

35 Historians and social scientists have been grappling with these questions for a very long time. See, for example, Ogburn (1926).

36 For a variety of perspectives on the deeply problematic US-Saudi alliance, see: Baer (2004), Lippman (2004), and Bronson (2006).

37 A sharply negative American view of Saudi trustworthiness is offered in Baer (2004).

38 For a biting critique of the 1970s-era United Nations, see Moynihan with Weaver (1978).

39 For a differing view, see Campbell (2007).

40 For a pessimistic view of the usefulness of international institutions for ensuring global stability, see Mearsheimer (1994–95).

41 The uncertainty and deep disagreement over what NATO should "be" is reflected in the post-Cold War period academic literature addressing the future role and structure of the alliance. See, for example: Borawski (1995); Art (1996); Cornish (1996); Croft *et al.* (2000); and Light *et al.* (2000).

42 See Bush and Scowcroft (1999) and Lampton (2001).

43 On the evolution of policy toward China in the Clinton administration see Mann (2000) and Lampton (2001).
44 On these events, see Scobell (2000).
45 In April 2001, a Chinese fighter collided with a US Navy EP-3E surveillance aircraft; the crew of the latter conducted an emergency landing on China's Hainan Island, while the pilot of the former was killed. The Chinese detained the crew of the US aircraft. However, the United States contended—accurately, by all appearances—that its aircraft was in international airspace at the time of the incident and that the accident was the fault of the PRC's pilot. The 24-person crew was released after Washington issued a letter expressing its regret for the death of the Chinese pilot and for the American pilot performing an emergency landing on Chinese soil without proper authorization. Although this ended the most acute portion of the crisis, tensions continued for several months as China negotiated the conditions under which the aircraft would be returned. Given the facts of the incident—including customary international law regarding emergency landings and sovereign property—it would be reasonable to describe the event as a major diplomatic humiliation for the United States. On the relevant international legal issues, see Kirgis (2001).
46 It would appear that many in Beijing give Washington much greater credit for strategic vision than is warranted. See Deng (2001).
47 See Jervis (2010).
48 See, among many other reports, Rosett (2006), Barron (2007), Hoge (2007), and Preston (2007).
49 On the failed 2006 *Al Qaeda* attack on the Abqaiq oil processing facility see Henderson (2006).
50 For a discussion of the sense of "drift" in US strategy in the early 1990s, see Miller (1994).

3 The slow drift: power without strategic clarity

1 See Luttwak (1994, 1999).
2 For very different viewpoints from the one stated herein, see Van Creveld (1991, 1999) and Mueller (2007).
3 If this hypothesis is wrong and a permanent era of great power non-violence has dawned, continued preparation for great power of course would be wasteful financially. However, happily, the world's peoples would still remain safe from global war: obviously, if great power conflict is impossible, specific acquisition and force structuring decisions are irrelevant to the likelihood of such wars occurring.
4 It should be noted that, at this point in history, the prevailing attitude in the EU is that future great power violence is extremely unlikely. See Kagan (2004).
5 Various terms were coined well before the 9/11 attacks, but as of yet no single phrase has been universally accepted as the one that should be used to describe differences between the terrorist threat presented in the past and the present. For various terminological usages, see Laqueur (1996, 2000), Schweitzer with Dorsch (1998), and Freedman (2002).
6 A good sense of the diversity of the "terrorism problem" confronting states throughout history can be derived from examining Chaliand and Blin (2007) and Burleigh (2009).
7 This is not to say that such attacks were completely unknown until recent times. The 1920 Wall Street bombing in New York, for instance, clearly was indiscriminate and done with the intention of killing substantial numbers of noncombatants. See Gage (2009).
8 On the PIRA strategy, see Moloney (2002) and English (2003).

9 Many Islamist terrorists—Osama Bin Laden having been a preeminent example—seem to view their terrorist campaigns as essentially "wars of maneuver" in which a sufficiently spectacular series of attacks will, somehow, result in final victory; after all, mere worldly disadvantages can be overcome if an omnipotent deity puts a thumb on the scales. As Michael J. Mazarr correctly notes, "Those fully in the grip of a fantasy ideology are in many ways lost to the ideology" (Mazarr 2007: 214).
10 See, for example, the comments, made by Hani Al-Siba'i, the Director of London's Al-Maqreze Centre for Historical Studies after the "7/7" bombings in the United Kingdom (Al-Siba'i 2005).
11 It should be noted that there is by no means agreement among *jihadists* as to what enemies they should focus on and how they would best defeat those opponents. See Kiras (2008: 274–275) and Brachman (2009).
12 See Lifton (1999).
13 For a good survey of biological weapons and their potential use by terrorist groups, see Guillemin (2005).
14 Walton (2008).
15 For varying assessments of the threat presented by nuclear terrorism, see Allison (2006), Levi (2007), Jenkins (2008), and Mueller (2009).
16 For a thoughtful work that recommends using US Cold War containment as a model for a reformed US counterterror strategy see Shapiro (2007).
17 Jones (2001).
18 An insightful work on anti-Westernism as a phenomenon is Buruma and Margalit (2005).
19 See, for example, Lichtblau (2003), Archibald and Kearns (2006), and Buckley and Rashbaum (2007).
20 Pew Forum on Religion & Public Life (2009).
21 Michael Burleigh paints a vivid portrait of the day-to-day activities of SA fighters in the 1920s:

> [T]he SA provided an opportunity for young men to display their anti-social proclivities in the service of an ideology and in uniform. In rural areas, what might have been gangs of under- or unemployed young men—say the sons of farmers, apprentices, and labourers—loafing menacingly outside bars and dance halls, regrouped in uniform under the control of older, more experienced agitators with lengthy records of paramilitary violence. The SA scene was superficially akin to any delinquent sub-culture. Gang members daubed slogans and swastikas on walls, then graduated via drunken brawling to semi-terrorism.... The SA were often drunk: for Nazi politics exuded stale beer, cigar smoke and sweat, a nightmare of a certain kind of masculinity, which in the Munich beerhalls routinely resulted what Patrick Leigh Fermor, the British travel writer, called "hoggish catalepsy."
>
> (Burleigh 2000: 111)

22 The revived Ku Klux Klan of the early twentieth century did not agitate for the overthrow of the government. Nonetheless, it is notable that, at the Klan's height in the early and mid-1920s, several million Americans belonged to an organization that was known to commit terrorist violence against US citizens.
23 A detailed account of the 1950 assassination attempt on Truman is offered in Hunter and Bainbridge (2007).
24 On the Weathermen and similar leftist terror groups, see Varon (2004).
25 McVeigh did not belong to any specific militia group, although his political views reflected those prevailing in the most extreme wing of the US militia movement. For discussions of that movement, see George and Wilcox (1996), Michel and Herbeck (2001), Crothers (2003), and Levitas (2004).

26 Thoughtful analyses of how and why terrorist groups "die" are offered in Harmon (2007) and Harmon *et al.* (2011).
27 On Michael Collins' role in the success of the IRA in bringing Britain to accept Irish independence, see Gray (2007a).
28 A classic meditation on violent movements and those who join them is Hoffer (2002).
29 Many critics of G.W. Bush argued that operations in Iraq were not part of the GWOT because Hussein appears not to have had any significant operational relationship with *Al Qaeda* (the latter contention itself having been the source of much controversy). This critique, however, failed to undermine the core point that the Bush administration conceived the Iraq War within a counter-terrorism context and saw it as part of the GWOT, even if Iraq itself had minimal ties to *Al Qaeda*. The administration always was careful not to limit the GWOT only to *Al Qaeda*, and the Iraq invasion clearly was seen within the administration both as a way to achieve goals specific to Iraq (such as the removal of Hussein and elimination of any Iraqi WMD programs that might exist) *and* to achieve larger gains relevant to the GWOT (particularly, "draining the swamp" that bred Islamist terrorism by spreading democracy in the Middle East).
30 This point in underlined throughout former President Bush's memoirs. For example:

> After al Qaeda killed nearly three thousand people in the United States, it was clear that the terrorists had interpreted our lack of a serious response [to previous attacks] as a sign of weakness. ... Dropping expensive weapons on sparsely populated camps would not break the Taliban's hold on [Afghanistan] or destroy al Qaeda's sanctuary. It would only reinforce the terrorists' belief that they could strike us without paying a serious price. This time we would put boots on the ground, and keep them there until the Taliban and al Qaeda were driven out and a free society could emerge.
>
> (Bush 2010: 191)

31 The Nixon administration provides a good example of this phenomenon. Rhetorically, Nixon—like every other Cold War president—treated human rights issues as being a legitimate foreign policy concern, but, in practice, he generally allowed other considerations to trump human rights matters. Thus, for instance, diplomatic reports of mass human rights violations by the Pakistani Army in East Pakistan (Bangladesh) in 1971—most famously, the "Blood Telegram" in late March of that year—essentially were ignored. This was because highlighting such reports could undermine Washington's relationship with Pakistan, damage US efforts to craft the "opening" toward China, which was very close to Pakistan, and, indirectly further Soviet goals in South Asia, as Moscow functionally was an ally of India.

> When President Nixon discussed the reports of atrocities in East Pakistan briefly with Kissinger in a telephone conversation on March 28, he agreed with the position taken by the [US Embassy in Islamabad]: "I wouldn't put out a statement praising it, but we're not going to condemn it either."
>
> (Library of Congress 2005)

32 However, this is an historical misperception. In fact, the United States was involved in many "limited" or "small" conflicts throughout its history, including in the early twentieth century. See Boot (2002).
33 It is notable that the period between the World Wars was a time of great debate and creativity in the (for most of this period, tiny) US Marine Corps. This intellectual activity subsequently paid enormous dividends in the Pacific War, as

Marine officers had been thinking for years about the difficulties which they would face in conducting amphibious warfare against Japan. See Steele (2005: 50–57) and Ballendorf and Bartlett (2010).

34 Of course, such an outcome is not guaranteed—the United States could make errors or experience unanticipated "blowback" that results in an increased probability of suffering a successful major attack—but for purposes of the present discussion this is not a relevant factor, as the *intended* outcome of counterterrorism-centered resource allocation is a decrease in the threat presented by terrorists.

35 On theory of victory as a concept, see Gray (2002b), Martel (2007), and Bartholomees (2008).

36 The Obama administration's understandable obsession with dealing effectively with the "AfPak problem" is chronicled in Woodward (2010).

4 The decider: the importance of presidential greatness

1 Quoted in Cloud (2006).

2 See, for example, Schlesinger (2004a, 2004b), and Savage (2007).

3 See Rudalevige (2005).

4 Congress did attempt to undermine the presidential prerogative to remove cabinet officials at will through the 1867 Tenure of Office Act, but the Act was repealed two decades later. Subsequently, the 1927 Supreme Court decision in *Myers v. United States* stated that the Act actually had been unconstitutional.

5 The reverse is also true: because it would constitute "civic blasphemy," no president would dare to publicly state the barely disputable fact that immediate democratization is not an appropriate remedy to that which ails many countries, and hastily constructed ramshackle democracies in troubled parts of the world have a tendency to collapse quickly and bloodily.

6 The latter career of Benito Mussolini makes this point nicely. See Knox (2009).

7 Depending on the security environment in which a state is operating—its geographical location, the prevailing attitude toward military aggression in the international community, and so forth—and specific historical circumstances, continuing survival as a fully independent, but relatively minor state, may, however, be possible. Sweden, for example, was able to manage its decline from great power status without suffering the conquest of its historical core, much less the complete loss of its national identity.

8 For a brief history of the Rebellion, see Fremont-Barnes (2007).

9 The rise and decline of this great power is detailed in Davies (2005: 125–411).

10 A thoughtful meditation on the mythology constructed around Washington in the Republic's early years is Brookhiser (1996).

11 Some of the most famous and important political figures in nineteenth century US politics never were elected president; this included all the members of the Great Triumvirate of the 1820s and 1830s: John C. Calhoun, Henry Clay, and Daniel Webster. Today, relatively few Americans can name more than a handful or US senators and representatives; even very powerful Congressional politicians tend to have little hold on the public imagination.

12 Obviously, there is no single embodiment of the people as a whole. Indeed, "the people" is an abstraction rather a simple fact; a specific group of bees may constitute a hive, but determining who is part of a particular human nation is rather more problematic. Yet, in myth symbolism and subjective perceptions are critical and the notion of a unified people has great resonance.

13 As Michael Mandelbaum points out, the president "is the nation's only military *and* civilian official" (Mandelbaum 1981: 200).

14 US Constitution, Article II, Section 2, accessed online at www.usconstitution.net/const.html#A2Sec2.
15 The history of Augustus' long, subtle effort to make himself the star around which the institutions of the Roman state orbited is well-recounted in Everitt (2006).
16 NSS (2002).
17 NSS (2006).
18 See, for example, Sadowski (1996).
19 On this impressively persistent American failing, see Walton (2007a: 205–206).
20 See, for example, Walton (2002b).
21 NSS (2010).
22 See, for example, Wright (2007).
23 NSS (2010: 44 and 45).
24 See Parker (2000, 2002).
25 A classic discussion of the concept of heroic kingship—and the argument that in the nuclear era leadership should be "post-heroic"—is offered in Keegan (1988).
26 In *The End of America*, author Naomi Wolf contends that after 9/11 the G.W. Bush administration placed the United States on the road to establishment of a fascist regime. President Bush later proceeded to hand over power peacefully to a member of an opposing political party and retire to the Dallas area, apparently having decided that imposing fascism in America would be too much of a bother (Wolf 2007).
27 On the civil–military relationship in the United States, see Cohen (1985) and Stevenson (2006).
28 On the struggle of wills between the two men—very different personalities, but each proud in his own fashion—see Pearlman (2008).
29 During the Kosovo War, White House interference in operational matters reached unsatirizable proportions:

> The most bitter objection that has been leveled at U.S. civilian leaders for the air war against North Vietnam was that they micromanaged the campaign by picking bombing targets themselves. By 1999, however, neither the Clinton administration nor the Europeans seemed concerned about this criticism. [Supreme Commander Europe General Wesley] Clark had to have every target approved not only by President Clinton but by [NATO Secretary-General Javier] Solana as well, along with American and European lawyers.
>
> (Betts 2001)

30 Cohen (2002).
31 Cohen (2002: 211).
32 The importance of public audit to military effectiveness, and the role of such oversight in the Western military tradition, is a major theme in Hanson (2001).
33 See Goodwin (1991) and Hershman (2002).
34 See Berke and Elder (2001).
35 See Nagourney and Elder (2003a, 2003b).
36 On the relationship between polling and presidential decision making, see Heith (2004), Newport (2004), and Canes-Wrone (2006).

5 Feet of clay: making inadequate strategists and war leaders

1 Roosevelt (1999).
2 See Thucydides (1998: 43).
3 The difficulties inherent in providing strategic education are explored in Gray (2009).

4 Surely Clausewitz's discussion of this problem is the most influential. The great theorist carefully attempts to describe the character of strategic genius, and arguably does so with as much success as one can hope for when addressing such an inherently misty concept. See Clausewitz (1984: 100–112).
5 Johnson's enormous skills as a legislative leader are exhaustively documented in Caro (1990, 2002).
6 When G.H.W. Bush was running for president in 2000, his boosters often pointed to the quality of his foreign policy advisors. And, indeed, once in office Bush largely filled the upper foreign policy ranks of his administration with exceptional individuals. Unfortunately, as a team they proved somewhat dysfunctional. See Mann (2004).
7 See, for example, Jervis *et al.* (1989).
8 See Coker (2007, 2008).
9 This theme is woven throughout Hill (2010).
10 Interestingly, however, President Clinton's reading of Kaplan (2005) supposedly initially discouraged him from actively intervening in the Bosnian conflict. See Harris (2005: 46–47). Whatever pessimistic lessons the president may have drawn from his reading, however, soon were overwhelmed by the bureaucratic, diplomatic, and media pressure to "do *something*."
11 At times, American statements even would veer into the fantastic. For instance, in a 1995 radio address, President Clinton claimed that: "At the end of the Cold War, Serbian nationalism forced the breakup of Yugoslavia. And ugly and dangerous war broke out in the heart of Europe, risking an even wider conflict in the Balkans which could have drawn the United States and many other countries in. Bosnia, a land in which Muslims, Serbs and Croats had lived together peacefully for centuries, was literally torn apart" (White House, Office of the Press Secretary 1995). The break-up of the Yugoslav Federation was not a simple process; to attribute it merely to Serbian nationalism ignores the fact that many non-Serbs, including various prominent politicians and intellectuals, long had desired national independence. More disturbingly, the statement regarding ethnic harmony in Bosnia ignored the deaths of vast numbers of Serbs, Jews, Roma, and others at the hands of Croatian and Muslim troops employed by the Ustaše government, which ruled most of the territory of Croatia and Bosnia during World War II.
12 See Walton (2009).
13 The vague character of US goals in regard to Kosovo is demonstrated in White House, Office of the Press Secretary (1999).
14 An interesting discussion of the uses and misuses of the "Munich analogy" is offered in Record (2007).
15 See Cohen (1990).
16 For a list of supposed Vietnam lessons—many of them banal and/or dubious—see McNamara (1996: 321–323).
17 Warfare was a major theme of Churchill's rich career, and one explored with admirable detail and thoughtfulness in D'Este (2010).
18 Robert Jervis notes that,

> Many presidents and cabinet officers come to the job with little education or experience with intelligence and with less time to learn once they are in power. Even presidents like Nixon who were more informed and who doubted CIA's abilities often held unreasonable expectations about what it could produce.
>
> (Jervis 2010: 158)

19 Eisenhower served in World War I, but his highest rank was as a brevet lieutenant colonel and he remained in the United States training troops throughout

the conflict. His involvement in the war contributed virtually nothing to his later political career. Truman did serve in combat during the war, and this was vital to his later political fortunes, but was only a junior officer.

20 A sharp critique of what the authors call the American "public culture" and the manner in which that culture shapes election discourse is offered in Rosefielde and Mills (2007).

21 Amusingly erroneous predictions concerning the 2008 race are provided in Morris and McGann (2005).

22 The 1988 Republican primary field was unusually rich in foreign and defense policy experience; the eventual Republican nominee of course was then-Vice President George H.W. Bush.

6 Lost wars, bleak peace: the tragedy of presidential weakness

1 Works challenging conventional academic views on Vietnam include Sorley (1999), Woodruff (1999), and Moyer (2009).

2 However, it should be noted that the Iraq War was not nearly as costly in lives as the Vietnam War—total American fatalities in that conflict were nearly sixty thousand. Also, there was no prospect of direct military intervention by a great power in Iraq, unlike in Vietnam, where there was a possibility that China would choose to provide ground troops to assist North Vietnam. It was never very likely that China would do this, and the likely military intervention of Chinese intervention was grossly exaggerated by skittish American policy makers, but the mere possibility of Chinese intervention encouraged Washington to place constraints on operations which undermined US military effectiveness.

3 Indeed, Francis Fukuyama goes so far as to describe the Hussein regime as being "totalitarian" (Fukuyama 2006: 138).

4 On these operations, see Cordesman (2003), West and Smith (2003), and Keegan (2004). An especially good "soldier's eye view" is offered in Fick (2005).

5 On the importance of Laos to the achieving of victory in Vietnam, see Hannah (1987).

6 In preparation for providing what would prove to be extremely controversial testimony to Congress, Gen. Eric Shinseki:

> asked historians on the Army's staff to research the number of peacekeepers used in Germany and Japan after World War II and after other conflicts. The data came back from the Army's Center of Military History: In Iraq the postwar peacekeeper force should probably number about 260,000 … That was the number in the back of his mind when he went to Capitol Hill and was pinned down on the issue.
>
> (Ricks 2007: 96–97)

As discussed below, however, even a force of 260,000 might have proven too small to speedily stabilize Iraq.

7

> Though loathe to admit it after the fact, the administration vastly underestimated the cost and difficulty of reconstructing Iraq and guiding it toward a democratic transition. In its internal prewar planning, the Pentagon evidently estimated that it could draw its forces down from the initial 150,000 to only 60,000 troops some six months after the end of active combat.
>
> (Fukuyama 2006: 115)

8 Vice-President Cheney is particularly notable in this regard; although now almost universally loathed by the American left, Bush's decision in 2000 to

name Cheney as his running mate was widely seen as a prudent and uncontroversial one. As one contemporary news article stated, Cheney was "a respected party elder" and Bush's decision was "a risk-free and respectable choice" (Mitchell 2000).

9 The large literature exploring the importance of group dynamics on foreign policy decision making includes such works as Builder (1989), Allison and Zelikov (1999), and Jervis (2010).

10 For the full text of the document, see Rumsfeld (2003).

11 On the development of US strategy in Iraq, see Ricks (2007, 2009), Metz (2008).

12 Dale R. Herspring offers a particularly blunt statement of this view: "Along with Robert McNamara, Donald Rumsfeld will go down in history as one of the worst U.S. secretaries of defense in the last forty odd years" (Herspring 2010: 77).

13 Even in a case of near-total war, great numbers of people must be convinced to act in a particular way; for instance, in World War II the population of Japan could have refused to surrender and instead chosen to die *en masse*. Indeed, there were some influential individuals in the Japanese government in 1945 who considered this preferable to defeat—and thousands of Okinawan women and children committed suicide rather than face an American occupation which they feared would be barbarously cruel. Fortunately, Emperor Hirohito eventually ordered his subjects to surrender, and the overwhelming majority of Japanese obeyed—but if he instead had demanded resistance to the bitter end, many surely would have acted accordingly.

14 The speech is reprinted in its entirety in Bush (2003).

15 See, for example, Tucker (2006), Gott (2007), and Pilger (2007).

16 Of course, one could contend that the speech was purely rhetorical and did not reflect the president's thinking, but the weight of publicly available evidence indicates that the address was not fundamentally mendacious. It appears, rather, that Bush sincerely believes in the general concepts behind the speech. It has, for example, been widely reported that he is a great admirer of the work of Israeli parliamentarian (and former Soviet dissident) Natan Sharansky, and the latter's views are quite compatible with those enunciated in the address to the American Enterprise Institute. See Sharansky with Dermer (2004) and Erlanger (2005).

17

> Our aims in Afghanistan are well known to the American people and this Committee. We seek to bring about an Afghanistan that is free of terrorists, that no longer is a source of poppy, and that allows its citizens—including an estimated five million refugees and an unknown number of internally displaced persons—to return to their homes and live normal lives in which opportunity replaces misery.
>
> (Haass 2001)

18 This point is discussed in Walton (2004: 303).

19 Bumiller (2001).

20 Precisely how blunt the United States was in this regard is a matter of dispute. In his memoir, Pakistan's President Musharraf claims that American Deputy Secretary of State Richard Armitage was menacingly frank:

> The choice was clear, Armitage told the director general of Pakistan's intelligence—America or the terrorists. And if Pakistan chose the terrorists, it should be "prepared to be bombed back to the Stone Age'." (Ajami 2007). Armitage, however, denies having made the threat.
>
> (Sanger 2006)

21 On the civil violence in the Democratic Republic of Congo see Clark (2002), Edgerton (2002), and Turner (2007).

22 This number may sound extreme, but a comparison with the early months of the US occupation in Germany is instructive:

> On V-E Day, Eisenhower had sixty-one U.S. divisions, 1,622,000 men, in Germany, and a total force in Europe numbering 3,077,000. When the shooting ended, the divisions in the field became the occupation troops, charged with maintaining law and order and establishing the Allied military presence in the defeated nation.... The occupation troops manned border control stations, maintained checkpoints at road junctions and bridges, sent out roving patrols to apprehend curfew and circulation violators, and kept stationary guards at railroad bridges, Army installations, [displaced person] camps, jails, telephone exchanges, factories, and banks. In the first months troops were plentiful and almost everything of importance—and some not so important—was guarded ... .[The occupation] was comprehensive and showed the Germans that they were defeated and their country occupied. This type of occupation was presumably capable of squelching incipient resistance since none was evident.
>
> (Zimke 1990: 320)

In addition to US personnel, of course, there also were enormous numbers of British, Soviet, and other Allied troops in Germany in the months following the end of the conflict.

23 Rather amazingly, even the question of precisely how the Iraqi Army was dissolved—the sort of matter that one might expect to be a simple matter of bureaucratic procedure—is disputed fervently. See, for example, Andrews (2007), Bremer (2007), and Gordon (2008).

24 An excellent exploration of the reasons why the United States chooses to use its military power as it does is offered in Kane (2006).

25 Thucydides (1998: 352).

26 On Alexander's practice of grand strategy, see Lonsdale (2007).

27 For a critical appraisal of the view that the United States is a "rogue superpower," see Walton (2007b: 58–62).

28 Gray (2004).

29 On China's rapidly growing military spending, see Office of the Secretary of Defense (2007).

30 Events such as the 1999 Kosovo War were on a small enough scale that they are considered minor for the purposes at hand. As of this writing, the US intervention in Libya fits into this category.

31 Special operations forces (SOF) are one area of particular US military strength, and when used properly may have a strategic effect far out of proportion to their numbers. See Kiras (2006).

32 Perhaps the most bizarre and nonsensical excuse by a Clinton administration official was provided by former Secretary of State Madeline Albright on *Meet the Press.* The program's host, Tim Russert, asked her, "[D]idn't North Korea develop a nuclear bomb on Bill Clinton's watch?" She replied:

> No, what they were doing, as it turns out, they were cheating. And the reason that you have arms control agreements is you don't make them with your friends, you make them with your enemies. And it's the process that is required to hold countries accountable. The worst part that has happened under the agreed framework, there was [*sic*] these fuel rods, and the nuclear program was frozen. Those fuel rods have now been reprocessed, as far as we know, and North Korea has a capability, which at

> one time might have been two potential nuclear weapons, up to six to eight now, we're not really clear. But in this period of time when there has not enough action been taken, I think that the threat from North Korea has increased.
>
> (NBC News 2004)

33 President Clinton bluntly stated at a press conference shortly after the Agreed Framework was signed that, "North Korea will freeze and then dismantle its nuclear program" (Anonymous 1994).

34 Moreover, though the Iranian government is no respecter of personal liberty, it does have some limited democratic characteristics, and it appears that some reasonable percentage of Iranians favor nuclear acquisition, either as an expression of national pride or for other reasons. However, it is difficult to determine just how great this support is. For an analysis arguing that support for actual nuclear acquisition (as opposed to, say, reprocessing of nuclear fuel for peaceful purposes) probably is not very high, see Herzog (2006).

35 This point is discussed in Walton (2006: 9[B)].

36 See Gittings (2006), Kinzer (2007), Krugman (2007), and Podhoretz (2007).

37

> A military strike against Iranian facilities would be much harder to conduct than the 1981 Israeli strike against the Iraqi facility at Osiraq. Key Iranian nuclear facilities such as Natanz are hardened, ringed by air defense, and buried deep underground. Others are reportedly in or very near populated urban areas. While the U.S. could probably knock out many of the Iranian nuclear facilities using bunker-busting munitions, there would be heavy civilian casualties — probably in the thousands. America would face international censure, including from many of its closest allies. Even if the strike were militarily successful, it would only slow—but not halt—the Iranian nuclear effort. Iran would probably accelerate its drive to acquire nuclear weapons, this time without any pretense of complying with international rules and restrictions. Moreover, the political costs would be very high. A military strike would unleash a wave of nationalism and unite the Iranian population behind the current regime, ending any prospect of internal change in the near future and ensuring decades of enmity from the Iranian middle class and youth, who are largely opposed to the current regime. It would also provoke outrage in the Muslim world, probably making any attempt to obtain the support of moderate Muslims in the war on terror impossible.
>
> (Larrabee 2006)

38 It is, however, notable that US anti-terrorist efforts during the 1990s were so risibly cautious and legalistic that Osama Bin Laden repeatedly escaped Washington's clutches. A government truly serious about fighting terrorism would not have refused numerous opportunities to seize or kill Bin Laden because it was waiting for a *perfect* opportunity in which to accost the *Al Qaeda* leader with guaranteed success. See Coll (2004: 371–396 and 438–452).

39 Sciolino (1992).

40 See, for example, Ross (1999).

41 See Bernstein and Munro (1997) and Mosher (2000).

42 See Green (2006).

43 For an argument that China is not in fact seeking hegemony in the Asia-Pacific, see Taylor (2005).

44 Huntington (1996).

45 Gray (2007b: 283).

46 See Taranto and Leo (2004).

47 For instance, while most of the individuals polled no doubt are knowledgeable about administrations that are recent and/or "popular" (such as those of Washington and Lincoln), one might doubt whether most of those polled are intimately familiar with the details of the presidencies of, say, Rutherford B. Hayes and John Tyler.

48 A considerably more generous assessment of Carter's ability as a strategist is offered in Auten (2008).

49 See Kriger (2003) and Meredith (2007).

50 See, for example, Carter (2003, 2006).

51 Carter (1996).

52 Carter (2007).

53 Ford of course could have chosen to disobey existing (albeit arguably unconstitutional) law and attempted to exercise his authority as commander-in-chief to order US aircraft to support the South Vietnamese against the North's invaders, but such an order surely would have resulted in a severe constitutional crisis. He certainly cannot be faulted for failing to undertake a "semi-coup" that would have profoundly stressed the US constitutional system and forced military officers to obey either the Legislative or Executive branch.

54 Such possibilities are discussed at length in Walton (2002a: 132–150).

55 A particularly bitter and angry example is Voorhis (1972).

56 For a literary treatment of this aspect of Reagan's life, see Morris (1999: 232–246.

57 On the operational aspects of the US intervention in Lebanon, see Hammel (2005), Lowther (2007: 82–101), and Geraghty (2009).

58 It is difficult to find much fault in Bush's handling of the conflict itself, although the triumph was marred somewhat by the decision to encourage Shia and Kurdish uprisings during the conflict and then not to support them after the conflict ended. Iraqi Kurds and Shia paid a terrible price for this cold decision and the United States possibly missed an opportunity to bring the Hussein regime to an end without the direct involvement of its own ground troops. Of course, Hussein's removal would have resulted in some degree of sectarian and ethnic conflict and, perhaps, the splintering of Iraq, which the cautious Bush administration legitimately feared. Yet looking with hindsight at the history of 1991 to the present, there is a compelling argument that, from both the perspective of US national interest and humanitarian concern, even the division of Iraq would have been far preferable to what actually has transpired.

59 The former president and his national security advisor explain the reasoning underlying the administration's policy in Bush and Scowcroft (1999).

60 Of course, every presidential campaign is unique, and G.H.W. Bush might well have won reelection in 1992 if not for the third-party campaign of the eccentric billionaire H. Ross Perot or, alternately, if he had faced a Democratic opponent less talented at campaigning than was Bill Clinton, a politician possessed of enormous charisma and related gifts.

61 On the role of energy in the Russian economy, see Goldman (2010).

62 See LeVine (2009).

63 Vannevar Bush, one of the twentieth century's most accomplished scientific administrators, argued very early in the Cold War that communist polities were incapable of energetic scientific progress over the long term:

> The weakness of the Communist state resides in its rigidity, in the fact that it cannot tolerate heresy, and in the fact that it cannot allow its iron curtain to be fully penetrated. All these things, vital to totalitarianism whether right

> or left, are fatal to true progress in fundamental science. They are not nearly so fatal to the application of science, but they are a severe deterrent to even the healthy growth of this along novel lines.
>
> (Bush 1949: 200)

There probably is much truth in his observation—Bush merely (and, given the time when he was writing, understandably) did not anticipate that communist governments might be capable of slowly "de-totalizing" and becoming, if not democratic, then at least free enough to allow scientists the intellectual space required to advance their fields of study.

64 This theme is developed in more detail in Walton (2007b: 88–100).

65 For a grim view of possible future developments in artificial intelligence and the possibility of a sort of "super-intelligence arms race," see Iklé (2006).

66 See Singer (2009).

67 See Altmann (2006).

68 The validity of the RMA concept itself is hotly contested. For a thoughtful defense of the utility of the concept and discussion of the RMAs that have occurred historically, see Gray (2002a).

69 The WikiLeaks phenomenon demonstrated how vulnerable US classified data is to unauthorized disclosure; non-democratic powers, however, may still feel somewhat confident in their ability to prevent the revelation of their secrets (except of course in those cases where they are interacting with the sieve-like US government). Inadvertently, Julian Assange and his associates demonstrated one of the potentially powerful advantages that some authoritarian governments may possess in the technological environment of the twenty-first century: compared to their democratic competitors, they may prove better able to keep their secrets uncompromised; more capable of minimizing the domestic political consequences of any information that is disclosed; and, finally, more credibly willing to use rough methods to punish leakers and demonstrate to potential future troublemakers that they do not respond fecklessly to actions that harm their interests.

70 See Luttwak (2001).

71 On the character of government entities, see Wilson (2000).

Conclusion

1 On the development of strategic studies in the United States up to the early 1980s, see Gray (1982).

2 Kennedy (1987).

3 There are many thoughtful works addressing the relationship between the two, including Kennedy (1987), McNeill and McNeill (2003), Christian (2005), Turchin (2006), and Pagden (2008).

References

Acheson, Dean, *Sketches from Life of Men I Have Known* (New York: Harper, 1961).

Acheson, Dean, *Present at the Creation: My Years at the State Department* (New York: W.W. Norton, 1987; originally published 1969).

Adelman, Jeremy and Stephen Aron, "From Borderlands to Borders: Empires, Nation-States, and the People in Between in North American History," *The American Historical Review* 104/3 (June 1999): 814–861.

Ajami, Fouad, "With Us or Against Us," Review of *In the Line of Fire: A Memoir*, by Pervez Musharraf, *New York Times* online edn., 7 January 2007.

Aldrich, George H., "The Taliban, *Al Qaeda*, and the Determination of Illegal Combatants," *The American Journal of International Law*, 96/4 (October 2002): 891–898.

Aldrich, John H., John L. Sullivan, and Eugene Borgida, "Foreign Affairs and Issue Voting: Do Presidential Candidates 'Waltz Before a Blind Audience'?," *American Political Science Review* 83/1 (March 1989): 123–141.

Alexander, Bevin, *Lost Victories: The Military Genius of Stonewall Jackson* (New York: Henry Holt, 1992).

Allison, Graham, *Nuclear Terrorism: The Risks and Consequences of the Ultimate Disaster* (London: Constable, 2006; originally published 2004).

Allison, Graham and Philip Zelikov, *Essence of Decision: Explaining the Cuban Missile Crisis*, 2nd edn. (New York: Longman, 1999).

Al-Siba'i, Hani, Excerpts from an Al-Jazeera television interview aired on 5 July 2005, MEMRI Special Dispatch #932, 12 July 2005, accessed online at http://memri.org/bin/articles.cgi?Page=archives&Area=sd&ID=SP93205.

Altmann, Jürgen, *Military Nanotechnology: Potential Applications and Preventive Arms Control* (London: Routledge, 2006).

Anderson, Fred, *Crucible of War: The Seven Years' War and the Fate of Empire in British North America, 1754–1766* (New York: Vintage, 2000).

Andrew, Christopher and Vasili Mitrokhin, *The World Was Going Our Way: The KGB and the Battle for the Third World* (New York: Basic Books, 2005).

Andrews, Edmund L., "Envoy's Letter Counters Bush on Dismantling of Iraqi Army," *New York Times* online edn., 4 September 2007.

Anonymous, "Excerpts from President Clinton's Session with Reporters," *New York Times* online edn., 22 October 1994.

Archibald, Rabdal C. and Jeff Kearns, "In California Terror Case, a Mistrial for a Father, but a Son is Guilty," *New York Times* online edn., 26 April 2006.

Arkin, Marc M., "The Federalist Trope: Power and Passion in Abolitionist Rhetoric," *Journal of American History* 88/1 (June 2001): 75–98.

Arquilla, John and María Moyano Rasmussen, "The Origins of the South Atlantic War," *Journal of Latin American Studies* 33/4 (November 2001): 739–775.

Art, Robert J., "Why Western Europe Needs the United States and NATO," *Political Science Quarterly* 111/1 (Spring 1996): 1–39.

Auten, Brian J., *Carter's Conversion: The Hardening of American Defense Policy* (Columbia, MO: University of Missouri Press, 2008).

Baer, Robert, *Sleeping with the Devil: How Washington Sold Our Soul for Saudi Crude* (New York: Three Rivers Press, 2004).

Bailyn, Bernard, *The Ideological Origins of the American Revolution*, enlarged edn. (Cambridge, MA: Harvard University Press, 1992; original edn. published 1967).

Ballendorf, Dirk Anthony and Merrill L. Bartlett, *Pete Ellis: An Amphibious Warfare Prophet, 1880–1923* (Annapolis, MD: Naval Institute Press, 2010; originally published 1996).

Barron, James, "South Korean Gets Five Years for Dealings with Iraqis," *New York Times* online edn., 23 February 2007.

Bartholomees, J. Boone, "Theory of Victory," *Parameters* 38/2 (Summer 2008): 25–36, accessed online at www.carlisle.army.mil/usawc/parameters/Articles/08summer/bartholo.pdf.

Beisner, Robert L., *Dean Acheson: A Life in the Cold War* (New York: Oxford University Press, 2006).

Berke, Richard L. and Janet Elder, "Poll Finds Support for War and Fear on Economy," *New York Times* online edn., 25 September 2001.

Bernstein, Richard and Ross H. Munro, *The Coming Conflict with China* (New York: Knopf, 1997).

Betts, Richard K., "Compromised Command," review of Wesley K. Clark, *Waging Modern War*, *Foreign Affairs* 80/4 (July/August 2001), accessed online at www.foreignaffairs.org/20010701fareviewessay4999/richard-k-betts/compromised-command.html.

Bialer, Seweryn, *Stalin's Successors: Leadership, Stability, and Change in the Soviet Union* (Cambridge: Cambridge University Press, 1980).

Bialer, Seweryn, ed., *The Domestic Context of Soviet Foreign Policy* (Boulder, CO: Westview Press, 1981).

Biddle, Stephen, "Victory Misunderstood: What the Gulf War Tells Us about the Future of Conflict," *International Security* 21/2 (Autumn 1996): 139–179.

Black, Jeremy, *Britain as a Military Power, 1688–1815* (London and Philadelphia: University College London Press, 1999).

Black, Jeremy, *America as a Military Power: From the American Revolution to the Civil War* (Westport, CT: Praeger, 2002).

Black, Jeremy, *Great Powers and the Quest for Hegemony: The World Order Since 1500* (London: Routledge, 2008).

Blight, James G. and Peter Kornbluh, eds., *The Politics of Illusion: The Bay of Pigs Invasion Reexamined* (Boulder, CO: Lynne Rienner, 1998).

Boot, Max, *The Savage Wars of Peace: Small Wars and the Rise of American Power* (New York: Basic Books, 2002).

Borawski, John, "Partnership for Peace and Beyond," *International Affairs* 71/2 (April 1995): 233–246.

Borneman, Walter R., *Polk: The Man Who Transformed the Presidency and America* (New York: Random House, 2008).

Boyd, Julian P., *The Declaration of Independence: The Evolution of the Text* (Washington, DC: Library of Congress, 1943).

Brachman, Jarret M., *Global Jihadism: Theory and Practice* (London: Routledge, 2009).
Brands, H.W., *The Reckless Decade: America in the 1890s* (Chicago: University of Chicago Press, 2002; originally published 1995).
Bremer, L. Paul III, "How I Didn't Dismantle Iraq's Army," *New York Times* online edn., 6 September 2007.
Bronson, Rachel, *Thicker Than Oil: America's Uneasy Relationship with Saudi Arabia* (New York: Oxford, 2006).
Brookhiser, Richard, *Founding Father: Rediscovering George Washington* (New York: The Free Press, 1996).
Brzezinski, Zbigniew, *The Geostrategic Triad: Living with Europe, China, and Russia*, CSIS Significant Issues series (Washington: Center for Strategic and International Studies, 2000).
Brzezinski, Zbigniew, *The Choice: Global Domination or Global Leadership* (New York: Basic, 2005).
Buckley, Cara and William K. Rashbaum, "6 Men Arrested in a Terror Plot Against Fort Dix," *New York Times* online edn., 9 May 2007.
Builder, Carl, *The Masks of War: American Military Styles in Strategy and Analysis*, RAND Corporation Research Study (Baltimore, MD: Johns Hopkins University Press, 1989).
Bumiller, Elisabeth, "A Nation Challenged: The President," *New York Times* online edn., 11 November 2001.
Burleigh, Michael, *The Third Reich: A New History* (New York: Hill and Wang, 2000).
Burleigh, Michael, *Blood and Rage: A Cultural History of Terrorism* (New York: HarperPerennial, 2009).
Burnard, T.G., " 'Prodigious Riches': The Wealth of Jamaica Before the American Revolution," *Economic History Review* 54/3 (August 2001): 506–524.
Buruma, Ian and Avishai Margalit, *Occidentalism: The West in the Eyes of Its Enemies* (New York: Penguin, 2005).
Bush, George H.W. and Brent Scowcroft, *A World Transformed* (New York: Vintage Books, 1999).
Bush, George W., "Threats and Responses," *New York Times* online edn., 27 February 2003.
Bush, George W., *Decision Points* (New York: Crown, 2010).
Bush, Vannevar, *Modern Arms and Free Men* (New York: Simon and Schuster, 1949).
Calhoun, John C., ed. by Ross M. Lence, *Union and Liberty: The Political Philosophy of John C. Calhoun* (Indianapolis: Liberty Fund, 1992).
Campbell, Kurt, "What Holiday from History?" *New York Times* online edn., 23 November 2007.
Canes-Wrone, Brandice, *Who Leads Whom?: Presidents, Policy, and the Public* (Chicago: University of Chicago Press, 2006).
Caro, Robert A., *The Years of Lyndon Johnson, Vol. II: Means of Ascent* (New York: Knopf, 1990).
Caro, Robert A., *The Years of Lyndon Johnson, Vol. III: Master of the Senate* (New York: Knopf, 2002).
Carter, Jimmy, *Why Not the Best?: The First Fifty Years* (Fayetteville, AR: University of Arkansas Press, 1996; originally published 1975).
Carter, Jimmy, *The Nobel Peace Prize Lecture* (New York: Simon & Schuster, 2003).

Carter, Jimmy, *Palestine: Peace Not Apartheid* (New York: Simon & Schuster, 2006).

Carter, Jimmy, "Undermining Peace," *Guardian* (London) online edn., 9 September 2007.

Chaliand, Gérard and Arnaud Blin, eds., trans. by Edward Schneider, Kathryn Pulver, and Jesse Browner, *The History of Terrorism: From Antiquity to Al Qaeda* (Berkeley and Los Angeles: University of California Press, 2007).

Chambers, Whittaker, *Witness* (New York: Random House, 1952).

Chang, Jung and Jon Halliday, *Mao: The Unknown Story* (New York: Anchor Books, 2006).

Chau, Donovan C., "Assistance of a Different Kind: Chinese Political Warfare in Ghana, 1958–1966," *Comparative Strategy* 26/2 (March 2007): 141–161.

Christian, David, *Maps of Time: An Introduction to Big History* (Berkeley: University of California Press, 2005).

Clark, John F., ed., *The African Stakes of the Congo War* (New York: Palgrave Macmillan, 2002).

von Clausewitz, Carl, *On War*, indexed edn., ed. and trans. by Michael Howard and Peter Paret (Princeton, NJ: Princeton University Press, 1984; originally published 1976).

Cloud, David S., "Here's Donny! In His Defense, A Star is Born," *New York Times* online edn., 19 April 2006.

Cohen, Eliot A., *Citizens and Soldiers: The Dilemmas of Military Service* (Ithaca, NY: Cornell University Press, 1985).

Cohen, Eliot A., "Why We Should Stop Studying the Cuban Missile Crisis" in Benjamin Frankel, ed., *In the National Interest: A* National Interest *Reader* (Lanham, MD: University Press of America, 1990), pp. 49–64.

Cohen, Eliot A., *Supreme Command: Soldiers, Statesmen, and Leadership in Wartime* (New York: The Free Press, 2002).

Coker, Christopher, *The Warrior Ethos: Military Culture and the War on Terror* (London: Routledge, 2007).

Coker, Christopher, *Ethics and War in the Twenty-First Century* (London: Routledge, 2008).

Coll, Steve, *Ghost Wars: The Secret History of the CIA, Afghanistan, and Bin Laden from the Soviet Invasion to September 10, 2001* (New York: Penguin, 2004).

Conway, Stephen, "To Subdue America: British Army Officers and the Conduct of the Revolutionary War," *William and Mary Quarterly* 43/3 (July 1986): 381–407.

Cooper, William J., *Jefferson Davis, American* (New York: Vintage, 2001).

Cordesman, Anthony H., *The Iraq War: Strategy, Tactics, and Military Lessons* (Washington, DC: Center for Strategic and International Studies, 2003).

Cornish, Paul, "The End of Architecture and the New NATO," *International Affairs* 72/4 (October 1996), 751–769.

Croft, Stuart, Jolyon Howorth, Terry Terriff, and Mark Webb, "NATO's Triple Challenge," *International Affairs* 76/3 (July 2000): 495–518.

Crothers, Lane, *Rage on the Right: The American Militia Movement from Ruby Ridge to Homeland Security* (Lanham, MD: Rowman and Littlefield, 2003).

Current, Richard N., "God and the Strongest Battalions," in David Herber Donald, ed., *Why the North Won the Civil War* (New York: Touchstone, 1996; originally published 1960), pp. 21–37.

Dallek, Robert, "National Mood and American Foreign Policy: A Suggestive Essay," *American Quarterly*, 34/4 (Autumn 1982): 339–343.

Davies, Norman, *God's Playground: A History of Poland, Vol I: The Origins to 1795*, rev. edn. (New York: Oxford University Press, 2005).

Deng, Yong, "Hegemon on the Offensive: Chinese Perspectives on U.S. Grand Strategy," *Political Science Quarterly* 116/3 (Autumn 2001): 343–365.

D'Este, Carlo, *Warlord: The Fighting Life of Winston Churchill, From Soldier to Statesman* (London: Penguin, 2010).

Donald, David Herbert, "Abraham Lincoln and Jefferson Davis as Commanders in Chief," in Gabor Boritt, ed., *The Lincoln Enigma: The Changing Faces of An American Icon* (New York: Oxford University Press, 2001), pp. 72–85.

Draper, Theodore, *A Struggle for Power: The American Revolution* (New York: Times Books, 1996).

Duggan, William, *Coup D'Oeil: Strategic Intuition in Army Planning* (Carlisle Barracks, PA: US Army War College/Strategic Studies Institute, November 2005).

Dunne, Michael, "US Foreign Relations in the Twentieth Century: From World Power to Global Hegemony," *International Affairs* 76/1 (January 2000): 25–50.

Durschmied, Erik, *Blood of Revolution: From the Reign of Terror to the Rise of Khomeini* (New York: Arcade, 2001).

Dusinberre, William, *Slavemaster President: The Double Career of James Polk* (New York: Oxford University Press, 2007).

Edgerton, Robert B., *The Troubled Heart of Africa: A History of the Congo* (New York: St. Martin's Press, 2002).

Eisenhower, John S.D., *Agent of Destiny: The Life and Times of General Winfield Scott* (New York: Free Press, 1997).

Eisenhower, John S.D., *So Far from God: The U.S. War with Mexico, 1846–1848* (Norman, OK: The University of Oklahoma Press, 2000; originally published 1989).

Ellis, Joseph, *Founding Brothers: The Revolutionary Generation* (New York: Knopf, 2000).

Ellis, Richard and Aaron Wildavsky, "A Cultural Analysis of the Role of the Abolitionists in the Coming of the Civil War," *Comparative Studies in Society and History* 32/1 (January 1990): 89–116.

Elman, Colin, "Extending Offensive Realism: The Louisiana Purchase and America's Rise to Regional Hegemony," *American Political Science Review* 98/4 (November 2004): 563–576.

English, Richard, *Armed Struggle: The History of the IRA* (Oxford, UK: Oxford University Press, 2003).

Erlanger, Steven, "A Compliment Sharansky Can't Refuse," *New York Times* online edn., 2 February 2005.

Etcheson, Nicole, *Bleeding Kansas: Contested Liberty in the Civil War Era* (Lawrence, KS: University Press of Kansas, 2004).

Everitt, Anthony, *Augustus: The Life of Rome's First Emperor* (New York: Random House, 2006).

Fainsod, Merle, *How Russia is Ruled* (Cambridge, MA: Harvard University Press, 1953).

Fatovic, Clement, "Constitutionalism and Presidential Prerogative: Jeffersonian and Hamiltonian Perspectives," *American Journal of Political Science* 48/3 (July 2004): 429–444.

Fick, Nathaniel, *One Bullet Away: The Making of a Marine Officer* (New York: Houghton Mifflin, 2005).

Fleming, Thomas, *The Illusion of Victory: America in World War I* (New York: Basic Books, 2004).

Freedman, Lawrence, ed., *Superterrorism: Policy Responses* (Oxford, UK: Blackwell, 2002).

Freedman, Paul, Michael Franz, and Kenneth Goldstein, "Campaign Advertising and Democratic Citizenship," *American Journal of Political Science* 48/4 (October 2004): 723–741.

Fremont-Barnes, Gregory, *The Indian Mutiny, 1857–58* (Oxford, UK: Osprey, 2007).

Frum, David and Richard Perle, *An End to Evil: How to Win the War on Terror* (New York: Random House, 2003).

Fukuyama, Francis, *America at the Crossroads: Democracy, Power, and the Neoconservative Legacy* (New Haven, CT and London: Yale University Press, 2006).

Gage, Beverly, *The Day Wall Street Exploded: A Story of America in its First Age of Terror* (New York: Oxford University Press, 2009).

Gallagher, Gary W., *The Confederate War: How Popular Will, Nationalism, and Military Strategy Could Not Stave Off Defeat* (Cambridge, MA: Harvard University Press, 1997).

Gellately, Robert, *Lenin, Stalin and Hitler: The Age of Social Catastrophe* (London: Vintage, 2008; originally published 2007).

George, John and Laird Wilcox, *American Extremists: Militias, Supremacists, Klansmen, Communists, and Others* (New York: Prometheus, 1996).

Geraghty, Timothy J., *Peacekeepers at War: Beirut 1983—The Marine Commander Tells His Story* (Dulles, VA: Potomac, 2009).

Gittings, John, "If the Unthinkable Happens," *Guardian* (London) online edn., 30 August 2006.

Glantz, David M., *Colossus Reborn: The Red Army at War, 1941–1943* (Lawrence, KS: University Press of Kansas, 2005a).

Glantz, David M., *Companion to* Colossus Reborn*: Key Documents and Statistics* (Lawrence, KS: University Press of Kansas, 2005b).

Goldman, Marshall I., *Petrostate: Putin, Power, and the New Russia,* rev. edn. (Oxford: Oxford University Press, 2010).

Goodheart, Lawrence B. "Abolition, the Northern Churches, and Social Change," review of John R. McKivigan, *The War Against Proslavery Religion: Abolitionism and the Northern Churches, 1830–1965* (Ithaca, NY: Cornell University Press, 1984), *Reviews in American History,* 13/1 (March 1985): 54–59.

Goodwin, Doris Kearns, *Lyndon Johnson and the American Dream* (New York: St. Martin's Griffin, 1991; originally published 1976).

Gordon, Michael R., "Fateful Choice on Iraqi Army Bypassed Debate, *New York Times* online edn., 17 March 2008.

Gott, Richard, "Revolutionary Leadership," *Guardian* (London) online edn., 9 January 2007.

Grant, David, "Uncle Tom's Cabin and the Triumph of Republican Rhetoric," *The New England Quarterly* 71/3 (September 1998): 429–448.

Grant, Michael, *The History of Rome* (London: Faber and Faber, 1993; originally published 1978).

Grant, Ulysses S., *Personal Memoirs* (New York: Modern Library, 1999; originally published 1885).

Gray, Colin S., "National Style in Strategy: The American Example," *International Security* 6/2 (Autumn 1981): 21–47.

Gray, Colin S., *Strategic Studies and Public Policy* (Lexington, KY: University Press of Kentucky, 1982).

Gray, Colin S., *House of Cards: Why Arms Control Must Fail* (Ithaca, NY: Cornell University Press, 1992).

Gray, Colin S., *Modern Strategy* (Oxford, UK: Oxford University Press, 1999).

Gray, Colin S., *Strategy for Chaos: Revolutions in Military Affairs and the Evidence of History* (London: Frank Cass, 2002a).

Gray, Colin S., *Defining and Achieving Decisive Victory* (Carlisle Barracks, PA: US Army War College/Strategic Studies Institute, 2002b).

Gray, Colin S., *The Sheriff: America's Defense of the New World Order* (Lexington, KY: The University Press of Kentucky, 2004).

Gray, Colin S., "The Anglo-Irish War, 1919–21: Lessons from an Irregular Conflict," *Comparative Strategy* 26/5 (October 2007a): 371–394.

Gray, Colin S., *War, Peace and International Relations: An Introduction to Strategic History* (London and New York: Routledge, 2007b).

Gray, Colin S., *Schools for Strategy: Teaching Strategy for 21st Century Conflict* (Carlisle Barracks, PA: US Army War College/Strategic Studies Institute, 2009).

Gray, Colin S., *The Strategy Bridge* (New York: Oxford University Press, 2010).

Gray, Colin S., *Harry S. Truman and the Forming of American Grand Strategy in the Cold War, 1945–53* in Williamson Murray, Richard Hart Sinnreich, and James Lacey, eds., *The Shaping of Grand Strategy: Policy, Diplomacy, and War* (New York: Cambridge University Press, 2011).

Green, Michael Jonathan, "The Strategic Implications of the Burma Problem," Testimony before the Senate Foreign Relations Committee Subcommittee on Asia Pacific Affairs, 29 March 2006, available at www.senate.gov/~foreign/testimony/2006/GreenTestimony060329.pdf (accessed 21 August 2007).

Greenstein, Fred I., *The Hidden-Hand Presidency: Eisenhower as Leader* (Baltimore: Johns Hopkins University Press, 1994; originally published 1982).

Guillemin, Jeanne, *Biological Weapons: From the Invention of State-Sponsored Programs to Contemporary Bioterrorism* (New York: Columbia University Press, 2005).

Guins, George C., "Soviet Culture: Old Trends and New," *Russian Review* 7/1 (Autumn 1947): 24–32.

Haass, Richard N., Director of the Office of the Policy Planning Staff, and US Coordinator for the Future of Afghanistan, *Testimony Before the Senate Committee on Foreign Relations*, 6 December 2001, "Future of Afghanistan," accessed online at www.state.gov/s/p/rem/6757.htm.

Halberstam, David, *The Coldest Winter: America and the Korean War* (New York: Hyperion, 2007).

Hammel, Eric, *The Root: The Marines in Beirut, August 1982–February 1984* (St. Paul, MN: Zenith Press, 2005; originally published 1999).

Hanna, Kathryn Abbey, "The Role of the South in the French Intervention in Mexico," *Journal of Southern History* 20/1 (February 1954): 3–21.

Hannah, Norman B., *The Key to Failure: Laos and the Vietnam War* (Lanham, MD: Madison, 1987).

Hanson, Victor Davis, *Carnage and Culture: Landmark Battles in the Rise of Western Power* (New York: Random House, 2001).

Harmon, Christopher C., *Terrorism Today*, 2nd edn. (London: Routledge, 2007).

Harmon, Christopher C., Andrew N. Pratt, and Sebastian Gorka, *Toward a Grand Strategy Against Terrorism* (New York: McGraw-Hill, 2011).

Harris, John F., *The Survivor: Clinton in the White House* (New York: Random House, 2005).

Heith, Diane, *Polling to Govern: Public Opinion and Presidential Leadership* (Stanford, CA: Stanford University Press, 2004).

Henderson, Simon, "Al-Qaeda Attack on Abqaiq: The Vulnerability of Saudi Oil," The Washington Institute for Near Eastern Policy, PolicyWatch #1082, 28 February 2006, accessed online at www.washingtoninstitute.org/templateC05.php?CID=2446.

Herrera, Ricardo A. "Self-Governance and the American Citizen as Soldier, 1775–1861," *Journal of Military History* 65/1 (January 2001): 21–52.

Hershberger, Mary, "Mobilizing Women, Anticipating Abolition: The Struggle Against Indian Removal in the 1830s," *Journal of American History* 86/1 (June 1999): 15–40.

Hershman, D. Jablow, *Power Beyond Reason: The Mental Collapse of Lyndon Johnson* (Fort Lee, NJ: Barricade Books, 2002).

Herspring, Dale R., "Rumsfeld as Secretary of Defense" in Stephen J. Cimbala, ed., *The George W. Bush Defense Program: Policy, Strategy, & War* (Dulles, VA: Potomac Books, 2010).

Herzog, Michael, *Iranian Public Opinion on the Nuclear Program: A Potential Asset for the International Community*, Policy Focus #56 (Washington, DC: The Washington Institute for Near East Policy, 2006), accessed online at www.washingtoninstitute.org/pubPDFs/PolicyFocus56.pdf.

Hill, Charles, *Grand Strategies: Literature, Statecraft, and World Order* (New Haven, CT: Yale University Press, 2010).

Hoffer, Eric, *The True Believer: Thoughts of the Nature of Mass Movements* (New York: Perennial Classics, 2002; originally published 1951).

Hoge, Warren, "U.N. Body Plans to End Investigation of Contracts," *New York Times* online edn., 21 December 2007.

Hoig, Stanley W., *The Cherokees and Their Chiefs: In the Wake of Empire* (Fayetteville, AR: University of Arkansas Press, 1998).

Hoover, Herbert, *The Ordeal of Woodrow Wilson* (New York: McGraw-Hill, 1958).

Hopkins, William B., *The Pacific War: The Strategy, Politics, and Players that Won the War* (Minneapolis: Zenith Books, 2008).

Howe, Daniel Walker, *What God Hath Wrought: The Transformation of America, 1815–1848* (New York: Oxford University Press, 2009; originally published 2007).

Hunter, Stephen and John Bainbridge, Jr., *American Gunfight: The Plot to Kill President Truman—and the Shoot-Out that Stopped It* (New York: Simon & Schuster, 2007).

Huntington, Samuel P., *The Clash of Civilizations and the Remaking of World Order* (New York: Simon and Schuster, 1996).

Huston, James L., "Property Rights in Slavery and the Coming of the Civil War," *Journal of Southern History* 65/2 (May 1999): 249–286.

Iklé, Fred Charles, *Annihilation from Within: The Ultimate Threat to Nations* (New York: Columbia University Press, 2006).

Isaacson, Walter, and Evan Thomas, *The Wise Men: Six Friends and the World They Made* (New York: Simon and Schuster, 1986).

Jaffa, Harry V., *Crisis of the House Divided: An Interpretation of the Issues in the Lincoln-Douglas Debates*, rev. edn. (Chicago: University of Chicago Press, 1999; originally published 1959).

Jaffa, Harry V., *A New Birth of Freedom: Abraham Lincoln and the Coming of the Civil War* (New York: Rowman and Littlefield, 2000).

Jamieson, Kathleen Hall, *Packaging the Presidency: A History and Criticism of Presidential Campaign Advertising*, 3rd edn. (New York: Oxford University Press, 1996).

Jayne, Allen, *Jefferson's Declaration of Independence: Origins, Philosophy, and Theology* (Lexington, KY: University Press of Kentucky, 1998).

Jenkins, Brian Michael, *Will Terrorists Go Nuclear?* (New York: Prometheus Books, 2008).

Jervis, Robert, *Why Intelligence Fails: Lessons from the Iranian Revolution and the Iraq War* (Ithaca, NY: Cornell University Press, 2010).

Jervis, Robert, Richard Ned Lebow, and Janice Gross Stein, with Patrick M. Morgan, and Jack L. Snyder, *Psychology and Deterrence* (Baltimore: Johns Hopkins University Press, 1989; originally published 1985).

Johnson, Timothy D., *Winfield Scott: The Quest for Military Glory* (Lawrence, KS: University Press of Kansas, 1998).

Jones, Archer, *Civil War Command and Strategy: The Process of Victory and Defeat* (New York: The Free Press, 1992).

Jones, Terry, "Why Grammar is the First Casualty of War," *Daily Telegraph* (London) online edn., 1 December 2001.

Jordan, David, James D. Kiras, David J. Lonsdale, Ian Speller, Christopher Tuck, and C. Dale Walton, *Understanding Modern Warfare* (Cambridge, UK: Cambridge University Press, 2008).

Kagan, Robert, ed., *Present Dangers: Crisis and Opportunity in Foreign Policy* (San Francisco: Encounter, 2000).

Kagan, Robert, ed., *Of Paradise and Power* (New York: Vintage, 2004).

Kaiser, David, *American Tragedy: Kennedy, Johnson, and the Origins of the Vietnam War* (Cambridge, MA: Harvard University Press/Belknap Press, 2000).

Kane, Thomas M., *Theoretical Roots of US Foreign Policy: Machiavelli and American Unilateralism* (London: Routledge, 2006).

Kaplan, Robert D., *Balkan Ghosts: A Journey through History* (New York: Picador, 2005; originally published 1993).

Kastor, Peter J., "'Motives of Peculiar Urgency': Local Diplomacy in Louisiana, 1803–1821," *The William and Mary Quarterly* 58/4 (October 2001): 819–848.

Keegan, John, *The Mask of Command* (London: Penguin, 1988).

Keegan, John, *The Iraq War* (New York: Knopf, 2004).

Keeley, Lawrence H., *War Before Civilization: The Myth of the Peaceful Savage* (New York: Oxford University Press, 1997).

Kennan, George F., *Memoirs, 1925–1950* (Boston: Atlantic-Little Brown, 1967).

Kennan, George F., ed. by Giles D. Harlow and George C. Maerz, *Measures Short of War: The George F. Kennan Lectures at the National War College, 1946–47* (Washington, DC: National Defense University Press, 1991).

Kennedy, Paul, *The Rise and Fall of the Great Powers* (New York: Random House, 1987).

Kinzer, Steven, "The New Drumbeat on Iran," *Guardian* (London) online edn., 11 July 2007.

Kiras, James D., *Special Operations and Strategy: From World War II to the War on Terrorism* (London: Routledge, 2006).

Kiras, James D., "Irregular Warfare," in David Jordan, James D. Kiras, David J. Lonsdale, Ian Speller, Christopher Tuck, and C. Dale Walton, *Understanding Modern Warfare* (Cambridge, UK: Cambridge University Press, 2008).

Kirgis, Frederic L., "United States Reconnaissance Aircraft Collision with Chinese Jet," *ASIL Insights,* American Society of International Law, April 2001, accessed online at www.asil.org/insights/insigh66.htm.

Kissinger, Henry, *Does America Need A Foreign Policy? Toward a Diplomacy for the 21st Century* (New York: Simon and Schuster, 2001).

Knox, MacGregor, *Hitler's Italian Allies: Royal Armed Forces, Fascist Regime, and the War of 1940–43* (Cambridge, UK: Cambridge University Press, 2009).

Kolchin, Peter, "In Defense of Servitude: Russian Proserfdom and American Proslavery Arguments, 1760–1860," *The American Historical Review* 85/4 (October 1980): 809–827.

Kornbluh, Peter, ed., *Bay of Pigs Declassified: The Secret CIA Report on the Invasion of Cuba* (New York: The New Press, 1997).

Kotkin, Stephen, *Armageddon Averting: The Soviet Collapse, 1970–2000* (New York: Oxford University Press, 2001).

Kriger, Norma J., "Robert Mugabe, Another Too-Long-Serving African Ruler: A Review Essay," *Political Science Quarterly* 118/2 (Summer 2003): 307–313.

Krugman, Paul, "Scary Movie 2," *New York Times* online edn., 12 February 2007.

Kupchan, Charles A., *The End of the American Era: U.S. Foreign Policy and the Geopolitics of the Twenty-First Century* (New York: Vintage, 2003; originally published 2002).

Lampton, David M., *Same Bed, Different Dreams, Managing U.S.-China Relations, 1989–2000* (Berkeley and Los Angeles: University of California Press, 2001).

Larrabee, F. Stephen, "Defusing the Iranian Crisis," *Orange County Register* (CA), 9 March 2006, accessed online at www.rand.org/commentary/030906OCR.html.

Laqueur, Walter, "Postmodern Terrorism," *Foreign Affairs* 75/5 (September/October 1996): 24–36.

Laqueur, Walter, *The New Terrorism: Fanaticism and the Arms of Mass Destruction* (New York: Oxford University Press, 2000).

LeBlanc, Steven A. with Katherine E. Register, *Constant Battles: The Myth of the Peaceful Noble Savage* (New York: St. Martin's Press, 2003).

Leckie, Robert, *Strong Men Armed: The United States Marines Against Japan* (New York: Da Capo Press, 2010; originally published 1962).

Leonard, Mark, *Why Europe Will Run the 21st Century* (London: Fourth Estate, 2005).

Leonard, Thomas M., *A Clear and Unquestionable Destiny* (Lanham, MD: Rowman and Littlefield, 2000).

Levi, Michael A., *On Nuclear Terrorism* (Cambridge, MA: Harvard University Press, 2007).

LeVine, Steve, *Putin's Labyrinth: Spies, Murder, and the Dark Heart of the New Russia* (New York: Random House, 2009).

Levitas, Daniel, *The Terrorist Next Door: The Militia Movement and the Radical Right* (New York: St. Martin's Griffin, 2004).

Lewy, Guenter, *Peace and Revolution: The Moral Crisis of American Pacifism* (Grand Rapids, MI: William B. Eerdmans, 1988).

Library of Congress, Manuscript Division, Kissinger Papers, Box 367, Telephone Conversations, Chronological File, reprinted in Louis J. Smith, ed., *Foreign Relations of the United States, 1969–1976, vol. XI: South Asia Crisis 1971* (2005) p. 34, accessed online at www.state.gov/documents/organization/45582.pdf.

Lichtblau, Eric, "Trucker Sentenced to Twenty Years in Plot Against Brooklyn Bridge," *New York Times* online edn., 29 October 2003.

Lifton, Robert Jay, *Destroying the World to Save It: Aum Shinrikyō, Apocalyptic Violence, and the New Global Terrorism* (New York: Metropolitan, 1999).

Light, Margot, Stephen White, and John Lowenhardt, "A Wider Europe: The View from Moscow and Kyiv," *International Affairs* 76/1 (January 2000): 77–88.

Lincoln, W. Bruce, *The Conquest of a Continent: Siberia and the Russians* (New York: Random House, 1994).

Lippman, Thomas W., *Inside the Mirage: America's Fragile Partnership with Saudi Arabia* (Boulder, CO: Westview Press, 2004).

Lonsdale, David J., *Alexander the Great: Lessons in Strategy* (London: Routledge, 2007).

Lowther, Adam B., *Americans and Asymmetric Conflict: Lebanon, Somalia, and Afghanistan* (Westport, CT: Praeger, 2007).

Luttwak, Edward, *The Grand Strategy of the Soviet Union* (New York: St. Martin's Press, 1983).

Luttwak, Edward, *The Endangered American Dream: How to Stop the United States from Becoming a Third-World Country and How to Win the Geo-Economic Struggle for Industrial Supremacy* (New York: Touchstone, 1994).

Luttwak, Edward, *Turbo-Capitalism: Winners and Losers in the Global Economy* (New York: HarperCollins, 1999).

Luttwak, Edward, *Strategy: The Logic of War and Peace*, rev. and enlarged edn. (Cambridge, MA: Harvard University Press/Belknap Press, 2001; original edn. published 1987).

Lynch, Grayston L., *Decision for Disaster: Betrayal at the Bay of Pigs* (Washington, DC: Potomac Books, 1998).

Mandelbaum, Michael, *The Nuclear Revolution: International Politics Before and After Hiroshima* (New York: Cambridge University Press, 1981).

Mann, James, *About Face: A History of America's Curious Relationship with China, from Nixon to Clinton* (New York: Vintage, 2000; originally published 1998).

Mann, James, *Rise of the Vulcans: The History of Bush's War Cabinet* (New York: Viking, 2004).

Martel, William C., *Victory in War: Foundations of Modern Military Policy* (New York: Cambridge University Press, 2007).

Martinez, Jenny S., "Hamdi v. Rumsfeld. 124 S.Ct. 2633," *The American Journal of International Law* 98/4 (October 2004): 782–788.

Marshall III, Joseph M., *The Day the World Ended at Little Big Horn: A Lakota History* (New York: Penguin, 2007).

Mazarr, Michael J., *Unmodern Men in the Modern World: Radical Islam, Terrorism, and the War on Modernity* (New York: Cambridge University Press, 2007).

McDonald, Forrest, ed., *Empire and Nation: Letters from a Farmer in Pennsylvania (John Dickinson) and Letters from the Federal Farmer (Richard Henry Lee)*, 2nd edn. (Indianapolis: Liberty Fund, 1999), accessed online at http://oll.libertyfund.org/title/690/102300.

McGinnis, Joe, *The Selling of the President, 1968* (New York: Penguin, 1988; originally published 1969).

McNamara, Robert S. with Brian VanDeMark, *In Retrospect: The Tragedy and Lessons of Vietnam* (New York: Vintage, 1996).

McNeill, J.R. and William H. McNeill, *The Human Web: A Bird's-Eye View of History* (New York: Norton, 2003).

McPherson, James M., "Lincoln and the Strategy of Unconditional Surrender," in Gabor S. Boritt, ed., *Lincoln, The War President* (New York: Oxford University Press, 1992): 29–62.

McPherson, James M., *Battle Cry of Freedom: The Civil War Era* (New York: Oxford, 2003; originally published 1988).

McPherson, James M., *Tried By War: Abraham Lincoln as Commander-in-Chief* (New York: Penguin Press, 2008).

Mearsheimer, John J., "The False Promise of International Institutions," *International Security* 19/3 (Winter 1994–95): 5–49.

Meier, Christian, trans. by David McLintock, *Caesar* (New York: HarperCollins, 1995; originally published in German 1982).

Meredith, Martin, *Mugabe: Power, Plunder, and the Struggle for Zimbabwe's Future* (New York: PublicAffairs, 2007).

Metz, Steven, *Iraq and the Evolution of American Strategy* (Washington, DC: Potomac Books, 2008).

Michel, Lou and Dan Herbeck, *American Terrorist: Timothy McVeigh and the Oklahoma City Bombing* (New York: Harper, 2001).

Miller, Linda B., "The Clinton Years: Reinventing Foreign Policy?" *International Affairs* 70/4 (October 1994): 621–634.

Millett, Alan R., *The War for Korea, 1945–1950: A House Burning* (Lawrence, KS: University Press of Kansas, 2005).

Millett, Alan R., *The War for Korea, 1950–51: They Came from the North* (Lawrence, KS: University Press of Kansas, 2010).

Millett, Allan R. and Peter Maslowski, *For the Common Defense: A Military History of the United States of America*, rev. and expanded edn. (New York: Free Press, 1992).

Mitchell, Alison, "The 2000 Campaign: The Running Mate," *New York Times* online edn., 25 July 2000.

Moloney, Ed, *A Secret History of the IRA* (New York: Norton, 2002).

Morris, Dick and Eileen McGann, *Condi vs. Hillary: The Next Great Presidential Race* (New York: HarperCollins, 2005).

Morris, Edmund, *Dutch: A Memoir* (New York: Random House, 1999).

Mosher, Steven W., *Hegemon: China's Plan to Dominate Asia and the World* (San Francisco: Encounter Books, 2000).

Moyer, Mark, *Triumph Forsaken: The Vietnam War, 1954–1965* (Cambridge, UK: Cambridge University Press, 2009).

Moynihan, Daniel Patrick with Suzanne Weaver, *A Dangerous Place* (Boston: Little, Brown, 1978).

Mueller, John E., *The Remnants of War* (Ithaca, NY: Cornell University Press, 2007; originally published 2004).

Mueller, John E., *Atomic Obsession: Nuclear Alarmism from Hiroshima to Al Qaeda* (New York: Oxford University Press, 2009).

Murray, Williamson, Richard Hart Sinnreich, and James Lacey, eds., *The Shaping of Grand Strategy: Policy, Diplomacy, and War* (New York: Cambridge University Press, 2011).

Nagourney, Adam and Janet Elder, "Support for Bush Surges at Home, but Split Remains," *New York Times* online edn., 22 March 2003a.

Nagourney, Adam and Janet Elder, "Americans See Clear Victory in Iraq, Poll Finds," *New York Times* online edn., 15 April 2003b.

Nash, Gerald D., *The American West Transformed: The Impact of the Second World War* (Lincoln, NB: University of Nebraska Press/Bison Books, 1990; originally published 1985).

NBC News, *Meet the Press*, transcript for 12 September 2004, accessed online at www.msnbc.msn.com/id/5981265/.

Newport, Frank, *Polling Matters: Why Leaders Must Listen to the Wisdom of the People* (New York: Grand Central, 2004).

Nichols, Thomas M., *Winning the World: Lessons for America's Future from the Cold War*, Humanistic Perspectives in International Relations series (Westport, CT: Praeger, 2002).

Nitze, Paul H., with Anne M. Smith and Stephen L. Rearden, *From Hiroshima to Glasnost: At the Center of Decision: A Memoir* (New York: Grove Weidenfeld, 1989).

NSS (*The National Security Strategy of the United States*), September 2002, p. 1. Accessed online at www.globalsecurity.org/military/library/policy/national/nss-020920.pdf.

NSS (*The National Security Strategy of the United States*), March 2006, p. 1. Accessed online at www.iwar.org.uk/military/resources/nss-2006/nss2006.pdf.

NSS (*The National Security Strategy of the United States*), March 2010, p. 20. Accessed online at www.whitehouse.gov/sites/default/files/rss_viewer/national_security_strategy.pdf.

Offer, Avner, "Morality and Admiralty: 'Jacky' Fisher, Economic Warfare and the Laws of War," *Journal of Contemporary History* 23/1 (January 1988): 99–118.

Office of the Secretary of Defense, *Annual Report to Congress: Military Power of the People's Republic of China, 2007*, accessed online at www.defenselink.mil/pubs/pdfs/070523-China-Military-Power-final.pdf.

Ogburn, William Fielding, "The Great Man Versus Social Forces," *Social Forces* 5/2 (December 1926): 225–231.

O'Neill, William L., *A Better World: The Great Schism: Stalinism and the American Intellectuals* (New York: Touchstone, 1982).

O'Shea, Stephen, *The Perfect Heresy: The Life and Death of the Cathars* (London: Profile Books, 2001; originally published 2000).

Ottanelli, Fraser M., *The Communist Party of the United States: From the Depression to World War II* (New Brunswick, NJ: Rutgers University Press, 1991).

Pagden, Anthony, *Worlds at War: The 2,500-Year Struggle Between East and West* (New York: Oxford University Press, 2008).

Parker, Geoffrey, *The Grand Strategy of Philip II* (New Haven, CT: Yale University Press, 2000; originally published 1998).

Parker, Geoffrey, *Success is Never Final: Empire, War, and Faith in Early Modern Europe* (New York: Basic Books, 2002).

Payne Jr., Samuel B., "The Iroquois League, the Articles of Confederation, and the Constitution," *The William and Mary Quarterly* 53/3 (July 1996): 605–620.

Pearlman, Michael D., *Truman and MacArthur: Policy, Politics, and the Struggle for Renown* (Bloomington, IN: Indiana University Press, 2008).

Peterson, Paul E., "The President's Dominance in Foreign Policy Making," *Political Science Quarterly* 109/2 (Summer, 1994): 215–234.

Pew Forum on Religion & Public Life, *Mapping the Global Muslim Population: A Report on the Size and Distribution of the World's Muslim Population* (Washington, DC: Pew Research Center, October 2009), p. 24, accessed online at http://pewforum.org/newassets/images/reports/Muslimpopulation/Muslimpopulation.pdf.

Pierson, Michael D., "'All Southern Society is Assailed by the Foulest Charges': Charles Sumner's 'The Crime Against Kansas' and the Escalation of Republican Anti-Slavery Rhetoric," *The New England Quarterly* 68/4 (December 1995): 531–557.

Pilger, John, "Reality Check," *Guardian* (London) online edn., 28 March 2007.

Pipes, Richard, ed., *The Unknown Lenin: From the Secret Archive* (New Haven, CT: Yale University Press, 1996).

Pipes, Richard, ed., *Communism: A History* (New York: Modern Library, 2003; originally published 2001).

Podhoretz, Norman, "The Case for Bombing Iran," *Commentary* 123/6 (June 2007): 17–23.

Porter, Patrick, *Military Orientalism: Eastern Warfare Through Western Eyes* (London: Hurst, 2009).

Posner, Richard A., *Not a Suicide Pact: The Constitution in a Time of National Emergency* (New York: Oxford University Press, 2006).

Preston, Julia, "Former Chief of U.N. Effort Faces Charges of Corruption," *New York Times* online edn., 17 January 2007.

Pry, Peter Vincent, *War Scare: America and Russia on the Nuclear Brink* (Westport, CT: Praeger, 1999).

Purifoy, Lewis M., "The Southern Methodist Church and the Proslavery Argument," *Journal of Southern History* 32/3 (August 1966): 325–341.

Ravel, Jean-Francois, trans. William Byron, *How Democracies Perish* (New York: Doubleday, 1984).

Read, John H., *Majority Rule Versus Consensus: The Political Thought of John C. Calhoun* (Lawrence, KS: University Press of Kansas, 2009).

Record, Jeffrey, *The Specter of Munich: Reconsidering the Lessons of Appeasing Hitler* (Washington, DC: Potomac, 2007).

Ricks, Thomas E., *Fiasco: The American Military Adventure in Iraq* (New York: Penguin, 2007).

Ricks, Thomas E., *The Gamble: General David Petraeus and the American Military Adventure in Iraq, 2006–2008* (New York: Penguin, 2009).

Robinson III, Charles M., *General Crook and the Western Frontier* (Norman, OK: University of Oklahoma Press, 2001).

Roosevelt, Theodore, *The Naval War of 1812, or, The History of the United States Navy During the Last War with Great Britain: To Which is Appended an Account of the Battle of New Orleans* (New York: Da Capo, 1999; originally published 1882).

Rosefielde, Steven, *Russia in the 21st Century: Prodigal Superpower* (New York: Cambridge University Press, 2005).

Rosefielde, Steven and D. Quinn Mills, *Masters of Illusion: American Leadership in the Media Age* (New York: Cambridge University Press, 2007).

Rosett, Claudia, "Central Park," *Wall Street Journal* online edn., 20 July 2006.

Ross, Robert S., "The Geography of the Peace: East Asia in the Twenty-First Century," *International Security* 23/4 (Spring 1999): 81–118.

Rowny, Edward L., *It Takes One to Tango* (Washington, DC: Brassey's, 1992).

Rudalevige, Andrew, *The New Imperial Presidency: Renewing Presidential Power After Watergate* (Ann Arbor, MI: University of Michigan Press, 2005).

Rumsfeld, Donald H., 16 October 2003 memo, accessed online at www.globalsecurity.org/military/library/policy/dod/d20031016sdmemo.pdf.

Sadowski, Yahya, "'Just' a Religion: For the Tablighi Jama'at, Islam is not Totalitarian," *Brookings Review*, Summer 1996, accessed online at www.brookings.edu/articles/1996/summer_islamicworld_sadowski.aspx?p=1.

Sanger, David, "Musharraf Defends Deal Made with Tribal Leaders," *New York Times* online edn., 23 September 2006.

Saunders, Jr., Charles W., "Jefferson Davis and the Hampton Roads Peace Conference: 'To Secure Peace Between Our Two Countries,'" *Journal of Southern History* 63/4 (November 1997): 810–811.

Savage, Charlie, *Takeover: The Return of the Imperial Presidency and the Subversion of American Democracy* (New York: Little, Brown, 2007).

Schlesinger, Jr., Arthur M., *The Imperial Presidency* (New York: Mariner Books, 2004a; originally published 1973).

Schlesinger, Jr., Arthur M., *War and the American Presidency* (New York: W.W. Norton, 2004b).

Schroeder, Paul W., *The Transformation of European Politics, 1963–1848* (New York: Oxford University Press, 1994).

Schweitzer, Glenn E. with Carole C. Dorsch, *Superterrorism: Assassins, Mobsters, and Weapons of Mass Destruction* (New York: Plenum Press, 1998).

Schweitzer, Peter, *Victory: The Reagan Administration's Secret Strategy that Hastened the Collapse of the Soviet Union* (New York: The Atlantic Monthly Press, 1994).

Schweitzer, Peter, *Reagan's War: The Epic Story of his Forty-Year Struggle and Final Triumph Over Communism* (New York: Doubleday, 2003).

Sciolino, Elaine, "C.I.A. Casting About for New Missions," *New York Times* online edn., 4 February 1992.

Scobell, Andrew, "Show of Force: Chinese Soldiers, Statesmen, and the 1995–1996 Taiwan Strait Crisis," *Political Science Quarterly* 115/2 (Summer 2000): 227–246.

Seigenthaler, John, *James K. Polk* (New York: Times Books, 2003).

Shapiro, Ian, *Containment: Rebuilding a Strategy Against Global Terror* (Princeton, NJ: Princeton University Press, 2007).

Sharansky, Natan, with Ron Dermer, *The Case for Democracy: The Power of Freedom to Overcome Tyranny & Terror* (New York: PublicAffairs, 2004).

Singer, P.W., *Wired for War: The Robotics Revolution and War in the 21st Century* (New York: Penguin, 2009).

Sloane, William M., "The World Aspects of the Louisiana Purchase," *The American Historical Review* 9/3 (April 1904): 507–521.

Sondhaus, Lawrence, *Strategic Culture and Ways of War* (London: Routledge, 2006).

Sorley, Lewis, *A Better War: The Unexamined Victories and Final Tragedy of America's Last Years in Vietnam* (New York: Harcourt, 1999).

Spector, Ronald, *Eagle Against the Sun: The American War Against Japan* (New York: Free Press, 1985).

Staiger, C. Bruce, "Abolitionism and the Presbyterian Schism of 1837–1838," *Mississippi Valley Historical Review* 36/3 (December 1949): 391–414.

Steele, Brett, *Military Reengineering Between the Wars* (Santa Monica, CA: RAND Corporation, 2005).

Stephanson, Anders, *Kennan and the Art of Foreign Policy* (Cambridge, MA: Harvard University Press, 1992; originally published 1989).

Stevenson, Charles A., *Warriors and Politicians: US Civil-Military Relations Under Stress* (London: Routledge, 2006).

Stevenson, David, *Cataclysm: The First World War as Political Tragedy* (New York: Basic Books, 2004).

Stocker, David, *The Grand Design: Strategy and the U.S. Civil War* (New York: Oxford University Press, 2010).

Streeby, Shelley, "American Sensations: Empire, Amnesia, and the US-Mexican War," *American Literary History* 13/1 (Spring, 2001): 1–40.

Sutherland, Daniel E., "Lincoln, John Pope, and the Origins of Total War," *Journal of Military History* 56/4 (October 1992): 567–586.

Symonds, Craig L., *Lincoln and His Admirals* (New York: Oxford University Press, 2008).

Taranto, James and Leonard Leo, *Presidential Leadership: Rating the Best and Worst in the White House* (New York: Wall Street Journal Books/The Free Press, 2004).

Taylor, Brendan, "Towards Hegemony? Assessing China's Asian Ambitions," *Security Challenges* 1/1 (November 2005): 21–25.

Thompson, Hunter S., *Fear and Loathing on the Campaign Trail '72* (New York: Warner, 1983; originally published 1973).

Thompson, Nicolas, *The Hawk and the Dove: Paul Nitze, George Kennan, and the History of the Cold War* (New York: Henry Holt, 2009).

Thucydides, Robert B. Strassler, ed., *The Landmark Thucydides: A Comprehensive Guide to the Peloponnesian War* (New York: Touchstone, 1998; originally published 1996).

Torres-Reyna, Oscar and Robert Y. Shapiro, "Trends: Defense and the Military," *Public Opinion Quarterly* 66/2 (Summer 2002): 279–303.

Tucker, Calvin, "Sticks and Stones...," *Guardian* (London) online edn., 15 November 2006.

Tucker, Robert W. and David C. Hendrickson, *The Fall of the First British Empire: Origins of the War of American Independence* (Baltimore: Johns Hopkins University Press, 1982).

Tucker, Robert W. and David C. Hendrickson, *Empire of Liberty: The Statecraft of Thomas Jefferson* (New York: Oxford University Press, 1990).

Turchin, Peter, *War & Peace & War: The Life Cycles of Imperial Nations* (New York: Pi Press, 2006).

Turner, Thomas, *The Congo Wars: Conflict, Myth, and Reality* (London: Zed Books, 2007).

Tzu, Sun, trans. Ralph D. Sawyer, *The Art of War* (New York: Barnes & Noble Books, 1994).

Valenta, Jiri, and William Potter, *Soviet Decision Making for National Security* (London: Unwin Hyman, 1981).

Van Creveld, Martin, *The Transformation of War* (New York: The Free Press, 1991).

Van Creveld, Martin, *The Rise and Decline of the State* (Cambridge, UK: Cambridge University Press, 1999).

Vandervort, Bruce, *Indian Wars of Mexico, Canada and the United States* (London: Routledge, 2006).

Varhola, Michael J., *Fire and Ice: The Korean War, 1950–53* (New York: Da Capo, 2000).

Varon, Jeremy, *Bringing the War Home: The Weather Underground, the Red Army Faction, and Revolutionary Violence in the Sixties and Seventies* (Berkeley and Los Angeles: University of California Press, 2004).

Vázquez, Carlos Manuel, "The Military Commissions Act, the Geneva Conventions, and the Courts: A Critical Guide," *The American Journal of International Law* 101/1 (January 2007): 73–98.

Vidal, Gore, *Dreaming War: Blood for Oil and the Cheney-Bush Junta* (New York: Thunder's Mouth Press/Nation Books, 2002).

Voorhis, Jerry, *The Strange Case of Richard Milhous Nixon.* (New York: Paul S. Eriksson, 1972).

Walton, C. Dale, "Europa United: The Rise of a Second Superpower and its Effect on World Order," *European Security* 6/4 (Winter 1997): 44–54.

Walton, C. Dale, "The Decline of the Third Rome: Russia's Prospects as a Great Power," *Journal of Slavic Military Studies* 12/1 (March 1999): 51–63.

Walton, C. Dale, *The Myth of Inevitable Defeat in Vietnam* (London: Frank Cass, 2002a).

Walton, C. Dale, "Beyond China: The Geopolitics of Eastern Eurasia," *Comparative Strategy* 21/3 (July–September 2002b): 203–212.

Walton, C. Dale, "The West and its Antagonists: Culture, Globalization, and the War on Terrorism," Review essay, *Comparative Strategy* 23/3 (July–September 2004): 303–312.

Walton, C. Dale, "Get Used to It: Iran Will Have Nukes," *St. Louis Post-Dispatch*, 13 April 2006.

Walton, C. Dale, "Triumph over Illusion: William Van Cleave and the Battle Against Conventional Wisdom," in Bradley A. Thayer, ed., *American National Security Policy: Essays in Honor of William R. Van Cleave* (Fairfax, VA: National Institute Press, 2007a).

Walton, C. Dale, *Geopolitics and the Great Powers in the Twenty-First Century: Multipolarity and the Revolution in Strategic Perspective* (London: Routledge, 2007b).

Walton, C. Dale, "Weapons of Mass Destruction," in David Jordan, James D. Kiras, David J. Lonsdale, Ian Speller, Christopher Tuck, and C. Dale Walton, *Understanding Modern Warfare* (Cambridge, UK: Cambridge University Press, 2008), pp. 296–299.

Walton, C. Dale, "The Case for Strategic Traditionalism: War, National Interest and Liberal Peacebuilding," *International Peacekeeping* 16/5 (November 2009), pp. 717–734.

Washington, George, "The Farewell Address: Transcript of the Final Manuscript," *The Papers of George Washington: Documents* (1796), accessed online at http://gwpapers.virginia.edu/documents/farewell/transcript.html.

West, Bing and Ray L. Smith, *The March Up: Taking Baghdad with the First Marine Division* (New York: Bantam, 2003).

Westwood, Howard C., "After Vicksburg, What of Mobile?" *Military Affairs* 48/4 (October 1984): 169–173.

Wheelan, John, *Invading Mexico: America's Continental Dream and the Mexican War, 1846–1848* (New York: Carroll and Graf, 2007).

White House, *The National Security Strategy of the United States*, September 2002, accessed online at www.globalsecurity.org/military/library/policy/national/nss-020920.pdf.

White House, *The National Security Strategy of the United States*, March 2006, accessed online at www.iwar.org.uk/military/resources/nss-2006/nss2006.pdf.

White House, *The National Security Strategy of the United States*, March 2010, accessed online at www.whitehouse.gov/sites/default/files/rss_viewer/national_security_strategy.pdf.

White House, Office of the Press Secretary, "Radio Address by President Clinton to the Nation," 23 September 1995, accessed online at http://clinton6.nara.gov/1995/09/1995–09–23-radio-address-on-prospects-for-peace-in-bosnia.html.

White House, Office of the Press Secretary, "Address to the Nation by the President," 11 June 1999, accessed online at http://clinton4.nara.gov/WH/New/html/19990611.html.

Williams, T. Harry, *Lincoln and His Generals* (New York: Vintage, 2011; originally published 1952).

Wilson, James Q. *Bureaucracy: What Government Agencies Do and How They Do It*, new edn. (New York: Basic Books, 2000).

Wolf, Naomi, *The End of America: Letter of Warning to a Young Patriot* (White River Junction, VT: Chelsea Greene, 2007).

Wood, Gordon S., *The Radicalism of the American Revolution* (New York: Knopf, 1991).

Woodruff, Mark W., *Unheralded Victory: The Defeat of the Viet Cong and the North Vietnamese Army, 1961–1973* (Arlington, VA: Vandamere Press, 1999).

Woodward, Bob, *Bush at War*, rev. edn. (New York: Simon and Schuster, 2005).

Woodward, Bob, *Obama's Wars* (New York: Simon & Schuster, 2010).

Woodworth, Steven E., *Jefferson Davis and His Generals: The Failure of Confederate Command in the West*, Modern War Studies (Lexington, KS: University Press of Kansas, 1992).

Wright, C. Ben, "Mr. 'X' and Containment," *Slavic Review* 35/1 (March 1976): 1–31.

Wright, Lawrence, *The Looming Tower: Al-Qaeda and the Road to 9/11* (New York: Vintage Books, 2007).

Yoo, John, *The Powers of War and Peace: The Constitution and Foreign Affairs After 9/11* (Chicago: University of Chicago Press, 2005).

Young, Mary E., "Indian Removal and Land Allotment: The Civilized Tribes and Jacksonian Justice," *The American Historical Review* 64/1 (October 1958): 31–45.

Zabecki, David T., *The German 1918 Offensives: A Case Study in the Operational Level of War* (London: Routledge, 2006).

Zhang, Shu Guang, *Mao's Military Romanticism: China and the Korean War, 1950–53* (Lawrence, KS: University Press of Kansas, 1995).

Zimke, Earl F., *The U.S. Army in the Occupation of Germany, 1944–1946*, Army Historical series (Washington, DC: Center of Military History, US Army, 1990; originally published as 1975-CMH Pub 30–6).

Zimmermann, Warren, *First Great Triumph: How Five Americans Made Their Country a World Power* (New York: Farrar, Straus and Giroux, 1992).

Index